TRIPTYCH

Gifts of the Spirit
The Way Through
The Illumined Road

TRIPTYCH

Gifts of the Spirit
The Way Through
The Illumined Road

by

DANE RUDHYAR

SERVIRE – WASSENAAR
The Netherlands

Most of the material used in this book was printed as three series of articles, entitled respectively "Gifts of the Spirit", "Challenges of the Earth" and "The Illumined Road" in the magazine "American Astrology" during the years 1945 to 1949; but whatever has been used here has been completely revised and modified in many ways, new chapters added, etc. "Gifts of the Spirit" was published in book form in 1956 by the New Age Publishing Co., Los Angeles, California -- a firm no longer existing. This book has been out of print now for several years.

FOREWORD

To become whole by assimilating that which completes our particular being -- to realize that individual existence is a process of repeated emergence out of a number of typical conditions which test the individual's strength, resilience and faith, and having realized this, to be victorious over the negative trend which is met at every step of the way -- and, having established ourselves in our own identity and consciousness, willingly to surrender this inevitably limiting sense of particular identity and consciousness and to begin the great "adventure in consciousness" which leads us to a state of total illumination, because the divine Whole is then focusing clearly the plenitude of Its Light upon our transfigured selfhood: these are the three basic phases of the great ritual which constitutes the spiritual unfoldment of the human being.

The three sections of this volume refer to these three phases. Each must be experienced. There are no short-cuts. Yet, to speak of three phases does not mean that they are separate and that they unfold in strict chronological sequence. There is a constant interrelation between them. It is all one process. Nevertheless anyone will court serious and, in a sense, perhaps fatal danger who, being fascinated by the apparent end of the process -- often unwisely seen as "the" mystical experience -- rushes to the path of self-transcendence, only too ready to surrender what in fact he has not yet built within his total person. To such a one the Illumined Road may turn into a very dark pathway filled with obsessions and irremediable deviations or perversions.

When dealing with what transcends the commonplace and the intellectually definable areas of our normal and safe everyday existence as personalities conditioned by our culture and our particular social environment, the use of symbols is inevitable. There are many systems of symbolism. Each religion and each culture has its own. Modern mathematics also constitutes such a system; every language does likewise. Perhaps the oldest and most universal type of symbolism can be said to be astrology -- not an astrology that deals almost exclusively with prediction, character-analysis, or worse still unabashed fortune-telling, but the kind of astrology which finds in the regular and cyclic motion of discs and dots of lights in the sky the materials for a symbolism that reveals to us the universal order and the unceasing -- because all-encompassing -- harmony of existence when perceived and felt in its totality and plenitude.

It is with this type of astrology that I have been essentially concerned. It is a l a n g u a g e;* and all languages are systems of symbols. It is also a kind of applied mathematics because the order of the universe appears to us as being based upon numbers, proportions and geometrical forms. Most, if not all, of the secret traditions of the past are related to it and indeed very often derived from it.

Astrology has been called the mother of all sciences, because it was presumably the primordial way in which human beings were able to sense and realize the cyclic order manifesting in the universe; and, because of this order, the possibility of predicting the results of actions attuned to this cyc-

*As it was impossible in preparing this book for offset printing to use italics, and rather than underlining words which are meant to be emphasized (which disturbs the look of the page as a whole) these emphasized words are printed with more widely spaced letters -- a procedure which has been used at times in Europe.

8

lic order. All sciences are actually attempts at predicting
events on the basis of known "laws of nature" -- an awkward
term to speak of the myriad of ways in which universal order can be rigorously analyzed and described.

What the type of astrology I have been concerned with des-
cribes symbolically are phases in the process of unfoldment
and concrete existential actualization of the potentialities inherent in the birth-moment of an individual person's existence. In this book, there is no technical reference to the various elements constituting the language of astrology. Nevertheless the astrological student will no doubt realize that the
first section, "Gifts of the Spirit", deals with the characteristics of the twelve signs of the zodiac, though in a rather
inverted manner -- i.e. it speaks not so much of what the
temperament of a person is in whose birth chart a zodiacal
sign is emphasized in one way or another, as of what this type
of person needs in order to achieve a state of fullness of
existence. The second section, "The Way Through", has as
basic reference the twelve houses of the astrological chart;
these being considered as twelve fields of experience, each
of which is related to the development of one human power or
capacity in terms of dealing with one of the basic aspects of
individual existence. The third section, "The Illumined Road"
uses the sequence of the planets away from the sun as a symbolic means to elucidate the relationship existing between phases on that Road -- which leads to at-one-ment with the Power that orders our whole universe ("God") -- and corresponding phases in our bio-psychological and social development as human beings.

In this way the astrologically aware reader should gain
from this book a deeper sense of the relationship between the
three basic factors used in astrology: zodiacal signs, houses
and planets. Yet the person who has no interest in astrology
needs not be concerned or antagonized by the occasional mention of signs or planets -- no more than by the symbolic cor-
relation, in Sufi mystic poetry, between wine and spiritual

experience, or between the emotional rapture of love for an earthly beloved and union with God.

The use of symbols cannot be avoided entirely whenever we seek to depict or interpret experiences dealing with q u a l i t i e s o f b e i n g and not with intellectually measurable and exclusively rational q u a n t i t a t i v e values. In an age hyp- notized by quantity, by success measurable by the amount of money a person owns or by the amount of noise produced by the laughter induced by a joke, or by the "gross national pro- duct", it has become more than ever necessary to stress the meaning, value and power of symbols which are not merely "signs" or indicators, but instead which can move, arouse and condition human action and personal unfoldment. Alas, sym- bols too are being used for negative purposes, i. e. in order to force upon other persons one's ego will or the thirst for profit of a particular group; witness political and commercial slogans, and all advertising pressures.

Negative factors always appear where positive values are most needed. Because people today have no longer faith in the great Images of their now mainly obsolescent culture, and be- cause their conscious worship of quantity, money and gadgets has produced a collective psychic disequilibrium, there is in most human beings a deep unconscious longing for allegiance to new, or at least totally renewed and transformed, Images or symbols. It is on this longing that dictators, advertising agencies and promoters of all kinds capitalize.

This book does not seek to promote or force upon anyone's consciousness anything. It simply points out a way of life by describing and interpreting cyclic patterns of human unfold- ment that are potential in every human being. It reformul- ates a wisdom which has its root in the very structure and purpose of Man, hoping thereby to be an antidote against self- intoxication with the ambiguous techniques and the illusive promises of easy, too easy ways to sublime experiences.

Christmas, 1967

CONTENTS

GIFTS OF THE SPIRIT
-To each type of man according to his need-

THE WAY THROUGH
-Twelve basic challenges and tests of individual existence-

THE ILLUMINED ROAD
-Planetary stations on the way to the Star-

GIFTS OF THE SPIRIT

To each type of man
according to his need

TO NICAELA

May her life be blessed, and a blessing—
a gift of the spirit!

D. R.

SPIRIT AND HUMAN NEEDS

SPIRIT AND HUMAN NEEDS

Throughout the past centuries philosophers and wise men, pondering over the many and varied ways in which human beings react to their experiences, have sought to define a few basic types of men according to the characteristic nature of their most familiar responses. Today psychologists and biologists, anthropologists and endocrinologists propound in great detail their own classifications of human types. But what these new categories have gained in precision and analytical subtlety does not suffice to make obsolete the ancient classification of twelve zodiacal types of human beings, with its deep root in a metaphysical and cosmological understanding of the universal patterning of the tides of life and of the creative answer of spirit to human needs.

We do not know where the concept of a twelve-fold cosmos appeared for the first time. We find it abstractly and geometrically defined by Pythagoras and Plato, who probably had inherited it from Egypt or Chaldea, perhaps from still more ancient civilizations. It is logical to assume that the men of the "vitalistic" era of culture and religion, completely absorbed by problems resulting from the cultivation of the land and the raising of yearly crops, found it obvious, in their attempt at grasping the secret of periodicity in nature, to consider the solar year and the cycle of the moon's phases as a basis for calculation. On these two cycles, agricultural man established his calendars; which in turn gave him a sense of mastery over time and seasonal activity -- a sense that he had become able to fathom the rhythmic pattern of all crea-

tive processes in nature. Having acquired the power to har-
ness the life-force in crop-raising and cattle-breeding, the
next step was for him to extend his understanding of nature's
rhythm to human nature, for he believed that the universe
was one organic whole controlled by divine Powers, and that
humanity was an inseparable part of the harmony of this whole.

Because man's universal experience showed him a basic
contrast between the ordered pageant of dots and discs of light
in the sky and the confused, unpredictable and fearful happen-
ings so frequent in the jungle, the forest, or the plains men-
aced by storms and inundations, the wise men of old quite log-
ically thought that the realm of the sky was the habitat of those
Powers ruling over the ordered creative processes of life.
Because agricultural communities had come naturally to worship all that related to the propagation of life, men were led
to regard the two "Lights" of the sky, the Sun and Moon, as
the focal points for the release of the two great creative poles
of the universal life-force, male and female. The combina-
tion of their yearly and monthly cycles of displacement and
transformation gave thus an approximate basis for a twelve-
fold pattern: the twelve soli-lunar months.

The Sun, as the male polarity, symbolized the creative
power of spirit; the Moon, whose countenance forever varied
and, thus varying, seemed to be related to periodical phenomena in the biological and emotional behavior of women and
all receptive organisms, was the symbol of organic needs in
nature. Twelve times during the year, the Moon vanishes,
absorbed as it were in the radiant being of the Sun. Each New
Moon came thus to represent a time of spiritual fecundation,
when nature was being impregnated by spirit in answer to nature's need. Twelve acts of fecundation -- twelve basic needs
that had to be filled by appropriate solar "gifts". The progeny of these creative acts was life on earth; but as well the
ebbs and flows of feelings, moods, impulses and inner realizations which sway the inner nature of human beings.

This was the origin of the solar Mystery cults vhich superseded the older lunar rites. Chaldea may have been the place where the solar pattern of the creative processes gained first its most definite ascendancy; where the solar year prevailed over lunar calendars, and the twelve-fold zodiac to which the Western world has become heir was finally developed. The twelve signs of the zodiac were considered as the twelve gates through which the creative power of the Sun flowed, each gate defining a phase of the total power necessary in the creation of any "microcosm", that is, of any organic whole.

In these ancient days the earth as a whole was considered the microcosm -- a small concentrate of the entire universe. Humanity, as a kingdom of earth-nature, was the soul of this microcosm; and humanity had to be likewise twelvefold -- twelve types of men corresponding to the twelve zodiacal signs. Each type was considered necessary for the development and the harmony of the social whole. Each type had a creative solar function to perform; and this function could be determined by the season of birth of this individual -- that is, by the position of the Sun at birth with reference to the spring equinox, symbol of all creative beginnings.

This constitutes the foundation of astrology, in its simplest form. But we are not concerned here with astrology and the problems it poses to the rationalistic intellect or the credulity of modern man. We are dealing only with psychological symbolism in its most universal and most ancient aspect, with man's attempt to understand human nature and to bring some order in the multiplicity of its responses to life and experience. We are dealing with great Images which are deeply rooted in man's collective unconscious; with universal ideas or archetypes so vital that our Western intellectualism and all the scorn of the modern scientific rationalism have not been able to dim their significance in the eyes of countless millions. We are dealing with spiritual processes which every man can experience if he chooses to open his consciousness to their fecundating and exalting power.

Every human individual, in so far as he can be considered

truly a complete and relatively independent whole, is in himself a zodiac. In him can be found all types of human responses to life. In him the characteristic qualities of each of the twelve zodiacal signs operate in varying degrees. However, one, or a very few, of these qualities -- these modes of response to the demands of bio-psychic living on earth -- predominate. It is such a predominance which determines the type to which the individual belongs -- his dominant zodiacal type -- just as it is the predominance of similar traits of character which makes of him an extrovert or introvert, a thinking, feeling, sensation or intuition type, according to the psychological classification presented by Carl Jung.

Because each type demonstrates the preponderance of some kind of reaction to life and of some mode of behavior, feeling and thinking, there is always a tendency in every type to exaggerate its characteristic attitudes. This produces disharmony through over-emphasis, illness of body or soul through congestion and malformation caused by the over-development of one function and the resulting under-development of a complementary function. A region of extreme fullness finds itself compensated for by one of emptiness. Brilliancy of mind may cause dullness or darkness of feelings. Health, psychological and biological, can only be regained if some power seeks to re-establish the disturbed functional balance of the total organism of personality by vivifying the under-developed function. This power, in its essential and original manifestation is spirit.

Spirit, as we use the term in this book, is the active outpouring of That which is wholeness, harmony, absolute equilibrium. Spirit is the power whose character it is to seek forever to re-establish harmony and functional balance wherever these have been disturbed; and this power thus must operate wherever there are "wholes" -- which means, everywhere. Spirit is that which must always attempt to fill all zones of emptiness, to bring together and integrate through an adequate structure the polarities of being which had drifted apart.

In its most deeply and vitally experienced aspect, spirit is the answer to all human needs. It flows toward every human being who has need of it, as electricity flows from higher to lower potential, as wind rushes from zones of greater pressure to zones of relative emptiness, as water seeks to reach a common level.

Thus, spirit is to be experienced always where the need is greatest. It must be sought where the mind and the heart have known to their utmost the torment of emptiness, the crucifixion of despair -- yet where also the mind and the heart have refused defeat and hopelessness, have kept active and expectant through the deepest agony; for nothing that is of the spirit can happen to the man who does not believe in the possibility of it happening. Faith alone can open the empty vase of personality to the influx of that which emanates from the absolute Fullness -- this Fullness which man, failing to grasp its infinity, hides from his blinded vision under the many names of God.

Faith is like an act of conscious breathing. Why breathe? Why the effort to expand the chest and open lungs to something that cannot be seen? Yet, there is air; and without opening lungs to its inrush, there can be no biological living. There is likewise spirit; and without acts of faith and of deep psychic inhalation, there can be no spiritual life in integrity, in selfhood and in truth.

Every human type, simply by the very fact that, as a type, it stresses a particular creative function, tends inevitably to demonstrate an equally basic need. And to every human type spirit seeks to bring a gift according to this basic need -- a gift that is meant to fill the emptiness produced by the type's characteristic emphasis.

Twelve gifts of the spirit thus can be seen to balance the twelve essential traits which define the make-up of the twelve zodiacal types of men. They are the healing virtues which alone can restore functional balance and harmony in the corresponding types of men. They are the blessings for which man should ever pray, and in faith open his whole being to their inflow. For only he who asks shall receive. Spirit is everywhere. The fullness of God is everywhere. Yet no man can be filled who keeps his gates rightly shut, his conscious mind cramped in egoism, pride or fear. Spirit can only press from everywhere upon that man -- and the pressure ultimately must kill him who refuses to be healed and made whole.

The twelve great gifts of the spirit to be described in this book are for every individual to receive and to use; because every individual is potentially a complete zodiac, a sphere of living wholeness within which the central Sun radiates in all directions forever. Yet the individual will attract to his being only that of which he has a vital need. To a man in whom the "Aries" type of activity is strongly accentuated the spirit will bring mainly the gift which can fill the need caused, in this man, by the constant use of this type of activity. But man as a mature individual is a concentrate of all powers. And as the use of each power produces the very condition which calls forth the corresponding gift of the spirit, to every man the spirit proffers a multitude of gifts, according to his multitudinous need -- if there is in this man faith and openness to the gift.

To live in faith is to live in wholeness and harmony. It is to release the fullness within, while welcoming gratefully into one's emptiness the abundance of divine being, the healing spirit. Then, inward and outward tides are balanced. God reaches into the heart of man, as man reaches to the place and the work that are his by inherent destiny. There is no exhaustion and no disease, no lack and no congestion. The dynamic process of world-existence operates in and through the individualized consciousness in harmonic strength, beauty and creativeness. Every moment and every act is fulfilled in peace, and man grows forever into the immortality of always more inclusive levels of being, from fulfillment to fulfillment, from everlasting to everlasting.

THE TWELVE GIFTS

ADAPTABILITY

Every cycle has a beginning. Every act of living requires a release of energy to break through the inertia of the past. And among men there are those whose main function is to initiate action, to start cycles unfolding, to release the kind of power that enables new ideas and new plans to manifest in the consciousness of men. These men who can see ahead and push ahead with Promethean vision and compassion belong to the "adventive" type of men, the Aries type. The zodiacal sign of early spring, Aries, is indeed the hieroglyph of all Advents, of all Annunciations.

To such a type of men, and to every individual who feels within him surging the impetuosity and the power of initiative leadership which Aries symbolizes, the spirit has a gift to offer, most precious among all gifts: the power of adaptability. It is a fundamental gift because all new departures in order to be successful must be adapted to the conditions of life in which they occur and, as well, to the essential purpose directing and giving meaning to the initiatory act.

Without the ability to adapt there can be no fulfilled organic existence; neither can there be any spiritual results, for the latter imply that something has been accomplished which met a vital need, and no need can be filled by any kind of behavior which is not adjusted to the conditions which brought forth the need. The plant or animal which is not able to adapt itself to its environment is condemned to rapid extinction. The individual person who likewise cannot fit into the surrounding social conditions, either by adjusting itself to them happily or by establishing firmly a s i g n i f i c a n t attitude of protest and rebellion against them -- such a person must experience sooner or later a physical, psychological or moral breakdown. In solidly structured societies, or where a Christian humanitarian attitude actually prevails, the chances of a complete breakdown of personality are relatively small, but in the realm of vegetable and animal nature the power of adaption is a matter of life or death.

This power manifests in many strange ways; the strangest perhaps being the ability for an organism to camouflage itself, that is, the ability to live unnoticed in a basically hostile environment. As all environments are potentially hostile, especially to the organism which represents a finer state of sensitiveness in its response to life, this ability to be inconspicuous and not to attract attention is in many cases an absolute requirement for survival. Thus we see insects painting themselves in the colors of their surroundings or modifying their forms to blend with the familiar shapes of twigs and leaves; we find animals changing the color of their fur or skin according to seasons, or, as the chameleon, able to harmonize swiftly with the shades of nearby groups of objects.

Do we not preach also: "In Rome, do as the Romans do"? Is not the ability to be at ease in any environment a proof of excellent social manners, and one which modern education increasingly stresses? And do we not hear, in accounts of the lives of those men who embody a finer and wider response to spiritual values -- the true mystics and occultists -- that they usually seek to attract as little attention as possible, so as to be let free to cultivate their supernormal psychological characteristics?

In many cases, the individual ahead of the evolutionary state of the average person of his day needs indeed to have recourse to deliberate "camouflage". He "covers his tracks" while he travels; he performs useful social functions, perhaps of the humblest nature, behind which, as it were, he lives his truly significant life. In other cases, however, there is no such effort at being inconspicuous. And this is so particularly where the individual has a creative message to bring forth, when he is of the "genius" type; in which case he resembles the kind of biological organism -- tree or animal -- which achieves perpetuation against all odds through either the prodigious abundance of its seed -- which allows for a vast margin of waste -- or by giving this seed a very remarkable power of survival.

Humanity as a whole does behave like any other species of life. It protects itself by means of very complex mechanisms of compensation. Where the birth-rate is very high, wars and epidemics are frequent -- or else birth-control becomes popular. Where the number of births declines, medical discoveries and hygiene help nearly every infant to live and prolong the life-expectancy. After wars, the majority of the children are born males -- and when the possibility of accidents increases or savage warfare maims millions, surgery makes wonderful strides. Indeed man learns to rebuild what man had first destroyed; thus, knowledge and consciousness develop in the typical human manner -- through suffering and disharmony.

This is what we have called up to this day: civilization. He alone survives who, either can adapt himself to strain and external danger or pressure, or else is able to bring forth a socially significant or world-transforming "seed", thus fulfilling the need -- at first, mostly subconscious -- of his race, his culture, and, broadly speaking, humanity.

In this latter case the individual person acts as an instrumentality for the spirit. He survives as a person -- even if survival entails severe tribulations! -- because that personality is a vehicle required by the spirit for the fulfillment of humanity's need. He is saved by "God", because "God" needs him as a transformer and releaser of new Images and new social impulses.

Such a person can dare at times to take great risk, because whatever in him is of value to the spirit will be prot-

ected. Because he is identified with his spiritual "seed" --
his power to fecundate humanity toward a new birth of the
spirit -- he will survive, however tragic the survival. Yet
this represents a relatively unusual possibility; and even here
we can speak of adaptability of a sort, for the genius and the
leader must strangely adapt themselves to the requirements
of their "destiny" and of their public.

As the Aries type of person is, above all, an individual
who releases into acts (most often in a spontaneous manner)
instinctual impulses or spiritual ideas, he is usually very poor
in the usual kind of adaptability. He exists predominantly in
what he lets out of himself. He is not essentially
interested in retaining for himself any part of the energy,
biological or spiritual, which he released; but neither does he
care very much about the end-results of the release. He identifies himself with fecundative acts. He lives in the act itself
rather than in or for the fruits of this act. If he seems selfish, it is not because he seeks to accumulate benefits for an
uncertainly realized self, or to exact a price from those he
contacts; it is simply that what matters most to him is to be
able to act again and again -- just for the sake of releasing
some "seed", be it life-seed or spirit-seed. He may go to
extremes of apparent selfishness in order to gain, retain or
increase this ability to act and to fecundate; but he will do so
as one who is merely the releaser of some power over which
he has no control and which he often does not even particularly
care to understand.

For this reason his normal reaction to the problem of adaptability is that, as long as he does his part in releasing the
life-seed or the spirit-seed, it is up to "Life" or to "God" to
take care of the rest, and, thus, to protect him. This cooperation with the spirit very often works; nevertheless it allows for a great deal of waste and of usually avoidable suffering. As long as the Aries type operates at the biological
or the entirely unconscious level, this may not mean much,
for physical nature is indeed prodigal of seed. But when the

realm of the individualized and conscious person is reached, Aries' need for adaptability becomes of great consequence, for conscious individuals who can act as releasers of new spiritual Images are as yet too rare to be recklessly expendable. They therefore must learn to adapt themselves; thus, to protect their spiritual seed and to direct their creative impulses and activities into socially acceptable channels, or channels which mean the least possible amount of friction and waste of power.

This type of social adaptation, however, should not be such as to divert or muddy the flow of the release of power. It should not alter the quality of the projected Images, or cloud the vision they convey. Thus, the truly creative Aries person is constantly confronted with the necessity of accepting the kind of adaptations which save from waste or permanent personal injury, while rejecting those which mean compromise and adulteration of seed.

This is a difficult task of discrimination! To be adaptable, yet to retain the purity and total integrity of one's vision and one's ideal; to accept detours, yet not lose the direction of the goal; to be understandable and acceptable to those who need the spiritual arousal, yet not distort or lower the character of the message; to use the values born of the past, yet not sell short the future to the uncertain present; to be kind to men, yet uncompromisingly true to the spirit -- such are the problems which the creative Aries person will constantly meet, in one form or another.

The line of least resistance for his temperament will be to stress directness of release regardless of cost or results; but the spirit within him will offer him a gift he should not fail to accept: the gift of adaptability. Ultimately he must come to realize that his activity, if it is to be true to the law of spirit, must be conditioned by compassion rather than by the sheer joy of creative release. He must learn to act not only from some vaguely sensed spiritual source, but as the spirit; thus, always in answer to a need. And so to act

means obviously to consider the results of an action as supremely important.

The act must be adapted to the need, if it is a spirit-conditioned act. It must have a character of inherent necessity
and it must meet necessary conditions. To be truly compassionate is to adapt oneself to the necessary conditions of
one's environment, while pouring forth what the environment
calls forth from one's fullness of being. It is to learn to live
with those who asked to be stirred, led or fecundated; and this
implies above all to accept their problems and their frustrations, even as these place barriers and peculiar conditions
around one's creative release.

To take in careful consideration the results of one's acts
upon those who call forth those acts is not enough. The power
of adaptability is not to be applied only in relation to the recipients of the creative energy or the spiritual vision; it should
also refer to the creator's relationship to the source of that
energy -- to life, or to the spirit. This means that whoever
finds himself acting according to the patterns characteristic
of the Aries type should not "take for granted" that life or
spirit will be available to satisfy his desire for action and
creative release. He should, on the contrary, learn as fully
as he can the nature of life or spirit, and the laws of their
operation. He should learn to be a trustable manager of life-
energy and spirit-power. He should account for his seed, and
use it wisely according to the cyclic character of the moment.

Both life and spirit operate rhythmically. Rhythm is the
first attribute of the universal creative Power. The impulsive and initiative type of individual has much to learn when it
comes to proper timing and proper accentuation. His tendency is to be spasmodic, tense, uncontrolled; or to waste his
power in long stretches of activity without regard for the necessary pauses of cyclic recuperation.

In short, he who acts in the way of Aries must learn to
adapt his releases to the natural rhythm of biological and spi-

ritual ebbs and flows, as well as to the character of the human need which these releases strive to satisfy. He should not only act, but act the part which is his by right of destiny, and his performance should follow the cues presented to him by the other actors of the play. It must be an "organic" performance, enacted in the name of the whole and not merely for the un-rhythmic or wasteful release of the energy stored in only one part, organ or function of this whole.

The individual who is consecrated and true to the spirit acts as the spirit, in terms of human needs. Turning toward humanity or toward those few it is his privilege to serve, the man of initiative will say: "Your need be filled". And, bowing reverently and gratefully to the source whence comes all creative power, he will add: "Thy rhythm will lead me". Performing thus the acts of the spirit, carrying forth the dynamic purpose of life, the individual will know fulfillment and harmony. He will know it as the cyclic linking of God and of man within the creative act. He will know it as the lightning knows the earth, as the wind feels the sea, as light experiences the worlds it stirs out of space.

DETACHMENT

There was a time in India when a strong and beautiful type of social organization prevailed under the power of Brahmanical law. The fabled law-giver, Manu, had established a pattern of society based on a very remarkable grasp of the differences inherent in the various levels of human nature, and of the characteristics of the various phases of a human life. According to this code of laws every human being was theoretically to perform at any time the tasks which were the most natural to him; that is, which followed along the normal and expectable "line of least resistance" of his organic, glandular or bio-psychological faculties.

Obviously, such a principle of conduct could easily lead to social chaos and anarchy if human beings let themselves be motivated by the typical selfish desires of their personal egos, which very often, especially in intellectually conditioned persons, rebel against natural rhythms and functions. Thus the clever person might force upon his less bright comrades many duties to which he finds himself superior, simply as a matter of wanting selfishly to escape their performance. Besides, there is in every organism a tendency to keep repeating forever pleasant (or even, at times, painful) acts, rather than go into a new and unfamiliar realm of experience. It was therefore necessary to establish norms of natural behavior; norms varying according as men were born out of one type or another of racial and social conditions, or showed one kind or another of biological and psychological charact-

eristics. The four "castes" of India, now known only in degenerate forms, were originally such "norms" of social-bio-
logical temperament and behavior. They constituted the regulating principles of social behavior and the foundation of a
thoroughly planned social and economic system.

The life of every man was also divided into four "ages".
To each age, or period, a general type of duty -- a certain
type of relationship between the individual and the community
-- was ascribed. Through his youth, the individual l e a r n t
from the elders and assimilated the results of the past of society. From his early twenties onward, the individual c o n-
t r i b u t e d to the substance of his community, providing it
with children and the physical products of agriculture, trade,
etc. Then, as a fully mature man whose children had reached
some degree of independence, the individual l e d the process of social and cultural development, working for society
as a whole rather than for his family. Finally, as a man in
old age, he turned his attention to the next step, death, and
learnt to prepare himself for death and the after-death by
d e t a c h i n g h i m s e l f f r o m a l l e a r t h l y c o n n e c-
t i o n s.

During this last phase of life the old man often took his
abode under a tree in the forest usually surrounding his vil-
lage or town, there to meditate upon the deeper realities of
life and of the beyond of embodied existence. The course of
these meditations led him n a t u r a l l y -- because of the glandular as well as psychological change in his personality -- to
a progressive retirement or detachment from the things which
had seemed so important to him while engaged in an active
biological and social existence. What was "breath of life"
came to be reinterpreted as "spirit" -- the name for both being often identical in ancient culture. What was "sex" became
to him the creative Power of the universe, Brahmā -- the
force of expansion. Thus, the old man, in his meditations,
progressively gave a n e w m e a n i n g to his familiar experiences: a transcendent, or ideal meaning.

In time there developed in India a type of men who, having thus retired into the forest to meditate upon death and release, formulated an attitude to life which eventually became the core of all later-date Hindu philosophies. The teachings of these Forest-Philosophers to the few disciples who gathered around them became formulated in a series of discourses generally called "Upanishads". These constitute the source of the transcendent, idealistic philosophy which has dominated the religious life of humanity ever since, flowering eventually in Christian mysticism after having reached a modified and more absolute expression in the teachings of Gautama the Buddha in the sixth century B.C. At the root of such a philosophy is the concept and the practice of "detachment".

It is very important for us to realize today that the society which developed under the caste-system of Manu was, for the time and in relation to the general evolution of mankind in India, as perfect a type of "planned society" as could be devised. Every social activity was not only planned, but ritualized and consecrated by religious practices, and enforced by occult-religious sanctions. "Nature" was enforced by divine authority. Everything (in theory, at least) was as it should be according to the rhythm of human and earth nature; but man's consciousness was thereby completely attached to these natural rhythms. Even when, in old age, individuals came to experience detachment and release, this still was according to plan.

However, in planning for an ultimate state of life in which men should seek release from the planning itself, the old Hindu society sowed the seeds of its dissolution. The Forest-Philosophers taught detachment and t r a n s c e n d e n t individualism to the few who were ready, according to plan. Buddha, however, taught detachment and p r a c t i c a l every-d a y individualism to every human being -- and freedom from the bondage to any plan, be it nature's plan or the Manu's laws. He taught detachment as a positive technique of living for every man to use at any time; a technique leading to a perfect state or condition of being which any man, whatever his birth, could attain. The revolutionary effect of his teaching was tremendous. It changed the course of human development and laid the foundation for Christian individualism and the Christian gospel of universal love.

Gautama, the Buddha, was born at the Full Moon of May; and, according to tradition, reached illumination and died at this same Full Moon. Whether it be fact or symbol, this in any case should be of capital significance to the student of zodiacal symbolism; for it places a strong emphasis upon the deep meaning of the sign, Taurus. Taurus signifies man's complete subservience to the natural rhythm of human activity. It is the symbol of "attachment". Attachment, here, does not necessarily imply a negative or compulsive bondage to nature; but it means a very deep identification with the energies of human nature, with the evolutionary processes operating, normally in a subconscious manner, within man and leading us to goals ordained by Life, or by God.

Historically speaking, the period of centuries which, according to the cycle of precession of the equinoxes is identified with the symbol of Taurus (third and fourth millenia B.C.) was the period of vitalistic religions, in which the powers of natural fertility were deified. Natural fertility is indeed the keynote of the Taurus type of human being. And the men of the great agricultural cultures of this Age believed that man could only grow through his attachment to the rhythmic powers of nature.

During the second millenium B.C. the attitude of detachment began very slowly to challenge the one of attachment. The Taurean Age had passed. But it was only with the Buddha that the new orientation was publicly formulated as a universally valid philosophy and a practical religious attitude which promised "salvation" from the suffering and the dying inherent in nature -- salvation from bondage to any planned society and ritualized religion as well as freedom from individual pain.

The old Hindu attitude of detachment was based on the fact that a time comes when we must let go of what we possess and enjoy, of body and life; when that time comes, we must learn to meet this unavoidable phase of detachment gracefully and with a quiet feeling of harmony and identification with the infinite. This, however, was a negative or passive attitude toward detachment. To it the Buddha sought to substitute a p o s i t i v e and deliberate attitude of detachment. He taught that it could be reached through an objective and rational understanding of the nature of ourselves as living personalities and of the world as a whole -- through total awareness, through a scientific analysis of all our reactions and of the cyclic series of causes and effects to be found wherever there are living organisms, through the control of desires.

This control was not to be obtained by means of will-ful acts of repression as much as by the focusing of the clear intelligence upon the process of formation, growth and unavoidable disappearance of all these desires, impulses and emotions which, if we identify our consciousness and ego with them, throw us into the tragic world of joy and sorrow, pleasure and pain.

Our attachment to the objects of natural desire must end in pain; our attachment to life must end in death. Why then not give up at the start, willingly and resolutely, what we will have to give up inevitably sooner or later in the midst of pain and anguish? To kill the seed of pain by withering the weed of desire with the fire of awareness and understanding: this is to be wise. This is to follow the Noble Path, Arya Dharma -- the "truth that sets all men free".

A l l men; not only the Brahmins or the Initiates in ritual Mysteries! There is no caste before the truth of the Buddha. There is no special age to learn the liberating secret of detachment. The sword of detachment and severance must be wielded by the strong mind and the noble soul; but these can be found in a low-caste barber (an outstanding disciple of the Buddha) as well as in the highly educated philosopher. This

sword cuts through the veil of nature, cuts through the mag-
netic-electrical polarities of life and death, love and hatred,
joy and sorrow, which are at the root of human nature -- nay,
of all nature. Aware of the essential meaninglessness of the
perpetual ebbs and flows of the vast ocean of universal life,
the Sage identifies himself neither with ebb nor with flow.
He follows the Middle Path, the Path of Equilibrium. Being
attached to neither polarity of life, desiring nothing in particular -- even n o t t o c e a s e d e s i r i n g! -- he enters a state
or condition of being which is beyond nature: N i r v a n a.

This word has been grossly misunderstood by Westerners
and by a vast number of Hindus themselves. It means symbolically "absence of vehicle". It refers to a state in which
the consciousness is free from attachments to the particular
mode of operation of a particular type of "vehicle", system,
organization, or natural organism. It is consciousness un-
conditioned by nature and its many "wheels", its fateful cycles of birth, death and rebirth. It is consciousness poised at
the hub of any and all wheels, where there is repose in the
midst of motion and emotion.

All compound things must come to decay. Every entity
finding its expression in a particular shape, name or set of
attributes will have to lose at some future time this shape,
name or set of attributes. That only escapes the universal
decay of complex substances -- thus, of nature -- which, being simple and single, finds its manifestation in any thing or
condition whatsoever.

What is "That"? The Buddha shunned to give answers to
all metaphysical questions. He was a practical realist, a tech-
nologist. He taught: Give up attachment to all desires and
you will be "That". Nirvana is a condition. It does not refer
to any being, however transcendent or divine, for any one to
worship. It is a practical condition for you to reach, n o w.
You can reach it. All men can reach it, if they dare to understand and to face the inevitable end of all things; if they
dare to uproot from their inner being and consciousness the

profound cause of all bondage and all suffering; if they dare to be free; if they not only dare, but perseveringly apply the technique of liberation. All else has no ultimate value or meaning.

This message of detachment is the answer to the Taurus type of personality, because Taurus, in the symbolical language of the Zodiac, identifies the type of person who lives fundamentally in its attachment to nature and to the ideal of natural growth and fulfillment in substantial, earth-born organisms. This attachment to, and identification with the rhythm of the universe can produce great beauty and an extraordinary richness of response to life and love; and in an age of mechanical artificiality, as ours is, the Taurean characteristics may be very precious. Taurus is a magnificent song of bondage to "life". It is the wondrous slave of a master great beyond all measure. Yet the Buddha came to show that greater still is the spirit within man.

This spirit is slave to no master; not even to life, to love, or to any god summoned by man's eternal desire for a universal Father upon whom to place the burden of the world's guidance or liberation. The spirit within every man is inherently free. It knows no decay. It knows no pain. The ebbs and flows of universes and cycles succeed one another along the rim of Time's endless wheel. All things return to whence they came. All beginnings are already deaths in disguise. But within the core of all human experiences there is that stillness and that peace which can be felt where all feeling ceases, which c a n be known in the failure of all knowledge.

To be that stillness and that peace -- this is the only "salvation"; this alone is freedom. Strive after it diligently, incessantly; yet...unhurriedly, serenely, without desire for its gifts. Strive after it; until there is no need any longer for striving; until there is no need whatsoever; until there is nothing whatsoever.

THE ART OF LETTING
THINGS HAPPEN

In the ancient cultures which history records, spirit was identified with all subtle and volatile things: the wind that eludes the grasp, the scent of flowers, and above all the breath, which, as it fails, reveals the coming of mysterious death. In later ages, when men who had pondered deeply upon this great mystery of death, sought not only to welcome it, but, with determined will to gain entrance even while alive to the realm of the beyond, spirit became a transcendent essence. These men taught that only through detachment from desire could the spirit be known. Therefore all definitions of the spirit had to be negative. It was not this, not that. It was neither this condition, nor its opposite; neither good nor evil, neither light not darkness. No one indeed could define the spirit, except by enumerating endlessly the limited things it was not. Even for the Christian mystic, God is not truly magnificence and all-encompassing glory; for the mystic has felt His presence within the "secret chamber" of the heart, where there is silence and nothing; and he speaks in faltering tones of God's "infinite poverty".

Today, however, a new Age of human development is dawning. In the far reaches of the consciousness, where mind and heart, action and contemplation, body and soul find themselves synthesized in a constant harmony of polar opposites, a new understanding of the spirit seeks adequate formulation. It may not find this formulation for centuries; and again, it is perhaps just now being precipitated into words and tones, into forms and deeds, somewhere where the need is greatest, the loss of all security most irretrievable. What is, then, this new understanding of the spirit?

Spirit as relatedness -- this might give a suggestion for a new definition of the spirit. Spirit as the light shining between all opposites that have come to face each other in understanding and in peace: that too may give a clue to the new revelation of the nature of the spirit. The Free Masons use in their essential symbolism two columns, Jachim and Boaz, each of which represents a polarity of being. Everywhere these two symbolic columns can be envisioned by the discerning mind, for everywhere there is duality and polarity. To the ancient thinker, spirit may have appeared as the wind that blows between these columns. To the transcendental mystic and idealist, spirit is the unfathomable mystery within the temple whose entrance is guarded by two columns. And today could we not say that spirit is the light of fulfillment radiating from the man who stands between these columns, accepting and unafraid, on his way toward ever more light and ever more inclusive fullness of being?

The zodiacal symbol of Gemini, II, is a conventionalized representation of two columns, linked above by the roof and, below, by the floor of the temple of which they mark the threshold. Gemini is the Gate which leads to the temple of human fulfillment. Through the Gate the wind of destiny blows. Beyond the Gate, the Holy of Holies is wrapt in mystery and glamor mixed with fear. At the Gate, the disciple pauses, facing the innermost in understanding and expectation; and also the priest stands, facing the outer world, blessing the multitudes.

At the Gate. . . This is the place to pause, to accept, and to know the peace which alone can insure to the seeker for spiritual reality success in his search. It is the place where confrontations have to be met; where, between the two towering columns which close in menacingly, the dreaded "Guardian of the Threshold" must be accepted and overcome -- our entire past concentrated in an experience of intense awareness, often bleak with despair and frightening in its horror. At the Gate, the youthful and unprepared soul, filled with excitement and eager curiosity, may wish to rush headlong into the mystery. Little does he care to wonder at the majestic columns. Blind to the haunting presence, he would force his way into the sanctuary. What would he find there? Nothing, save the avenging fury of his frustrations and his fears, save the aroused image of his darkest failures -- and he would reel back, stunned and blinded.

At the Gate. . . It is there, that the greatest need of the Gemini type of person is to be experienced. This type is filled with a vivid eagerness and curiosity for sensation and knowledge. Gemini, like the college youth which is its typical representation, feels that all experiences are his for the asking; that there is nothing not to be known, no secret door the lock of which cannot be forced. With candid ardor he seeks to link all facts, to classify all data, to catalogue the gods and stars of the entire universe, to engineer adventures to heaven and hell.

One thing he needs to learn: the art of letting things happen. He must learn to pause and to wait. He must learn to understand first, to act afterward. At the Gate of all experiences he has to stop and listen; and to bow as he meets the two great columns of life, for they are to teach him that all nature obeys laws which cannot be broken, and is structured by cycles whose rhythms compel all beings.

Action and reaction are found in all things and all conditions. The beat of life is measured by tides of destiny which control the unfoldment of events. It is true that every goal and event clearly envisioned and persistently sustained comes to maturity. Nevertheless, he who strives after the goal must learn to let the goal happen to him -- not in passive expectation and careless wishing, but in the silence and the pause which is peace. Peace compels all mysteries to reveal themselves. Bodies may be violated, but souls only open to him who can wait, in power and in strength. Eagerness is not enough; power out of understanding is necessary. What draws to itself all things? A vacuum contained within a strong vessel which no pressure can shatter.

There is an inner emptiness of mind which will draw to itself all knowledge. It is difficult for the typical Gemini person to see that such a statement can make sense. But to learn that it does make sense is perhaps Gemini's greatest need. "The art of letting things happen" is the greatest gift of the spirit to his eager curiosity and his passion for getting at knowledge and things in general. It is the gift from that which is totality of being to the person who overvalues his tense strivings to be "conscious" at all cost -- merely to be conscious.

One can stress too much the value and importance of conscious representations. One can stress the will to intellectual clarity and mental formulations to such a degree that all except the relatively few facts able to fit in the conscious structures of the mind are left unnoticed. One can strain one's power of perception and classification so much that there develops what Carl Jung called graphically and most accurately a "cramp in the conscious". Unless this cramp is resolved, unless man let life pour again within the relaxed structures of the mind, the seeker after reality will never find the spirit, however much he may think he knows. For the spirit is the constant and total relatedness between all objects, all persons and all events. Spirit, in terms of modern physics, is the entire patterning of the "world-lines" which constitute the essence of space, and the intersections of which we perceive as things and events.

To seek the spirit in true understanding is to gather in one's field of vision these world-lines as they weave their intricate cyclic patterns before the observer. It is to stand at the threshold of all experiences in intense awareness and positive openness of the mind, unhurried, serene, without strain or desire to fit the interweaving patterns of events into set formulas. It is to avoid cramping one's mind in such a manner that the unfamiliar or unwelcome event finds no admittance to the consciousness, and the feeling too overwhelmingly to be expressed is forced back into the tightened heart. It is to learn the difficult art of being positive and controlled, while letting things happen according to their own natural rhythm. It is to go forth with assurance and eager determination, yet force no issue until the proper rhythm operates between the two great columns at the Gate, and the shrine is revealed beyond the majestic figure of the welcoming hierophant of the Mysteries.

The columns, the floor and the roof of the temple form a mystic rectangle. Within this rectangle the candidate stands, erect, drawing to the center of his being -- where the diagonals of the figure intersect -- the power which emanates from the directions of space: north-east, south-west, south-east, north-west. Before him, the Initiator is revealed, who bids him enter. . .

This is, in the form of symbols, the pattern of all true experiences, as the seeker for spiritual understanding comes to meet them. Impatience and the eager rush of desire will only disturb the sacred performance. Wisdom is not to be rushed into: it is to be received from the wholeness of life by the wholeness of one's nature. Wisdom which is of the spirit is a gift. It is a gift because it comes to the recipient as a c o m p l e t e d   w h o l e. He does not piece it together, part by part, hurriedly putting forth a scaffold and throwing into it every bit of available material. Wisdom is a gift. One must not force the giving of gifts.

This truth is for Gemini to learn; and it, too, must be received as a gift. The heart will understand its meaning only if not rushed into acceptance of its seeming obviousness. All seeds mature slowly; wisdom and integration are of the nature of seeds. One must grow into them, effortlessly, serenely, in faith and in beauty.

KNOWING WHERE ONE BELONGS

Revolutions and wars have been fought in the tragic attempt to solve one of humanity's greatest problems: that of the relative value of individualism and collectivism. It is indeed a universal problem. All worlds and all conditions of existence are but varied answers to this question of questions. But while planets, trees and whatever may be meant by "angels" and the like are compulsive expressions of solutions defined by the Power that acts at the core of universal evolution, human beings find in themselves the god-like capacity to formulate and try out a variety of solutions. They can decide to quite a large extent -- yet, not as large perhaps as many imagine! -- the relative intensity in their lives of the trends toward individualism and toward collectivism. They can decide how great a value they will give to the rights of the individual, how deep their subservience shall be to the dictates of society or the state. And this possibility gives to all men a great responsibility -- a tragic responsibility.

We discuss today the merits of a collectivistic attitude to life in the economic and political fields, and many people believe that the struggle between individualism and collectivism occurs only in these fields. But all life is a basic conflict between the forces which seek to isolate a number of different elements, then to integrate them into a relatively unique and independent organism, and the forces which attempt to break down the insulation of the individual entity and to make of this entity one of the many units within a vaster whole, to the rhythm and purpose of which they are subservient. All modern psychologists recognize the importance of this basic life-conflict between what we call today "individual" and "society"; and they seek to transform the conflict into a harmonious marriage, or at least a workable compromise.

The twelvefold cyclic pattern of the zodiac is a remarkable tool for charting at any and all levels the different phases of the ever-renewed struggle between the trend toward individualization and the pull toward collectivization. This struggle gives to the periodic sequence of the seasons and to the yearly cycle of vegetation their essential meaning. Spring is the time when life seeks to become expressed in particular organisms as different from one another as the stage of their evolution allows. It is the season when all life-energies and chemical substances aim at becoming harmonized, blended or integrated within the exclusive field of a particular organism and an individual personality. And the summer solstice, the first point of the zodiacal sign, Cancer, represents the apex of this striving. The autumn, on the other hand, is the season when individualized characteristics tend to fade away with the fall of the leaves; when all that is not absorbed by the soil and the snow concentrates in the seed which is utterly dedicated to the task of preserving the collective values and energies of a species -- every seed being the very expression of the species as a whole and of the species' will to immortality.

The spring symbols of the zodiac identify types of human beings which, each in its own way, fervently desire to reach the status of individual. These men seek the fullest possible differentiation from the average; they see as their ultimate goal the attainment of a condition of personal integration and of individualized selfhood. The Aries type seeks this goal by personalizing the power of new creative impulses or ideas; the Taurus type, by bringing up human substance and human energies to a state of maximum responsiveness to the fecundant spirit of "Man", or of God. The Gemini type seeks personal integration through an increase of mental awareness and an ambitious striving for new values and a new sense of relationship.

Then, the summer solstice comes. The tide turns. The sun symbolically "stands still" and reverses its motion in declination. The sunsets begin to occur farther to the south. Integration on an individualistic and exclusivistic basis has reached its maximum degree. In the Cancer type of human person we see in operation, both, the purest or most "rugged" of individualism -- the greatest kind of insularity and isolationism -- and a peculiar sense of fear and resentment caused by the inescapable realization that the tide has turned and that society and its collective power will win eventually over the individual. The Cancer person is most consciously individualized, yet most fearful subconsciously of the unavoidable pressure of the demands which life, society, humanity as a whole, and ultimately God, must and will make.

The most concrete expression of these demands is: the child -- and the home which the child makes necessary. For a woman to be pregnant is to give up her hard won individuality of consciousness -- and of physical structure as well. For a man to become a provider for a home is to have been caught into the wheels of social duties, social respectability and social normality. Life has won over the mother; society has won over the head of the family. There is no turning back for either, at least for a long period. Yet, this victory of collective life and society over the individual also brings these individuals to personal fulfillment. Always, indeed, the apex of a curve is also the beginning of its decline. This fact is the solution of the riddle which a typical Cancer person presents -- to himself as well as to others.

Cancer is the symbol of personal, private integration. It represents the will to establish a foundation of selfhood and consciousness on a particular set of values, limited, well-defined in verbal formulations, and exclusive of others. It represents the will to establish a clear but narrow focus for the operation of life and mind; and, again, such a focus is exemplified by a child or a home -- my child and my home, each one theoretically quite unique an expression of its parents' supposedly unique personalities!

Yet, what is actually unique about most children and most homes? Are they not rather the obvious proofs of the triumph of collective patterns and traditions over the individualistic dreams of earlier years? Do they not often betray the subconscious, yet just as potent, resentment of the individuals against the fateful subservience to social normality -- a resentment which will turn back against the children in very subtle, possessive, almost revengeful ways, or flare up in later years as emotional conflagrations of an unsocial or even abnormal nature?

To avoid such subconscious reactions, immediate or delayed, is the greatest need of the Cancer type of person; and always spirit is ready to fill the vital need, if only the cup is ready to receive the spiritual downflow. To every need there is an answer; to every type of scarcity, a species of abundance which will utterly dissolve the shadow of want. But one must believe that the miracle of fulfillment is possible. One must not recoil before the entrance of divine beneficence, before the inrush of the spirit.

The need of Cancer, like every other need, can be met. It is met as the fear of the mysteriously oppressive idea of "losing oneself into a vast collective entity" is transformed into the realization of the p l a c e one occupies, by one's individual birthright, in such an entity. To find one's place in the vast organism of society or humanity is to feel that o n e b e l o n g s; and so to feel means the eventual disappearance of even the most unconscious fears and resentments.

This indeed is above all things the spirit's gift to the Cancer type of person: that he or she may k n o w where he or she belongs. And this means not a merely intellectual brain-knowledge; but a knowing in the roots of being, in the depths of feeling as well as in the heights of spiritual intuition. What is at stake here is not even the actual business of participating in the definite activities of one's group, community or nation.

This experience of active participation will come later, even though it is implied in the spirit's gift to Cancer. What the individual needs essentially at this Cancer stage of human development is to feel through and through that he belongs, and to realize that he has a definite place and a definite function, clearly his own, in the economy of society and in the life of whatever group is claiming him.

He needs to see clearly that place. He is no longer afraid of religion, if his church has a pew with his name inscribed on it. He ceases to resent traditional behavior and social tasks, if what he is expected to do can be imaged out clearly as belonging to a particular.spot of the vast pattern of society. But if these expressions of inner security are wanting, the Cancer person clings stubbornly to his individualism, to his old standards and his personal possessions.

All of which means that the vague forebodings of losing oneself into a collective immensity can only be appeased if this type of person can find anchorage in a clearly defined situation, function or locality which he can picture to himself. Therefore he has to develop the ability to make pictures, to see pictures; and this is the foundation for the psychic gifts of some of the Cancer personalities. Confronted with a new situation, they learn to visualize its meaning as a symbolic picture -- which is what most types of clairvoyance or psychism are. The symbol shows where the situation "belongs" -- and where one "belongs" in it. It p l a c e s the problem in reference to a definite set of values and symbolic experiences. The symbol is the gift of the spirit. It is an island of meaning in the vast unknown ocean of collective, universal life. It helps one to verify one's position and direction. It establishes a foundation for one's security among the fears of a perilous voyage.

The home is such a foundation. Moral respectability is another. A schedule of work, a clock to tell the exact time, a sign-post in the desert -- these also bring a sense of "belonging". Spirit in its wealth of kindness showers such "X

marks the spot" upon human travelers who see their feeble
individualities caught into the tide of vast open spaces without
boundaries and without names. Men die of fear where there
is no sound to be heard, no sight to be seen; where infinite
duration cannot be hammered into time-patterns by the pend-
ulum of a clock; where their egos feel themselves slipping into the sea of N i r v a n a. They must hold on to place and function, to form and name. They hold on tenaciously with crab-
like claws -- symbols of Cancer. They hold on, as every
man holds on to his achievements, in fear of the mysterious
unknwon in which he cannot distinguish his own place. . . even
though the unknown might be God.

It is strange indeed how every fulfillment brings to us,
human beings, a great fear -- the fear that we might have to
grow beyond it in entirely unfamiliar ways. We are willing
to give up the growth rather than face the mystery which reveals to us as yet no definite place or standard. It is so painful, so terrifying for us all, to set our course only by the
faith in our divinity. Is this not indeed proof that we do not
yet feel that we "belong" in God?

If only each of us could realize, deep in his most essential
roots of existence, "In God, I am. In God, I belong through
any and all conditions. . ." it would be easy to meet the on-
surging tide of the collective. Then, this vast tide would only
mean the promise of our entrance into a state of enduring participation in ever vaster wholes of being. As townsmen, we
would know there is a place for us in the metropolis. As cit-
izens of a nation, we would know there is a function for our
national existence in the great global organism of Humanity.
And as mortal bodies, we would know it is our privilege to
assume our place in the company of immortal souls who have
established themselves forever in their own conscious Iden-
tities.

There would be no need to fear. There is never any need
to fear, or be in want. Spirit is that which always answers
with abundance and plenitude the empty heart and the clean,

bare hands lifted up to the stars. All there is need to do is to lift up our hearts and our hands to the stars. All there is need to do is never to set up limits to our fulfillment, never to stop in fear of the receding tide. For spirit is that which moves from crest to crest, even though it fills the deepest abysses. For, in spirit, heights and depths are as one. All there is is movement, rhythm and forever harmony.

The sun "stands still" in the solstitial hour. But man does not need to stand still. It is man's eternal destiny to move through all crests and all depths, to move with the rhythm and the creative power of spirit. Man is spirit. And, as spirit, man goes on, ever on. And his path is glorious; for it is God's path made clear with consciousness, made fragrant with the scent of noble deeds.

SIMPLICITY

Through countless centuries men and beasts, trees and clouds have sung paeans to the sun. To him, whose powerful magic sustains all the things that breathe and compels all waters to rise, be it into leaves or clouds -- to him, effulgent one, source of warmth, bestower of life -- to him, all nature pays homage. In a myriad of voices and in gestures varied beyond all power of imagining, every creature stammers reverently its love in answer to the adorable gift of light and life.

To these gestures of plants we give the formidable name of "heliotropism" -- the sheer yearning of green leaves for the sun-light. As men turn toward the east to celebrate with prayers the daily resurgence of the sun, we speak of "devotion". And symbols have been built upon the ringing tones of Chanticleer, whose "clairsinging" accents are harbingers of the day to the animal world. Every life soars toward the sun; stretches stems, wings, arms and hands -- whatever can move and, thus moving, responds to light and to God. And these gestures, simple in the primitive forms of life, grow in complexity as more evolved modes of organization and consciousness appear. Until, with humanity, we find an over-abundance of gestures, and indeed a Babel of voices, each claiming excellence, each ready to assure all and sundry creatures that its way is the best -- the directly inspired, the only manner of worship.

As men develop in ever-increasing degrees their individualized consciousness, the natural "heliotropism" of their souls -- the spontaneous devotion of their living to the sun --

changes into the yearning for an exalted state of emotional and mental inner being. The devotee seeks identification with the radiant Essence toward which his worship rises in tumultuous waves of feeling. The sun appears to him not only as the Creator of the universe but, in a far more poignant and ecstatic sense, as the source of life, of identity and selfhood within the most intimate and personal core of his being. He himself becomes transfigured, glorified. He himself radiates with a solar countenance. Convinced beyond any possibility of doubt that he is, in reality and indeed, a sun to those who are as yet unable to experience this ecstasy of identification with the solar Essence, he comes to expect, and soon to demand, of these others that they turn toward him as to an incarnate sun.

Thus religions began. Men who have felt themselves illumined from within by solar ecstasy claim the privilege of being objects of worship; if not as incarnate suns, at least as necessary mediators between the sun and ordinary human beings, between the realm of effulgent, creative light and that of the earthly creatures, opaque and heavy with materiality. The one sun in the sky becomes the one divine Person, who comes down upon the earth into illumined personages who thereafter act "in His name". And we have the various series of solar Kings-Hierophants, the mystic line of Initiates who periodically transfer their spiritual energies and the one solar "Word" to a chosen successor.

In the natural process of human development, this ideal of divine-solar transfiguration comes down to levels of increasing diversity. It serves to vivify man's avidity for power, man's desire to increase the radius of his selfhood and the scope of his authority over other men. The hereditary privileges of kings and priests find in it the substance of their strength; and these privileges are challenged, age after age, by individuals who, having truly experienced the magic identification of their innermost self with the sun or with God, are able to draw to themselves the few or the many, and to wean them away from the binding matrices of organized religion or imperial power.

As men operate increasingly at the mental level and away from "life-instincts", religious Revelations become "ideologies", and the naive devotionalism of the primitive becomes a blind intellectual-emotional subservience to catch-words, formulas and propaganda. Heliotropism changes into "ideotropism". Ideas rule the world of men. Yet -- not ideas alone. To be effective, ideas must be able to touch the generic or the socialized wellspring of human life; the instincts, the primordial emotions, the deep collective Images of a race, culture or civilization. Ideas must be d r a m a t i z e d.

To the simple ritual of natural living -- the cosmic alternation of day and night, of life and death, of light and shadow -- succeed the infinitely varied, complex, and confusing dramas born of human imagination. All these dramas, expressed in myriads of words and gestures, in many lands, and through many tongues, have nevertheless their one root in the tragic fatality of the wedding of light and shadow -- a pair of opposites which must exist wherever the radiance of the sun meets the opacity of material objects.

The inevitability of shadows is the burden of the sunlight. It is likewise the burden of all divine personages, who have become identified with the solar Source of light and life, that they too must create shadow as well as illumination in the souls and minds of men; they must assume the responsibility of death within their very bestowal of life, the tragedy of hate answering to their gift of love. The light they shed upon a man's ego or the race's culture summons forth a shadow in the man's or the race's unconscious. The radiance that illumines the path to tomorrow fills the ways of yesterday with ghosts and with fears, with doubts and resentment.

Man can only move forward by making the emptiness behind him dark -- unless he reaches the state of t r a n s l u c -e n c y; unless his mind and his soul are trans-substantiated and made like crystal, as a lens to focus the glory of the sun upon all yesterdays. Until then, every man who seeks to reach ever so faint an approximation of solar being must come to understand that his very efforts will inevitably evoke a shadow within his psychic depth -- and he must be prepared to deal with it; as the would-be Initiate of occult lore has to be ready to meet the monstrous "Guardian of the Threshold".

This awesome confrontation may be experienced only by a very few men; but every person who has actually become an individualized ego must face the shadow cast within his subconscious by the radiance of his solar identity. Should he refuse to face it, the individual is almost inevitably led to project it upon another person who, in some way, has made himself or herself a ready screen for the reception of the dark image. All psychological processes of growth are marked, at some time, by such projections. Life moves forward by stepping over death. Every great love must ever be renewed out of the substance of ghosts overcome. And this is the eternal drama of light, of life, of power and of love.

Such a drama is experienced at white heat wherever the type of individual who answers to the characteristics of the zodiacal sign, Leo, is active. Aroused by the intensity of this feeling of light and shadow, yet unable to face the shadow within his own depths and reach the condition of t r a n s l u c - e n t   s e l f h o o d, the Leo personality strides dramatically across the world-stage filling receptive souls with the projection of his shadow, and burdening many of the most avid recipients of his light with his own dark images.

He erects temples to the sun, but the builders are made into slaves and die in dreary bondage. Half-glorious and half-slave, the more deeply oppressed the more glowing in its dream-palaces; such is, at first, the Leo world. And in order to hold the enslaved in willing subjection to the darkness of blind devotion, the Leo autocrat -- high-priest or king -- is compelled to stage one grandiose drama after another, to summon one glamorous fantasy after another. He fills his world with gestures and slogans, with heroics and betrayals of truth, with tumultuous triumphs and strident war-cries. His crusades to the sun advance over the piled remains of his wasted devotees.

Upon such a one what greater gift could the spirit bestow than s i m p l i c i t y? To such a heart throbbing with a power that has not yet learnt to know compassion, what blessing more wondrous could there be than s t i l l n e s s? To the mind for which every statement and every concept has value only in terms of its dramatic and devotion-rousing effectiveness, what else could the spirit offer save the g i f t o f t r u t h?

To meet the world with simplicity and with stillness of heart is to meet every soul with shadowless gifts. The essence of drama is complexity; the fatality of heroism is the need to overcome an enemy. The hero thrives on tragedy. Without tragedy, how could there be heroic deeds? Wherefore the sun-glorious ruler finds himself compelled to summon forth war. Some people, some group, some individual must be dark and evil, that, overcoming them, the great leader may prove his heroism. This is true as well in the realm of mind and ideas. There must be pagans condemned to the eternal shadow of hell, if the "man of God" is to show forth his inspired mind and his God-energized faith, either by converting the un-illumined, or by dying the martyr's death at their hands.

Even at the level of greatest sublimity, what would Jesus have been without a Judas to give him the great opportunity of overcoming death and fulfilling the Scriptures, thus proving his divinity? This is the mystery of the spirit in action, that there can be no spirit-born deed except in answer to a need, no incorporation of the spirit except for the purpose of illumining opaque objects or dense egos wedded indissolubly to the fatality of the shadow. Man must sin if God, by redeeming him through the gift of His son, is to prove His divinity.

A "dark saying", indeed, which has bewildered countless minds. Theosophical books likewise speak of "the inertia of spirit", and of the strange destiny of those "Sons of Lucifer"

-- Sons of Mind -- whose task it is, at the dawn of truly human evolution, to oppose spirit, in order to compel its manifestation. These Beings are the eternal Rebels who force humanity to realize its needs and, having thus become aware of a lack, to call to God for one who will fill this need. These Rebels, they are the dramatists of the universe; they act many parts to arouse the somnolent life within human nature. They are the "movers and shakers" of men; they bring tragedy in the form of ruthless awakenings. They dynamize the static; they fecundate the soil with lightnings and with vernal radiance that tear through the shells of seeds, releasing the dormant life within. And their penetration is tragic with the inevitable sequence of the shadow.

To these "first-born" of the universal God there must come at long last a song of peace. To them who have lived through eternal dramas of light and darkness, who have taken a multitude of forms to penetrate the closed gates of bodies and egos, who have spent themselves lavishly in phantasmagories of power and spectacles of greatness, there must come that stillness of heart, that restfulness in truth, that simplicity of action which transfigures and which soothes.

> "Be still, O my heart!
> Be still -- and know God. "

This is the poignant song of the Lucifers, the Bearers of Light, the Vibrant Ones who accept no rest, from eternity to eternity. To be still -- to be simple. For what is "simplicity", if not the overcoming of duality and of drama? To be simple is to be of one essence only. It is to be that which forever is what it is, and that only. Which also means "truth"; for to be "true", and to be "pure", is to be completely and solely what one is, without any adulteration, admixture or conflict. It is to be resolved into unity. . .which is peace.

> "Be still, O my heart!
> Be still -- and know God. "

The sun's power takes the earth in embraces of light. All things are moved thereby into living and dying, into love and the glamour of love, into growth and the wastefulness of seed. Emotion, dynamism, passion, greatness and evil surge luxuriously from the mating of sun and soil. But the time comes when the arc of the sun's journey at last bends low toward the horizon; and, as light vanishes within the folded robe of the western sky, stars appear in the east. Over the earth, stillness descends with the soft darkness of the night. Man's soul, released from the dramas of light, opens to the peace and the grandeur of star-studded skies.

For him who can meet the sun with simplicity and in truth, the same peace can bless every hour. Satisfied to be only what he is, standing erect and true at his work in the fields of this earth, the sun-illumined individual can know the stillness of the stars even at the high-noons of creative living. In utmost translucency of mind and of soul, letting-through the light in shadowless giving, he is indeed a lens for the rays of the sun. His path is light; and his words are true.

In his eyes, space spreads its infinitude in wondrous stillness. Men who dare look into these eyes see themselves amidst the stars. They enter the gates. In reverence, in simplicity, and in peace, they become themselves light. And the rhythm of life, in them, scans gently the silence -- still...oh! so very still!

TOLERANCE

To every man the spirit brings a gift according to his most characteristic need, for the spirit is that which fills all empty vases with the radiance of fulfillment. Each vase -- each type of human being -- calls from its very depths for that one priceless substance which will be as living waters for its thirst. Yet, many men estimate falsely their innermost need. They live at the surface of themselves, not in their depths. Their consciousness is moulded by the ornamentalities of the culture and the tradition which gave them words and symbols as tools for expression; they dare not immerse their agitated ripples of selfhood in the stillness of the essential container which gives form to their fundamental nature.

This occurs particularly in the case of the Virgo type of human beings, because in this type the very substance of conscious selfhood is in a "critical state" -- such a state as exists between ice and liquid water when solidity is hesitantly slipping into the unknown of liquidity, the static into the dynamic, the rigid into the multiform. Virgo marks the stage of metamorphosis in which the conscious ego feels the impact of the world of total relatedness and of participation in a greater whole of which it is to be only one among many parts. It feels this impact, and it recoils in fear or confusion, in anguish or in pain. Its depths shaken by mysterious upheavals, it seeks to explain, to formulate, to criticize, to escape, to invent many and wondrous substitutes, to become the devotee of exotic gods. It tries every possible way of keeping on the go, of thinking, of evaluating -- while the one thing necessary is simply to be still and silently to bear the pressure of evolution, the inevitability of the metamorphosis.

By maintaining a strained and over-eager type of mental activity the ego gives himself the illusion that his power is still supreme. He reassures himself as to his stability. If he criticizes this or that condition, is it not a proof that he is superior to these conditions? If he invents new techniques, and journeys on distant and difficult pilgrimages, is this not a testimony of his ability to meet new conditions and retain his control over circumstances?

Such a behavior indicates that the ego has, indeed, learnt and is willing to learn new ways of adjustment to experience. Yet all these attempts are still ego-controlled. They still refer to the upper layers of being, to the neck of the vase and not to its containing depth. They do not question the essential factor: the quality of the ego himself, the value and meaning of his authority or privileges. They are like the reforms granted by an autocratic king, believing himself ruler by "divine right", to his awakened and rebellious people. They seek to trans-form without trans-substantiating. They offer palliatives rather than a cure. They meet the tidal mutations of destiny with new devices, new techniques, new forms of worship or rules of conduct. By doing so, they are instruments of resistance against the fatality of metamorphosis. Through these efforts the ego seeks feverishly, withal unconsciously, to block the impending evolutionary change, to delay the inevitable. He frustrates life or God by inventing biological procedures or new gods.

Does this mean, then, that the ego is to abdicate and renounce its rule; that he should let the amorphous powers of the unconscious erupt to the surface of being and sweep away all the structures of his reign? In some cases, such revolutionary upheavals may be unavoidable. They should not, however, be considered the ideal solution; for they tend to create a vacuum, into which reactionary forces may rush, violently defeating the purposes of life. What is needed, during the crises which Virgo symbolizes, is "transfiguration" even more than "transformation". The substance of consciousness and selfhood is to be renewed; and with this renewal, undertoning it, goes necessarily a re-statement of purpose.

The structures of the ego may be retained, but the purpose of these structures and of the ego himself must be renewed; the dark and heavy contents of the consciousness must become effulgent and light. Social mechanisms -- from colleges to factories -- may likewise withstand the crisis that comes to a civilization at a certain stage of its development; but the purpose they serve and the use to which they are put in the total economy of society should be changed utterly. At such times, the elite may not experience the "purge" of revolutions; yet its achievements should be given new meaning and purpose. Ownership for the sake of the owner should change into management for the sake of the community -- just as the self-seeking and jealous attitude of the ego has eventually to be superseded by the compassionate and all-inclusive understanding of the Self.

The change, however, does not depend upon the invention of new devices and new forms of worship. It comes only as the substance of consciousness itself is changed. It comes through generalized and persisting new experiences, through the open-hearted acceptation of new relationships, through confrontation with new facts of life from which new symbols and new myths can be created by men of vision and understanding. It is true that new techniques and new machines serve to produce new experiences, to alter conditions of living, to force upon the inert minds commerce and communion with different minds. But the modern instruments of "progress" are only means to an end; and these means can easily be used by the ego or the selfish rulers of society to make their control more vicious and implacable -- thus defeating for a time the very purpose which brought them into being.

Whether we speak of "Fascism" or of the passionate rebellion of the ego against his transfiguration into the compassionate and inclusive Self, we refer to the same negative attitude toward a crisis which constitutes the main turning point in the evolution of humanity or of an individual person. In this century we are witnessing the "Civil War of Man" -- and likewise no individual can reach true maturity until he or she experiences within his or her total being such a "civil war". History and psychology reveal the same facts; and just as the old Hindu sages used the events of the "Great War" of several millenia ago to symbolize the spiritual crisis faced by the individual who dares to focus the evolution of the human race within his own personality, so, the day will come when inspired thinkers will present to their generations the various colossal struggles of our days as potent symbols of the individual crisis which makes mere men aspirants to divinity.

The Hindu "Great War" and its climax, the battle of Kurukshetra, saw the destruction for centuries of the "warrior caste" in India, and as a result the beginning of a great Age of Philosophy, which reached its culmination centuries later with the coming of the Buddha. Our global "Great Wars" will, we trust, lead likewise to an era of peace in which mankind will, at long last, meet creatively and joyfully the challenge of global maturity.

For this to happen, humanity must face squarely the vast evolutionary issues of this day and of days yet to come. And first of all, our generations must give up their belief in the illusion that our recent wars have been merely wars between nations -- for this illusion is the great psychological "escape" of our age, the tragic historical fallacy which could sap the very strength necessary for mankind to arise into a new stage of world-wide evolution. It is an illusion based on the heresy of "national sovereignty" and on the refusal to understand the necessity there is to transfigure the very substance of social relationships everywhere. Nationalism parallels egoism. Both can only remain as integral parts of the civilization of tomorrow if they are thoroughly transsubstantiated and utterly renewed in purpose and in will.

This is our crisis. This is our Virgo challenge. This is our need. And to this need the spirit answers with a word of profound, but little understood, meaning: Tolerance.

If anyone today speaks of tolerance, his hearers are likely to think of a kind of attitude of mind or feeling which is in contrast to the practice of sharp criticism and fanaticism. To be tolerant of the opinions, feelings and habits of others is indeed to allow every man the right to live and to think as he sees fit. But real tolerance goes far deeper than such an attitude of "live and let live" which often is not without a strong taint of smugness and self-centered indifference to anything but one's own truth.

Tolerance is not the absence of intolerance. It does not mean simply to give up finding fault with what everyone else thinks, feels or does. It means etymologically "to bear". To bear what? -- the burden of the necessity for change and for growth. To be tolerant is to bear the responsibility of an incessant quest for broader knowledge, less constricted feelings, and a more adjustable behavior. It means the ability to stand up in readiness and with open heart when God knocks at the door and summons the individual -- and the nation -- to their greater destinies. It is the ability to grow by becoming ever more inclusive.

Tolerance is not a negative virtue. It is a positive and conscious attitude which refers to oneself and one's beliefs far more than to some other person or opinion. With Virgo, the zodiacal hemicycle which began in Aries comes to an end. The gift of the spirit to the Aries type of activity is that of "adaptability". But at the Aries stage of human response to life adaptability operates essentially at the instinctive, or at least actional, level. It should become, at the Virgo stage, a clear realization that no truth is complete or even real which does not include its opposite -- and all that occurs in between!

This realization alone can be the foundation for true tolerance. Tolerance is the willingness to accept the crucifixions which are the unavoidable results of the acceptation of all opposites, the necessary prelude to inclusiveness and integration. It is the dynamic essence of man's conscious growth -- the path to divinity.

Tolerance, compassion and charity are the three great virtues whose gifts bless the path of the Virgo type of person -- and to a greater or lesser extent, of every human being. Tolerance is more of the mind, compassion more of the heart, charity more of the realm of action; yet all three are manifestations of the same deep root, the willingness to grow by experiencing and assimilating always more numerous and varied aspects of truth, of love and of sacrificial action.

To the intolerant, there can be no expansion of intelligence and understanding. To the man lacking in compassion, spiritual death must forever beckon -- death from a constricted heart. He who cannot face the future in a sacrificial relinquishment of his bondage to the past, can never reach the full stature of his inmost divinity.

These three great virtues bless the Virgo path, because on this path there is especially need of them. On this path of crisis and personal re-orientation, it is easy so to concentrate on the tribulations at hand that the obstacles to growth are magnified at the expense of the clear realization of the purpose which the crisis should reveal to the man who accepts it without resentment, rebellion or anguish. The Virgo type's preoccupation with details of work, with technique, with health and hygiene, with analytical vivisections of himself and others, is actually a focalization on negative values of crisis. All these traditional characteristics of the Virgo type should be shown clearly for what they are: palliatives and substitutes for the one great effort really needed.

Nietzsche once described cryptically the paradoxical nature of this effort when he spoke of the need to "jump beyond one's shadow." One might also speak of it symbolically as a peculiar process of drinking from a glass of water in which the glass itself is swallowed with the water.

What these two symbols mean essentially is that the great crisis of personal growth coming under the symbolism of Virgo implies not only a change in the c o n t e n t s of the body or ego, but an entirely new approach to the c o n t a i n e r itself. To purify the body or the ego is not enough. To absorb the shadow they cast, to "jump beyond" and thus resolve or dissipate it: such is the great problem to the solution of which the crisis of personal metamorphosis should be dedicated. Likewise, the spiritualized consciousness of the fully mature individual must not only illumine and assimilate the energies (the "water") of the ego. It must also a s s i m i l a t e t h e ego h i m s e l f (the "glass" containing the water).

This mysterious and puzzling operation underlies all lesser efforts characterizing the Virgo phase of human evolution. It is the "great work" of the true Alchemists. Men who at long last have reached this step in their evolution often recoil, be it in fear or lack of understanding. They seek teachers and "Masters" to solve for them this haunting mystery. They scrutinize every detail of their past, analyze their feelings and strive after "delayed reactions" in the vain hope that somehow, in some manner, they will find, or be given, a magic key. They seek everywhere. They look in all directions -- except one: the direction of their shadow. The path to divinity is through one's shadow. The way to assimilate all truth is to assimilate the ego that seeks to know all truth.

Words cannot say more. The crisis must be won by being lived. The rose ever blooms at the center of the cross. God is found where the divine in man has "assumed" that man -- and the shadow of that man.

EASE

All the signs of the zodiac are balanced around the equinoctial axis which links Aries and Libra. And all the gifts that spirit can ever make to the individual eager to participate as an individual in the vast ritual of cosmic activity revolve around two precious virtues: adaptability and ease. These are the two essential marks of the person in whom spirit acts, radiating thence in "gift-waves" of light. What "adaptability" is to the novice in spiritual living, "ease" is to the man of more mature experience ready to establish himself and his work among his peers.

At the beginning of the path, when the individual faces the challenges which necessarily meet his determination to emerge from the womb of the collective and to act from his own center, the greatest need is adaptability. He must, first of all, survive. He must not betray himself and his innermost goal to the powers of collective mankind which seek to reduce every individual to the average and the unconscious. He must not seek to ram with impatient eagerness and adolescent egocentrism the "defenses in depth" of society. He must learn to adjust and adapt himself to the over-all need of the times, to "camouflage" his purpose and to beat his will into pliable steel.

When half of the journey around himself -- and his world -- is made, he has learnt many a lesson. To his ever-changing needs, the spirit has answered with varied and wondrous gifts. He finds himself, now, rather sure of himself. But what of other men? Heretofore, he had seen them somewhat as dangers on the path, as material for conquest and over-

coming. Meeting them, he had felt, above all, he was en-
countering his own objectivized nature -- human nature. And
the last lesson he learnt has been that of "tolerance", the realization that total growth in selfhood meant giving up the limitations and the rigidity of ego-centered judgments and welcoming all that was different, yet assimilable.

Inclusiveness, however, is a great strain on the mind and
the feelings. Meeting with equals, with human beings who also
claim to have arisen as individuals from the womb of the collective -- meeting with them the better to work toward a goal
held in common, notwithstanding superficial differences, this
indeed presents serious difficulties. The self-assurance of
the youthful individual may vanish suddenly as he becomes
fully and vitally aware of the fact that society is not only something to take from; it is, in its higher expression, a form of
co-operation and of sharing -- a give-and-take in relationship.

Inclusiveness of unfamiliar points of view may be difficult;
but full relatedness with unfamiliar people is even less easy.
The delegate to an international conference may have been all
his life very tolerant of the peculiarities of thought of Asiatic
culture, but he may find himself rather embarrassed when
discussing, and even more sharing everyday living, with a
man who came from Tibet minus a European education!
But what of the intelligent and sensitive young man and woman finding themselves, with the usual lack of preparation,
faced with the personal problems of life together -- of cooperation in constant interchange? What greater blessing could
they ask from the spirit than the gift of "ease"?

This little word "ease" is rich with great depths of meaning. As it was with "tolerance", most definitions of it stress
only a negative meaning. But ease is not only freedom from
agitation, constraint, affliction, tension or fear. It is not
even merely a form of tranquillity or comfort, or facility in
performing this or that type of action. It is all these things;
but far more important still, it is the realization that "co-

operation" is more than mere "operation", that the whole is more than the parts and the sum-total of the parts. It is the sense of being lived by a greater life which embraces and contains all the components of a situation, or of a relationship of which one is a part.

The mystic seeking union with his God comes to realize the wondrous fact: "God lives me". God, the wholeness of the whole, operates in all the parts; and the mystic is at ease with the world, because as he meets the world he meets it within God. God does the meeting. If you and I vitally realize, and not only intellectually conceive, that we are both functioning parts of a whole, with the wholeness of which we have felt ourselves one -- how could there be lack of ease between us? What acts in us, is no longer I or you, but the created and the creating We; and, at the limit Man, or God. And this applies to every conceivable situation.

If I am a delegate of France and you are an Englishman in a world-conference, and if we meet in terms of the future world which it is our task to create, and not in terms of our pasts which we should forget, there will be ease between us. Ease is the absence of the ghosts of yesterday and the utter identification with an inclusive tomorrow. Ease is the refusal to be stymied by the things I do not know or have not done, and the utter conviction that if I and that new action to be performed are meeting in a particular situation, that situation includes me and the action, and will fulfill itself through me acting -- if only "I" am not interfering; the "I" that is full of ghosts.

Ease is an expression of totally accepted relatedness -- be it with an object, a situation or a person. It is the utter lack of mental reservation in approaching a relationship and the acts which this relationship demands; and a dancer is related to the floor, a speaker to his audience, a lover to his expectant mate, a participant in an international conference to humanity whose many faces he beholds around him. If any of these men holds for an instant a thought or feeling against his being related to whatever he faces, then, ease vanishes. Back of all resistances is some kind of fear. Selfishness is a form of fear; and so are most illnesses.

It is customary for people ever so little familiar with zodiacal symbols to speak of the fine social feelings of the Libra type of individuals. We should nevertheless realize that these feelings are in many cases attempts to hide fear. Deep inside of himself the Libra type could often find (if he only dared investigate) an unconscious, subtle but often most powerful, resistance against total relatedness. This resistance exists just because total relatedness is the step ahead for him. He senses subconsciously that it is so; and sensing it, fights it. If he attains social ease, it is essentially by overcoming this resistance and a sense of social inferiority -- just as the impulsive bravado of the Aries type is usually an over-compensation for a gnawing sense of personal insecurity.

Where the negative character of the Libra type has gained control, the sense of relatedness takes on exclusivistic and destructive forms. There is still a glorification of relationship, but of the type of relationship which is spiritual bondage, and, being inherently un-free, seeks subconsciously to bind and to absorb.

This occurs in relatively few cases, but one should realize that, in the Libra type of personality, real "ease" is not to be taken for granted. If it truly manifests, it is as a gift of the spirit -- and therefore, being a spirit-born manifestation, it both satisfies a vital need and has to overcome a subconscious fear. Where the overcoming takes place, the results are so much more radiant than in any other type of person; for what comes as a spiritual victory has always a creative and contagious quality found in no other way. Individual selfhood -- and, as well, history -- are never transformed except by victory; and there is no victory without struggle, and without faith in ultimate overcoming.

For many centuries, humanity has stressed and over-stressed the factor of "struggle" and the kind of faith in eventual victory symbolized by the tightened jaw and the clenched will. This strained performance has been understood, by most Westerners at least, to constitute "morality". It could hardly have been otherwise in a civilization that worshipped a crucified and bleeding Savior, whose agony and death redeems sins inherent in human nature! This concept of morality as the glorification of a desperately fighting will-to-be-good should nevertheless vanish under the dawning light of an age of abundance and plenitude of living, just as the image of a dying Christ should become superseded in the heart of men by that of the l i v i n g Christ whose yoke is easy, whose burden is light.

Morality as an expression of tenseness of mind and feeling leads to "dis-eases" of a constricted will, just as body illness inevitably follows physical strain and long-held cramped postures. Struggle may be necessary; but the one great struggle that brings health of soul and body is the effort to overcome inertia, spiritual indifference and the doubt that there will be a victory. Not a struggle a g a i n s t any particular entity, to be met with strained muscles, contracted heart and tightened will; but instead a struggle f o r understanding, inclusiveness, breadth of vision and greater light -- a struggle for an ever more relaxed sense of openness to life and to God. It is an effort, without it being a conflict. It is, more truly, a constantly deepening eagerness for identification of the ego with the greater Self.

The ego is what it is, and that only. The Self is all there is, focused for expression in the particular way defined by one's birth and environment. Egohood is exclusive. Selfhood is focalized wholeness. One can only grow in selfhood through inclusiveness; but through the degree of inclusiveness which matches one's capacity for a s s i m i l a t i n g what is being included and absorbed.

Assimilation is never satisfactory where there is tenseness, conflict and harsh pain. What is needed for tomorrow

are men who assimilate and put to constructive use the powers of the universe and of human nature; not men who fight
these powers. Men who tensely fight the world cannot creatively utilize the world. Men can only be free from nature by
fulfilling nature; by fulfilling it with ease, with elegance.

By "elegance" we mean that quality which the mathema-
tician has in mind when he speaks of "the elegant solution of
a mathematical problem" -- a solution which moves on with
extreme ease, with the utmost simplicity of means, with a
minimum of intermediate steps, with inherent logic. A red-
wood tree is likewise the elegant solution of the problem contained in its seed; a perfectly easy and logical development of
the life-potentialities inherent in this seed.

Natural growth of inherent potentialities, ease and logic
of development, elegance of unfoldment -- these are jewels of
the art of living; these are the tests of mastery. For the "Master" is the artist supreme in the noblest of all arts, the art
of living. And the art of living is the art of meeting all the
powers and all the challenges of human nature and of social-
collective living with ease, out of the fullness of a consciousness which is rich, serene and true to the seed-Self -- the end
and beginning of all human manifestation.

Such a living is the mark of the only aristocracy that matters; for the real aristocrat is the man who, being established
by tradition and a long ancestry in a full sense of participation
in the affairs of his nation or community, is a living expression of the basic type of adaptation-to-life of this nation or
community. He is a type, rather than an individual. He is
the collective whole expressing itself in an individualized body and mind. And how could that which represents the whole
display lack of ease while meeting the parts of this whole!

The true aristocrat can be servant as well as ruler. Like
Jesus he can wash the feet of his disciples with such ease and
inner elegance of feelings that the disciples, too, will find
themselves at ease. And this is the greatest proof of ease:
that everyone encountered will also be at ease, answering with

the fullness of his nature to the rich outpouring from the bestower of gifts.

Indeed the source of ease is to be found in every part of
the soul as of the body. Ease spreads from the center of being, only because the center has gathered to itself the harvest that has grown from the whole nature. Suppression, repression, a sense of inadequacy or of guilt, fea1, and the
pride born of fear -- all these products of a civilization theoretically stressing morality at all cost, and of a will burdened
with the belief in sin, are witnesses to a fundamental inability
to trust God and His promise of abundant living. They are
products of scarcity. Morality, as we traditionally know it, is scarcity of the spirit.

Gradually a morality of spiritual abundance will take form
among men. It will be a morality that is wholeness operating
through every part of the social organism; a morality refusing
to be haunted by the ghostly sins of individuals, and account-
ing every man responsible for every other man's failure; a
morality which will establish the spiritual priority of the whole
over the parts, and sing of relatedness fulfilled, where men
of old wailed for their individualized sins and frustrations.
The crowning glory of such a morality will be ease of living,
ease in being -- ease also in the antiphony of love.

Ease is the fragrance of a love so harmonious that the participants share one another wholly, in feelings and in deeds.
Ease is the fragrance of happiness. It is simplicity become
peace; peace singing to itself in the silence of consummated
living. As the vine unfolds its tendrils to reach for the light
and the sustaining tree, as the water flows gently through the
meadow it blesses with green abundance, as clouds dance in
the sky in multiform grace, likewise, their souls freed from
scarcity of love and poverty of spirit, their bodies joying in
the light and warmth of the sun, their minds gathering ideas
from gardens of divinity -- as bees gather the flowers' nec-
tar -- men and women of tomorrow shall know the wonder of
ease. They shall know it wholly; and knowing it, shall know
God.

NON-IDENTIFICATION

A moment comes in every life when the individual passion-
ately yearns to become identified with the beloved, and with
the togetherness that grows out of steady relationship and sustained group-feeling. Having perceived the ideal of comradeship glowing in the sky of social living, having accepted the
unknown that is beyond the landscaped gardens of the self, its
adventures and its promises, the human mind has become op-
en to the mighty winds that blow from the oceanic expanse of
the Unconscious. Above, is the soul and its great dreams;
below, the generic wholeness of humanity -- sky and sea,
ecstatic Images and tidal strength prolific with evolving lives.
The mind has caught the fever of immensity. The contagious
fervor of unity whirls through the safety-devices which insulated the precious mechanisms of the ego from the electric
potential of love. The one desire is now to be more than one
is by being different from what one is. To lose one's insularity and to blend with others; to give one's mind away in be-
trothal to the whole and to merge in the unity of souls; to fore-
go one's dreams and to flame forth with the vision of a Host
-- these are symptoms of the passion for identification that
seizes every individual in the wake of some crucial metamorphosis.

There are men who act this passion with such a compact
and compelling intensity that they become Avatars of Man-the-
whole, Incarnations of Man's divinity. There are men whose
being becomes so seized with the fecundant power of a great
human mutation, biological or spiritual, that they resound like

bells calling the multitudes to the new worship or the new advance. They are the prophets, the leaders and seers of humanity. But there are those also who are swept into elemental whirlpools that tear the very fabric of mind and body -- who sink into sexual disintegration and mental sadisms, eventually to become food for the dark Powers of the Unsouled.

In its simplest and most primordial form this great yearning for identification is known as sex -- and thus the zodiacal sign, Scorpio, has been traditionally linked with this basic activity in human experience. But sex -- in its conscious and human aspect -- is only the most elementary of the manifestations of an urge which sweeps through all the separate structures of the world of souls. Individual egos are just as susceptible to the passion for identification as biological organisms. The devotee who craves for complete self-surrender to his God, and the martyr who joyously dies in order to uphold the power of his Cause, give themselves just as surely to the objects of their loves as the woman in utter sexual abandon. The spirit of the moth goes into the flame which drew its passionate flight. Every soul is absorbed in that which it worships. Every consciousness becomes that with which it has consistently and fervently yearned to become identified.

The saying "As you think, so you become" is familiar to students of modern New Thought and of occult "metaphysics" in all ages. But a more accurate formulation would seem to be: As your passion for identification is, so will be the s u b - s t a n c e of your total being. To "think" is not sufficient a means normally to effect a total transformation of being. At the Libra stage of evolution men "think" and even "act out" comradeship. They see the great vision and step into the circle of the great Dreamers. But not until the individual has experienced the passion for identification and the fire of "union" can his thinking and his dreams become himself, and he become them.

Nor is the term "self-surrender" adequate to express this mystery ritual of the all-consuming Fire. What is being "surrendered" is not the self, but the desire of the ego to remain separate; and one should not confuse the d e s i r e to remain separate with the power to stand as a witness even to one's own fiery death. The owner of the house surrenders his ownership, but not the house. He becomes the manager and trustee for the new owner, Man -- or God. He surrenders the boundaries of his fears, and gains participation in the being of the universe. This, at least, is the goal; but few attain it. It is easier to die the death of the moth.

All spiritual living is a paradox. He who wishes to make his great dream live must become identified with the dream, and he who wishes to become divine must love God with all-consuming passion. Yet, the dreamer must remain a witness to his dream, if he is to avoid being absorbed by the very shadow of his ideal; and the devotee cannot "know" God except he remains as container of divinity. Identification can only succeed through the non-identification of the consciousness with the process of identification. To be consumed by the Fire, and nevertheless be tender of the flame -- this is the goal. And this goal can only be reached by using this most magical gift of the spirit: the power of non-identification.

At the level of biological function, identification is of rhythm with rhythm. From the sexual center the dynamic pattern of union spreads in concentric circles until every nerve and every cell is touched by the fire. At the level of personal being, we know this process of at-one-ment as love; identification is of psychic and mental substance. The self is absorbed into the relationship.

At the level of consciousness, the ego identifies itself with Images -- Images projected by great creative Intelligences, fed by the power of collective living, and enhanced by the devotion of a group of men, dead or alive. Some of these Images are entities with perennial lives within the collective Unconscious of nations, of religious groups and of humanity as a whole; and the power of these great Images can overwhelm the ego weary of the burden of its own selfhood. So many men, through so many centuries, have paid homage to these idols within the depths or the skies of collective mankind, have given to them the very substance of their souls! The images become indeed maelstroms of psychic energy.

A Mussolini dreams of power as a compensation for an acute and neurotic sense of social inferiority; and lo! his consciousness is drawn to the potent magnet of the Caesar Image. The barriers of his rational mind bend under the inflow of power. A people's unconscious, that for so long had gravitated in the dark toward the glory-Image, becomes massed for action as the Image is given once more conscious shape by the passion of a man whose ego, now, has become identified with the idol.

Here the identification is almost total and devastating. The devotee dies for his god, and with him, countless millions. But, if the god may be one fed by brutal power and by lust, he may be also an Image of light; he may be an amazing cosmic Being, such as have been worshipped by countless devotees of Star-Gods in ancient (and even modern) times. The greater the power of the Images, the greater the danger of total identification of the ego with this idol. And vast is the number of idols which draw to their hoary shrines the consciousness of weak or frightened, loving or desperate humans!

All men, women and children are living within a psychological sea teeming with countless Images with which they may become identified. Identification may signify weakness; it may reveal strength. Identification should be a stage of growth. The man established in spirit, secure in his individual Identity, journeys through it. Consciously, he enacts the part outlined by the Images. He is the fire, and he is the hearth. He is contained, and he is container. Though his entire being vibrates under the inrush of power, yet does he remain firm, knowing. He contains power as an engine contains explosive bursts of molecules. He enfolds and he uses that power which multitudes of lesser men have poured into the Image in passionate uncontrolled identification.

The power of non-identification bestowed upon man by the spirit is the power, not of self-containment, but of containment by the Self. Many definitions of the Self have been attempted, but the Self essentially eludes definition because only that which has a particular form can be defined, and the Self is the power to create at all times the form necessary to contain just the kind of power flooding a consciousness in the condition of identification with some Image of the Unconscious. The Self is the power to contain and to use any kind of power. It is the power not to be identified with the results of any and all identifications.

There must be identification if there is to be fullness of substance and power to use. Man must dare to lose his soul in order to reach the condition in which he can make use of the protean Soul of the Whole. He must dare to drink the glass as well as the water, and to find himself as nothing, before he may hope to gain the ability to utilize everything. This ability is the Self.

The Self is spirit in act, because spirit is that which acts wherever there is need for action -- which means, everywhere! The Self is the eternal Performer. It is "action through form" -- any necessary action through any available form. He who has the power to perform any necessary action through any available form, and the power to restrain from performing any action that is not necessary: such a one is Self. He is spirit in act. He is free from identification, because he can use the powers born of identification with any Image necessary for whatever performance is required of him.

To perform effectively the action required of a father a man has to become so identified with the Image of fatherhood that he appears to his children as the Father. The great lover is he who can incorporate in his being the eternal image of woman's desire. All spectacular living is living in the name of an Image, or a god; for only such a living can command the allegiance of groups and collectivities. It is the

Myth which triumphs, not the personality which has become invested with the power of the mystical Image. Great spiritual personages are, however, individuals who recast the form of the Myth into the mould of their own individual victories. They become identified with the Myth, but in them and from them, the Myth is born anew.

Jesus did incorporate the Image of "the Jewish Prophet". He became identified with it -- yet he remained separate. He gave to the Image a new meaning, a new purpose, from the creative center of Self; and this made him Christ. In Jesus we see the identification; in Christ, the spiritual power of non-identification. This is what is really meant, psychologically, by the double appellation, "son of Man" and "son of God". God can only be reached through Man and through unreserved identification with human destiny. But he only can reach God who remains established in his own spiritual Identity, even while being burnt in the fire of his identification with humanity. In this achievement the magic of the ideal Scorpio is fulfilled in perfection.

The technique which leads to this is essentially the technique of ritual performance. In this technique, forms are built which give to the individual, or the group, the ability to contain the power released during the process of identification with the great Images of the Unconscious. These forms (structures of behavior, verbal formulations, consecrated gest - ures, tone-sequences, etc.) acquire resistant strength through exact repetition. They become containers of psychic power. They bind the will and attention of men, as chemistry binds molecules in the making of plastics. They are -- if true to the spirit -- the means whereby individuals can dare to meet unreservedly the powers born of relationship -- social and international, as well as sexual and personal -- without being "un-selved" by these powers.

Such ritualistic processes may apply to a man-woman unit, to a group of ceremonialists, to a nation, to humanity at large. They are as varied as are the requirements of particular pro-

blems of human relationship. While they change with places
and eras, yet some fundamentals are found true anywhere and
at any time -- for these are expressions of the very structure
of generic man.

There are times, however, during which a strong stress
is placed upon the ritualistic e v o c a t i o n of Images and powers by human groups trained for this purpose; and during
such periods individuals are intent upon arousing latent powers into the over-conscious or over-stable average ego. At
other times there is no outstanding need for such an arousal,
because the Images are almost spontaneously breaking to the
surface of the consciousness. Then, the emphasis is placed
upon the i n v o c a t i o n of the spirit -- and the insistent demand of men is for the power of non-identification, which
alone can promise salvation from the tragic storms of the collective.

Evocative techniques lead to complex forms of rituals,
and involve the co-operation of groups, small or large. In-
vocative techniques stress the concentrated action of the individual, largely on the plane of the mind. The former manifest in ceremonials of all kinds -- in the fields of occult or
religious action, in politics, in business, in war or victory.
The latter operate mostly through what is known as prayer or
occult meditation, or through individual artistic-literary expression.

In essence, the "invocation" is a call to the spirit; and as
spirit always answers every vital need when the soul's gates
are kept open to the spiritual inflow, this call is most effective where the need is greatest and most acutely realized.
For this reason, the great saint is often a man whose early
life has known the fiercest tragedies of "sin"; and the creative
genius, a man whose personality poignantly lacks the very
elements which give greatness to his message.

This is the glory and the tragedy of the human individual
-- the mystery of man "before the threshold"; for man's power resides in his contrasts and his ability to will himself

whole while most crucially torn by conflicts or polarities of feeling. Thus the most profound act of will is the will to become empty, that the spirit may fill the poignant void -- the will to be earth, that God may answer with His sky and His lightnings -- the will to compel God into incarnation, thus integrating the highest heights and the deepest depths. Man is contrast and paradox, the eternal chiaroscuro of light and shade. He is at his greatest where his dynamic passion is most acute, yet his wholeness most inclusive; when, in his soul, opposites forever meet in rhythmic and creative interplay.

Man is the moving passion of the universe. There is nothing so deep he cannot yearn to experience in crucial identifications. And there is no depth that the spirit may not reach through the man poised in Self and serene at the core of all storms. Man is the fire and the hearth, the log and the sacrifice, the devotee and the sacrificer. All things are possible through man, evocator of power, invoker of power, invoker of God. All things are possible "with God".

COMRADESHIP:

THE ART OF LIVING TOGETHER

Consciousness develops in human beings on the basis of experience and of the feelings stimulated by experience. It develops through formulations of various kinds; through words, through conventionalized and meaningful gestures, through concepts and, in general, through the infinitely varied relationships of human society.

The state of living in society is, we believe, natural to human beings; nevertheless, the development of a truly s o - c i a l consciousness is gradual, both in terms of the historical growth of human communities and with reference to the slow unfoldment of the child's and adolescent's mentality. What comes first is the development of a p e r s o n a l consciousness which is based upon instinctual drives and biological-generic experiences. This phase corresponds to the first half of the sequence of zodiacal signs, from Aries to Virgo -- Virgo being a phase of readjustment and critical metamorphosis.

Aries and Taurus refer in astrological symbolism to those impulsions and urges in which the unconscious bio-psychic powers of human nature find their expressions. They correspond to the dawn of human history, to the tribal stage during which man's consciousness strives to emerge from its undifferentiated state of subjective identification with the universe and the energies of nature. The result of these strivings toward a more objective perception, classification and organization of the experienced world is the phase of human development represented by the zodiacal sign, Gemini -- the sign of intellectualized consciousness, of verbal formulations, and of all the mental activities through which the human being emerges as a more or less individualized person. The summer solstice symbolizes the acme of personal differentiation and the triumph of the will to be a separate ego, center of a small universe through the space of which it can spread in solar and self-sufficient glory.

While the spring quarter of the year symbolizes the trend toward individual differentiation and singularization, the fall quarter, on the other hand, suggests, by the very nature of the experiences it brings to men in northern temperate zones, the need there is for human beings to come together in terms of common requirements, collective aspirations, and communal cultural values. The fall is a time of withdrawal and ingathering. The fruits of spring and summer labors are collected to insure future livelihood. Work in the fields is brought to an end.

Then men begin to seek permanent shelter from nature -- physical nature, at first, but also psychic-emotional nature. They realize that the fact of being drawn together so as to withstand better the cold and darkness of long winters brings about progressively a new type of experiences and realizations. Out of the sharing of shelter and of food, then of plans, ideals and values, social consciousness is born.

We see the first realization of it during the Libra phase of growth, as the symbolic joining of hands.

In Scorpio, the joining of hearts and of creative powers is the substance of a new realm of experience; while, with Sagittarius, men reach the phase of the joining of minds. Social consciousness finds its own field of operation, and civilization emerges from nature. Within the framework of logic, concepts are abstracted from perceptions -- as wine and intoxicants are extracted from the fruits of the dark earth, their fermentation held within resistant containers.

Philosophical and abstract concepts, ideas and systems are the quintessence of generalized experiences. They are made possible by the creation of language, of words which hold and release the power generated by men's reactions to common experiences. Through words, the results of experiences become t r a n s f e r a b l e. These words make possible communication between men not immediately concerned by particular facts of their environment. Above all, language -- especially once it is r e c o r d e d -- becomes the means to "bind time" (Korzybsky) and to overcome death. Communication between successive generations, as well as between men of distant lands, is made possible. Civilization develops, characterized by a constant and insistent urge to link the most distant factors in human experience, even those that are still wrapped in the womb of imagined futurity.

This preoccupation with the distant, the future and the abstract is the mark of civilization, in the strictest sense of the term. Civilization is necessarily the overcoming of nature, because nature is always absorbed in immediate action and reaction; it is localized and personal. Even where a natural action is often repeated, each performance nevertheless reaches the consciousness of the purely "natural" being as a new and single phenomenon. This gives vitality to the performance -- a sort of life-and-death challenge -- but it binds to the particular; the results of the "natural" experience cannot be transferred verbally or abstractly, except through the memory of unusual deeds.

Civilization, on the other hand, deals with the t r a n s - f e r a b l e essence of experiences, with those factors which escape time-determination and the singular character of unique facts. Civilization is the organization of generalities and universal values. It is man's common humanity raised to the level of consciousness and meaning, formulated in symbols which are significant wherever human beings live and experience the world of total reality.

The universalistic and timeless character of civilization has however negative possibilities. The one limitation imposed upon civilization is its very challenge to limitations. The fact that it deals with universals makes it potentially destructive of the health and sanity of particular individuals. Its timelessness makes it impotent and disintegrating whenever the living core of an individual's experience is at stake. The transferability of its values, standards and achievements make them inadequate in any dealing with unique occasions in the lives of single individuals. Because they fit everywhere, at any time, they touch nowhere and at no time that center of reality in the individualized person which is quickened by the spirit.

Spirit, in its deepest expression, deals with individual persons, in an individual way, meeting individual needs. It speaks to human beings who have given an individual meaning to their humanity. It speaks within the soul. It is the One speaking to a one. All spirit-conditioned transfers are from the uniqueness of another self. The substance of the transfer belongs to all; it is universal. But the living act of transference is from individual to individual. There is no test-tube impregnation in the realm of the spirit! The gift of the deific power admits of no standardization. It is a personal gift -- however impersonal the substance of the gift and the power bestowed.

This is something which needs to be recalled often to a humanity who has gone, often with fanatical vehemence, to the side of civilization and of universal -- because intellectually abstract -- ideals. Big theories and world-wide schemes can be, and have often been, destructive of the welfare and of the lives of individuals. The most universalistic religions have been the most fanatical in their proselytic zeal. The most embracing truths have crucified the greatest number of people who either were not ready for them, or demanded the right to experience and formulate these truths according to their own individual temperament.

It is indeed easy for the civilizer and universalist to forget that the most exalted or most valid ideas must always reach
the core of individuals' experiences, if these ideas are to be
vital and spiritually radiant. To those who would thus forget
the humanity of the persons whom they seek to convert by any
means available to some great (or not-so-great) vision, the
most essential gift which the spirit can offer is the gift of
c o m r a d e s h i p.

Comradeship is the practice of cooperative and warm living with other human beings treated as h u m a n persons. It
is the art of living together -- with the accent upon the word
"living". To be a comrade to other individuals is to meet
them in terms of their individual needs and characters, at
the level, not of abstractions or dogmatic beliefs, but of concrete, actual, everyday living. It is to meet them as unique
persons through unique occurrences requiring unique forms
of cooperation and understanding. It is to meet them creatively -- the spirit in every one acting directly upon, and responding vitally and fully to, the spirit in all the others.

Etymologically, comrades are individuals who live and act
within one room (c a m e r a). They may work in one room, or
sleep in one room; but, whatever makes them comrades in
name, the essential fact of comradeship is the sharing of common activities and common everyday problems of living within a well-defined space. The space may be a small room, a
palace, a city, or the entire planet; but comradeship implies
living together within boundaries of some sort -- and, what is
more, living together, not because of a common past or ancestry, but above all because of common activities and, ideally, because of a common purpose.

Men who live together within a confining space must learn
to consider one another with essential respect and tolerance.
More than anything else, they must consider one another as
h u m a n beings, and not as automatons guided by abstract
principles or dogmas, repeating blindly words, ideas and gestures. They must learn to understand each other as individ-

ual persons, not as servants of some social Cause, or of a
jealous God and his priests.

True comradeship operates at a level where fanaticism
and narrow bigotry cannot exist. It operates where all relationships can be simple, direct and rich with an immediacy of
response to human feelings and individual needs; where there
is no pride of position, or pride of sex, or psychological ob-
structions thwarting the flow of sympathy from individual core
to individual core. The practice of comradeship is an art,
one of the finest and most exacting of all arts, because it demands of the comrades a creative approach to human relationships, a keen sense of attention to details, an objective
technique of mutual give-and-take, and a realization of meaning and purpose in those activities which have brought the comrades together in bed-room, army barrack, club, restaurant,
factory, or Parliament.

Comradeship demands essentially that no one of the comrades takes anything for granted in their relationship, or in himself! And this requirement alone makes of comradeship a most difficult among all arts.
Just as the creative painter, when confronted with a landscape,
is able to see every part of the scene as if he had never seen
any such object before, with a fresh and direct response to
the color and form of whatever he contemplates -- so the real
comrade is the person able to meet at every moment those
who share his activities and his "living space" as if they were
always new to him, always vibrant with fresh vitality, with
unique facets of humanity, with significant vistas and energizing responses to the challenge of common living.

Indeed, comradeship is a most exacting art; and whoever
acts according to set and conventional patterns, following rigid precepts or binding dogmas, or being stirred by fanatical
devotion to gods or ideas existing of themselves outside the
immediacy of the living situation, such a one cannot be a true
comrade. He may be a remarkably effective partisan or a
devotee capable of flaming martyrdom. He may be superbly

efficient as an individual worker, a boss or a servant; but he cannot be truly a "comrade".

Comradeship is both the apex of social consciousness and the spiritual antidote against the negative aspects of an over-civilized society.   To the constant drive of civilization to-ward abstract generalization and remote goals, contemptuous of the means used to reach these goals, comradeship answers with a profound respect for the dignity of every human person and for the values born of concrete interchanges and shared feelings.   It always seeks to base the struggle for distant re-sults upon the human foundation of neighborliness, friend-ship and a psychological understanding of those who are near. Comradeship is the glorification of the near in a world dedi-cated to the pursuit of far-flung goals and universal values. It is based on the intimacy of personal being in a society de-personalized by machines, apartment-houses, movies and 5-and-10 cent stores.   It is indeed the answer to the most poig-nant need of our Western civilization.

It is particularly the great gift of the spirit to whomever is filled with the impersonal intensity, the fanaticism or the ruthless efficiency so often associated with the type of behav-ior and consciousness signified by Sagittarius.   Jovial and fond of outdoor activities, the Sagittarian type of person may be, at times; but these expansive and social characteristics hide in a great many cases a stubborn drive toward the achieve-ments of social, religious or managerial results at the ex-pense of personal and human values.   Social goals are found to be more important than the welfare and freedom of indivi-duals.   Abstractions (or even verbalisms and formulas) are given prominence over living beings.   The religious leader is willing to destroy human personalities in order to "save their souls" according to his concept of salvation and spirituality. A nation is preserved, but millions in it die of hunger.   Aban-doned Asiatic children are rescued across thousands of miles of water, but the slums a block away are taken for granted as parts of a traditional social system.

This is the ransom of civilization and of Western man's restless quest for that which is always beyond: the Sagittarian quest for God -- or for gold. The Medieval period knew well this lure of the beyond. Its Conquistadores and its Inquisitors came mostly from a Sagittarian land, Spain. Seeking God, they destroyed human values. Dreaming of spiritual life, they tortured their bodies and distorted their essential humanity. And today, we too, on the whole, have forgotten the meaning of the simplest and most immediate human contacts, whether it be in our cities, our armies or our homes.

Once a prophet, whose voice rose at the beginning of an epoch of ruthless industrialization, sang to us, of the West, songs of comradeship and of faith in individuals. Walt Whitman is gone, but his magnificent voice still vibrates amidst our mechanized lives. The song of comradeship cannot, must not, die. It is an essential gift of the spirit. It is a blessing that we should all receive with hearts fresh and warm, vibrant with eternal human youth. Ours it is to become adept in the art of living together, as comrades and friends. Ours it is, at the dawn of the age of global civilization and atomic bombs, to radiate in our every day the love, the great love of the comrades. For however far man's mind may soar, it is the heart and the love of humans that is the indestructible foundation of creative tomorrows. Comradeship is the living substance of all civilization true to the spirit. It is the Divine singing at the core of human relationships.

PERSONAL INTEGRITY

At the winter solstice the trend toward collective action and socialization of feelings and of thoughts reaches its apex. Civilization, the organization of generalities and of universal values, triumphs. It is exalted in the average citizen of vast social organisms -- cities, states or confederations -- in which races and minds blend, and separate cultures are lost. Civilization makes for standardization and the catering to those desires, impulses and interests common to most men. Yet these common human factors are strangely perverted, thwarted and emasculated in our metropoles. What universality of thinking and behavior there is is reached at the cost of an indifference toward, or an effective suppression of the distinctions and contrasts which stimulate character and the use of creative powers. The transferable nature of all civilized values, while it makes them fit theoretically every person and every age, permeates the products of civilization with the vapid sentimentality of popular songs and motion pictures. Even man's loves become curiously transferable and un-individualized, reaching up blandly toward the "pin-up girl" ideal.

With the winter solstice, the zodiacal sign Capricorn begins. It is traditionally a symbol of political action; but it also witnesses the birth of the Christ. Caesarism and Christhood: the organization of empires or federated states, and the gospel of the inconquerable dignity and uniqueness of the human individual -- how deep and poignant the contrast, how significant a theme for our meditations! But no one can truly resolve these opposites of human evolution unless one comes

to the realization that, in man, two essential o r d e r s   o f
a c t i v i t y co-exist.   One of them refers to the progressive
evolution of personal and social "forms of living"; the other,
to the transforming and creative activity of spirit in response
to the need of the particles of humanity let loose and disintegrated as a result of this evolution. What we call so inadequately "human nature" is the result of the dynamic interplay
of these two life-streams.

The "psycho-mental" order has its origin, in terms of zodiacal symbolism, at the summer solstice and in the sign of
Cancer, ruled by the Moon; the "spiritual" order issues forth
during the Christmas period of the year from the sign of Capricorn.   Both types of activity operate throughout the year,
but with varying and compensatory degrees of intensity. Likewise in every one of the twelve types of "human nature" defined by the basic characteristics of the twelve signs of the
zodiac we find that the spirit-aroused and psycho-active traits
interact and seek outer expression in organic or social behavior in contrasting ways.

Man, in his psycho-mental being, is ceaselessly striving
toward more inclusive forms of organization; yet, as he does
so, he always takes in much more than he can actually assimilate and integrate, and he becomes the victim of the aroused
energies of his still undifferentiated or long repressed depths.
The organization becomes big, top-heavy with intellectual gen-
eralizations and standardizing regulations. It absorbs masses
of elements which but superficially respond to the integrative
rhythm of the organizing mind. In order to hold them in check ,
more regulations, more generalities, more formulas are produced, which apply to nothing in particular because they have
to apply to everything in general.   The over-conscious ruling
elite loses real touch with the rootless, aroused and demand-
ing, but fundamentally unconscious, masses; to their rest-
lessness it can give no vital and truly integrative solution --
only palliatives.

This is then the moment of greatest challenge to the spirit.

A new l o g o s, a new "word of power", a new creative meaning, a new quality of humanhood must be projected into the
seething chaos of those parts of human nature and of society
which cannot become actually integrated by the over-expanded
and over-generalized "form of living" constituting collectively
the state or the universal empire. The spirit must act with a
fresh momentum and impregnate the masses of a disintegrating organism. It must establish a new rhythm, a new era;
and, in order to do this, it must incorporate itself in those
few portions of human nature -- in those few individuals living
in the over-civilized society -- that can respond to this descent of the fecundative power and vision. Christ and his followers take birth in the Roman Empire of the Caesars.

    In the Capricorn type of human nature and temperament
we find at work the same precarious balance of forces which
characterized the early Roman Empire. Then, new types of
personal and social "forms of living" had reached their maturity, and the momentum of their growth was drawing into
them an enormous mass of really unassimilable human substance. The collective Roman mind which had created these
new "forms of living" had to stop creating, for it was over-
occupied with the problem of organizing the heterogeneous
materials (peoples, cultures, religions) it had absorbed. A
new creation had to come, in a polar relationship to the products of the Roman mind -- a creation of the spirit. The spirit of Christ's message was an answer to the need of the millions drawn into the Empire, yet unable vitally to accept the
Roman "forms of living", however much they might assent to
them intellectually and in outer behavior.

    This situation is at least partly duplicated by the one con-
fronting the world at this time. Anglo-American democracy
has produced "forms of living" (political and cultural) which
tend to spread all over the world. The peoples subjected to
this deliberate or matter-of-fact propaganda are asked to assent to and imitate these democratic "ways of life" which we
Americans feel sure are the best possible -- at least in so

far as their basic principles are concerned. Back of the asking is the power of America, which has been symbolized in the eyes of countless millions by the atomic bomb. Therefore, the world at large may have to answer as the Mediterranean and the Germanic world answered to the Rome of the Caesars.

Can our form of democracy fill the need of Asia or Africa? Did it fill the need of Germany, of Italy, even of France, after the first World War? What is giving power to our democratic institutions and way of life is the typical character of our people and of our past history; what has held Great Britain firm so long is the character and traditions of England. Transport these institutions to Africa or South Asia; and the relative chaos these lands know today will not be transformed automatically into order -- no more than the Roman philosophy of social organization and the Roman way of life brought real social order to Egypt, Syria, or to the countries of the Franks and the Teutons.

Man is essentially triune. In him there is a psycho-mental life which builds individual "forms of living" from small seeds of thought into mature ways of behavior and thought. In him, too, there is an instinctual physiological life and old half-repudiated ancestral traditions, which are filled with confusion, contradictory pulls, uncertainties and unconscious fears -- especially after the ebullience of youth has vanished.

This chaos will not become ordered and harmonized by the conscious mind and its individualized "forms of living"; the less so, the more the individual has expanded into a variety of fields and absorbed, but not assimilated, a great complexity of experiences. What is needed to bring about real personal integration is an act of the spirit, a divine Incarnation within the total personality. The need is not for better or more thoroughly organized "forms of living" -- more managers, more bureaucrats and stronger policemen of the individualized consciousness -- but rather for a new spiritual quality, a new logos.

The individual's "forms of living" may be of use -- and we know, for instance, how Roman Law remained the legalistic foundation of the Christian European world. But what regenerates and integrates, what stamps an essential character of order and purpose upon the future personality or society are not the slowly matured products of the psycho-mental or cultural life, but the rhythm and the living example of the incorporated spirit -- not the Roman "way of life" developed through five centuries of Roman history, but the gospel of Christ and the new quality of the spirit Christ incarnated and demonstrated as Jesus.

Today, once more the world of man is a chaos of disintegrating cultures, religious and political entities. The Anglo-American mind -- with its essential European, and particularly French, roots -- has produced a way of life, a typical kind of political structure (a universally copied Constitution, etc.), a democratic pattern of rights and culture. Yet this mind and its products have not in themselves the power to integrate the present world-chaos. The integration, which must become global in the centuries yet to come, can only be brought about by an act of the creative, divine spirit, by a new logos focusing a new potentiality of Man, activating new faculties.

That this is always and forever the case is the great lesson which man has to learn -- and particularly the Capricorn type of human individual. Capricorn symbolizes the stage of maturity of social "forms of living", the ultimate product of the mind of man having reached its full development (and the imperialism, mild or harsh, inevitably associated with an individual's maturity) through collective expansion, generalization, standardization, legalization and rationalization (all Sagittarian characteristics). In Capricorn the trend which began with Cancer, and was foreshadowed in the spring signs of the zodiac, comes to its fullest expression -- of which a characteristic symbol is the Roman Empire.

Every Capricornian type of man has in himself a potential Caesar Augustus, if not a Nero! Within him lurks the Roman

political machine of proconsuls and the power of Roman legions
seeking to hold in check a disintegrating and a barbaric world
-- the past and the unborn. And to every Capricornian and
his conflicts there may come, in the "night of his soul", a
Christ -- the light that alone integrates the chaos of the world.
This gift of the spirit, this Christ-l o g o s, is the one answer
to the need of a humanity blinded by the worship of the biggest,
the best and the most efficient political machine, state or federal structure -- blinded, yet yearning in its depths, for that
which no pattern of social organization and no planned society
can give: the clear realization by every individual and within
every individual of his essential identity.

Such a realization, operative in everyday life, is what
might be called t h e s e n s e o f p e r s o n a l i n t e g r i t y,
from which derives also a sense of personal responsibility
and individual destiny. Such an interior "sensing" may manifest in a number of ways. It may be a conscious, vibrant
realization; or it may be a dim awareness of essential selfhood, of the divinity within. But wherever there is such a vital feeling and knowing of that quality of "personal integrity",
there, also, we may say that the spirit is operative, that God
has acted and brought his most wondrous gift -- His "son" --
to a confused and oppressed human mentality.

This act of the spirit does not deal with the formation of
social-political institutions or with the thoughts-feelings of an
individual person. The spirit, in its essential aspect, does
not deal with the collective patterns of democracy, with Con-
stitutions and electoral systems, any more than Christ dealt
with the Roman magistrates. "Render unto Caesar what belongs to Caesar, and unto God what belongs to God", said the
Galilean. The forms of living which structure the social and
personal everyday life belong to "Caesar" -- that is, to the
state or the federation of states, and also to the ego which,
in every man, is the ruling power of the socially conditioned
conscious life. What belongs to "God" is the gift of the spirit, the divine spark which arouses, animates and sustains, in

every true individual person, the sense of personal integrity.

Identity, integrity, self -- these are words that touch the core of the activity of the spirit in man. They are Christ-words, utterances which centuries ago awakened from the limbo of human potentiality new tones of spirit-essence, new melodies of human living. These tones and melodies have made u s e o f the most sifnigicant forms of living and institutions that the Roman Empire had built, strengthening their new meanings and permeating them with a new goal and a new feeling of universal consecration to humanity as a whole, beyond geographical space and limiting centuries. But the sense of personal integrity transcends the realm of political-social or psycho-mental structures. It can operate in the Roman elite of old, in the slave hiding in catacombs, as well as in a Walt Whitman, or in a fighter of the French Movement of Resistance asserting the triumph of the power of the spirit over a ruthless political machines -- or in a Gandhi.

What adequate social institutions, or personal patterns of thinking and feeling, can do is to allow the sense of personal integrity to radiate and freely to permeate the fabric of civilization. Yet the contagion of spirit often works more powerfully under the pressure of an antagonistic and oppressive political system, or even of an uncooperative personal ego. And this is particularly true where the Capricornian type of human nature is concerned; for this type reveals more often than not a Herod frightened by the news of Christ-birth, an entrenched ruling class (or personal ego) clinging stubbornly to the structures of empire.

This clinging to the social mechanisms of power (or to traditional-cultural and religious forms of living) is caused by "spiritual deafness" as well as by psycho-mental inertia. Man is unable to hear, or refuses to hear, the voice of the spirit. What the spirit proclaims is that all forms of living are as nothing unless they be pervaded and in-spirited by the l o g o s -- the message -- of personal integrity. Dependence upon "free institutions" does not insure a real kind of individual freedom. Men are free only where they live in terms of personal integrity and personal responsibility.

How crucially the world needs at this time to realize such truths! Even from our own legislative and executive councils we have heard voices seeking to impose our democratic procedures and forms of living upon ancient nations or youthful societies, and some believed that we could monopolize the tremendous new power which a host of minds from all over the world had placed in our hands. Even though these voices did often ring with the tone of paternal beneficence and were free from the most obvious harshness of imperialism, yet they revealed a naive faith in the omnipotence of social institutions and forms of organization.

This faith is a delusion. Institutions alone will not, because they cannot, bring to Europe, Asia -- or even to ourselves -- the peace and the creative happiness men desperately need. What is needed is a new impregnation by the spirit, a new arousal within the hearts of countless individuals of the spiritual power of personal integrity, a contagious refusal to rely upon formulas or institutions, upon any systems of thinking and any traditional patterns. True, there are ways of life and social procedures which will allow better than others the outer and collective expression of the spirit of personal integrity. These, all men should study and assimilate. They should never take them for granted.

Man is a maker of forms. But these forms are prisons without the animating power of the spirit. They may compel; they will not integrate. They can destroy the decaying past -- as an atomic bomb, Hiroshima, city of lust and political decadence; they cannot breathe the life of tomorrow into anachronistic cultures. Our faith must not be placed in procedures or institutions; but, instead, in the spiritual contagion of our example. Nations will make of democracy a blessing in proportion as they create their own forms of living and refuse to accept ours; and they will hungrily seek to emulate our democracy, in proportion as we, ourselves, live democracy in terms of personal integrity and responsibility.

SERVICE

We are at the threshold of an age of power; and power cannot be used constructively and made operative in a human sense unless it is m a n a g e d. The fundamental task of humanity during the coming decades and centuries is therefore the development of a type of human being able to assume safely and constructively the responsibility which the management of power entails; to assume it with safety, for themselves as individuals, as well as for society as a whole. To assume this responsibility, not for their own individual or group advantage, but for the welfare of the whole; to assume it freely, consciously, joyously -- indeed, as gods-in-the-making -- this must be the way of men of tomorrow, if humanity is to survive.

According to the symbolic pattern derived from the nearly 26,000-year long cycle of the precession of the equinoxes, humanity is now at the threshold of the Aquarian Age, and about to bring to a conclusion the twenty-one centuries of the Piscean Age, which began most probably within the century prior to the birth of Jesus. As is always the case when a new cycle, a new religion, a new attitude to life and a new type of human being are appearing over the horizon of time, these seem to glow with extra-ordinary and wondrous light. They condense, by virtue of their novelty, the diffuse expectancy of all men dissatisfied with the present and impatient with the past. Upon them, all dreams are focused. They come as bearers of long promised gifts, as heralds of "glad tidings" so long suppressed.

Thus we are prone to idealize all characteristics related to the zodiacal symbology of Aquarius. We forget that the man or woman whose basic type is described by this hieroglyph of the sky has a great burden to carry and a grave responsibility to discharge; and the burden and the responsibility are not always assumed consciously and not often discharged successfully. That they should be so assumed and discharged a quality of the spirit is necessary, a quality which many are reluctant to exemplify, because it requires much from the exemplar.

A little and homely word, if properly understood, expresses the essential nature of this spiritual quality: s e r v i c e. The New Age humanity can only be true to its high destiny if the men and women who are to be roots and flower of its civilization succeed in incorporating within their lives and their philosophy the ideal of "service"; if they seek no greater glory than to be known as "servants" of humanity -- which means as well "servants of God", for through their service to humanity, God will become known. And He will be known as Man.

God, it is said, moves in strange and wondrous ways. Perhaps there was no stranger and more baffling way for Him of forcing to our attention the spiritual requirement of the Age about to come -- and, in a sense, already come i n   s e e d -- than to thrust open the gates of tomorrow by the explosive release of atomic energy. This explosion over Japan has shocked the sensibilities of many good people. But so was the figure of Jesus, chasing with a whip the merchants crowding the steps of the Temple, a shock to many "good people" among the Jews.

God, or spirit, is no respecter of goodness or sentiment. What has to be uttered, what has to be revealed, will be manifested. The Man of God accepts for himself the Cross, that thereby the truth of the incoming era may be dramatized and seared into the soul-substance of a new humanity. If humanity needs an atomic bomb to herald the coming of the spirit of the New Age and to burn into the human mind the message of

this spirit, then God -- the God of the whirlwind and the Burning Bush -- will announce His presence by stepping out in awesome majesty from the core of the atom.

How will we meet this God of Power? How are we meeting the challenge of atomic power? How are we facing the
fact that we, of the United States, are the only nation with
huge wealth and piled up surpluses when everywhere else on
this earth human beings are in want and often dying of hunger
and cold? How are we understanding our function as managers of this terrible power and enormous wealth placed in our
hands? Shall we seek to impose our will and our concepts
upon a resistant and sullen world, or shall we so act as "servants of humanity" that hearts and minds everywhere will turn
toward us in gratitude and renewed hope?

The answers to these questions do not depend upon sentiment, idealism or goodness -- or the lack of them. Only by
giving a meaning far broader than usual to the word "morality"
can it even be said that the challenge upon us is a moral challenge. It is a challenge thrust upon men who hold power, and
have access to the instruments for the release of power, by
the very nature of power itself -- just as the Cross was a
challenge thrust upon a man, in whom God had manifested,
by the very nature of divinity.

Whoever seeks to hold power for power's sake, or for the
self-centered use of power, finds himself thereby on the high-
way to destruction. Power can bring wholesome fruits only
to those who hold it in trust for the Whole and, with it, serve
the Whole. All kinds of monopoly on power are nothing but
certain means for eventual self-destruction.

Men have yet to learn thoroughly this lesson. They will
learn it only when this eventuality of self-destruction ceases
to be remote and vague; when the power used is so awesome,
and so swift the reaction to any attempt to monopolize it or
use it for profit and imperialistic expansion, that men will be
inwardly compelled into an attitude of service to the Whole.
Spirit does not compel; but facts do. It is therefore necessary

that facts be made so compelling that men at long last recognize that all power is of the Whole, belongs to the Whole, and is entrusted to individuals, only in order that they may manage its release with clear-cut and specialized efficiency for the sake of the Whole.

The issue reaches far beyond the military use of atomic bombs in one form or another. There is, at least in the long run, as much danger in the uncontrolled and monopolistic use of atomic energy in the hands of big business organizations as there is in the hands of an attacking army. If one nation could control for its own advantage or easy security the release of atomic power, the crime against the spirit would be no less great. But such a cornering of power is impossible, except for a very short time; this we know now! Everything that is basically human flows from the common root of our humanhood into the myriads of channels opened by the will, the vision and the skill of men of courage and of thought everywhere. Yet, to those that are first belongs the unparalleled opportunity to serve as vehicles for the original and originating downpour of the creative spirit, whence comes all power on earth as in heaven.

It is this downpour of the creative spirit which is the essential characteristic of the new era which carries the astrological signature of Aquarius. The one task of those among men who also carry this signature imprinted upon their individual selfhood is to gain the ability to release this power that flows down from high altitudes, be they physical or psychological; to release it not for profit, but in service, as the heart releases the blood which floods its left ventricle -- that the entire body be nourished with vital oxygen and with the potent chemicals of the endocrine glands.

To gain this ability to release power in service to the Whole means to reach psychological maturity. And the greatest enemy of maturity is: Fear. It is fear alone that keeps the adolescent in bondage to infantile attitudes. It is fear alone that keeps nations and the effective -- if not official --

rulers of nations from realizing that humanity as a whole is the one frame of reference with regard to which the achievements of any nation m a k e s s e n s e and acquire their full human worth. It is fear that causes aggression and twists men's minds into tortures -- fear, and the gnawing sense of frustration which is forever wedded to fear and engenders despair, then self-destruction.

With the coming of the Aquarian Age mankind should be reaching the threshold of its maturity. To be mature is to be able to assume the effective management of the power that is of man, and to fulfill one's trust as a true servant of the great Company, humanity. It has been said that the future belongs to the "managers"; but what has not been understood is that the spiritual issue for all of us is whether these managers will seek to rule, or will accept to serve. Will they form a new caste of autocrats, or a vast "Civil Service" dedicated to the welfare of a global society including all men?

This issue is t h e issue to be faced and solved during the next twenty centuries -- and, at least in seed, during the next twenty years. It is to be met primarily by men of the Western World and of white skin; because to them has come the secret of universal power and the ability to use it -- either as greedy owners, or as consecrated servants. It is a dilemma which confronts every predominantly Aquarian man, woman, and even child -- and in every human being there is a touch of the Aquarian. Indeed, it is t h e o n e HUMAN d i l e m m a; for man is that mysterious being filled with conflicts, with fears and with hopes, who must choose how to use power, because he c a n choose.

We spoke of atomic power, because with it man has come at last to the power within the root-reality of the world, the atom and the stars; and the challenge of that power is upon us, with the imminent and un-postponable choice of human maturity, or human disintegration. But older civilizations have also known how to tap root-power of one kind or another. The yogis of ancient India had their way of arousing the root-power which is the foundation of human consciousness and human evolution. They too had to choose the kind of use they made of this power once it could be released.

The main difference is that, in this Aquarian era, it is global Man who will be the yogi -- and not only a few daring individuals living lives either of sanctity or of senseless spiritual selfishness. Humanity now is to be judged. Humanity as a whole is to become "individualized", once it achieves an "organic" status on a global scale. The transcendent God in the heights is becoming Man, the God in the depths. Will we serve this God made human through the consecrated use of this root-energy of atom and star, or will we destroy the newborn divinity of Man by seeking to hoard and to profit individually or in group from the awesome revelation of the power that is everywhere in the vast spaces of the universe, and nowhere actually except in the mind of man?

A momentous decision! Both individuals and nations have to make it. It is an "Aquarian" decision because it is essentially within the scope of this Aquarian type of human being and of its characteristic attitude to life to make such a decision. When we see the socially-minded, perhaps over-zealous, idealistic or self-righteous reformer type of person who shows Aquarian traits, we are prone to see him or her as superb characters in whose hands the future of the world will be safely placed. We may wish there would be more of such a type. Yet we must realize that in most cases these persons have yet to meet their greatest test -- as we Americans, collectively and nationally, have still to meet our greatest test.

We have been in fact confronted with it during the decades which saw our nation grow ever more powerful, yet in the deepest sense aimless. We have been mostly aimless, in so far as we have been primarily concerned with restoring in an expanding manner the status quo and enjoying our wealth and our institutions, which have yet to withstand their cruelest trial. We remain aimless because in a world ploughed under by the release of a power beyond all imagination we have not yet decided what essential use we will make of that power. We have but superficially understood our responsibility to humanity and to God for having released it for use, any use.

Aquarius -- the symbolical Man of the zodiac -- is carrying upon his strong shoulders an urn filled with waters. Yet these waters may mean life or death for him who is loaded with the gift; for unless man has received within his own soul the baptism that forever makes it impossible for him to drink of the waters and let the earth thirst, may God have mercy upon him! Many are tempted and very few choose the Cross. Many know technique and management, but few have answered to their God the crucial challenge: What for?

As the hand is the servant of the brain, so should the manager be the servant of the spiritual purpose of the new humanity. All the idealism and the goodness of men -- indeed all their traditional morality and religious observances -- can be nothing when confronted with a crisis of power. What is needed is a spiritual purpose. What is needed is that individuals become conscious of the evolutionary goal next ahead for humanity -- call this goal, "God's Plan", if you will. What is needed is a total identification of the human imagination and will with this goal, and the faith that makes such an identification work.

Work and management -- these are the immediate Aquarian requirements. Power is here, upon us -- tremendous, awesome. It must be used. Its use must be managed; and the men of the New Age will know how to do the managing. But to what end? If we are open to the voice of the creative spirit within us, there can be but one answer: service. The Aquarian man in us all must reach that noble station of human development and become "the Servant". Humanity is the Great Orphan. It must be fed with power. Power must be given purpose. And there can be only one true purpose: peace.

Purpose, power and peace. He who lacks either will prove himself in centuries to come less than man. That we should incorporate all three in our personal and communal lives is demanded of all of us who can claim the right of survival in these tragic and wonderful decades of death and rebirth. This is the new Incarnation.

Because we have been so long blind to its glorious revelation, we have had to realize power in the embrace of death. But death can be deliverance, wherever it is true to purpose and a herald of peace. We shrink before the dreaded countenance only because we have failed to understand, to use and to manage power. Thus, power overcomes us. We clamor to heaven, simply because we are afraid. And we are afraid because our vision of the purpose of Man, and of the Living God within our own person, has been so faint, so paltry, so insignificant! We know ourselves condemned by our lack of vision, of purpose and of faith. We cling to power -- or to love, which is also power -- because we are blind to the potential of our tomorrows.

Power is not to be clung to, and neither is love. Power is to be used. Love is to be used. Life is to be used. All that is ours to touch, to feel, to experience is to be used, to be managed. And it must be managed to serve a purpose that is true, real, divine -- simply because it is an evolutionary purpose that alone makes sense. Nothing makes sense which does not go forward in greater, deeper, nobler, more inclusive creative activity; and all motion forward demands that power be summoned, used and managed.

Are we afraid of more power? Are we unwilling to exchange coal dust for clean atomic energy, cartels for peace, national selfishness for global organization, slavery for conscious service? Every individual or group is forever being judged by the use it makes of power. And we are being judged today by our collective refusal to transform our lives and our civilization to fit the new horizons which the new power tore open.

The gates of the New Age have been blown open. Men of little faith can see through the gaping space only the horror of death. But to those whose hearts and spirit have assumed the responsibility of creating the future; to those who have accepted the joy and the martyrdom that come with the true station of world-service, that space curves skyward into a threshold. Beyond it, there is God become Man; Man, bearing on his shoulders the urn of infinite power, as Jesus once bore his cross; Man pouring -- oh, profusely pouring -- upon all that have need and yearning for it, the joy, the wealth, the plenitude that can be ours if only we dare accept the challenge of power and peace. our whole nature singing in service to the Whole.

COURAGE

To men of "the Last Day", to men whose nature is attuned to the rhythm of closing cycles and incorporates the deep challenge of twilights between night and day, winter and spring, what else can the spirit proffer as its most bounteous gift but the power to overcome the disintegration of all things and the pressure of memories, regrets or resentments -- the power to emerge into the New Day? What gift could be greater than the bestowal of c o u r a g e!

It is easy to romanticize about the meaning of these last moments of any and all cycles, and to become enthralled by the Neptunian glamour so often identified with the symbolism of Pisces, the last winter sign of the zodiac. Psychism and passivity to the unconscious, boundless compassion and the rapturous openness of the mystic to the unknown beyond can indeed characterize some of the manifestations of the Piscean type of human being. But if one stresses these transcendent and elusive traits, which are secondary results rather than basic attributes, one tends to ignore the very factual and unavoidable confrontations experienced by conscious and thinking men whose temperaments make them eminently sensitive to the problems inherent in periods of transition and renewal.

All transitions coming under the symbol of Pisces are potential passages between death and rebirth, and not only escapes into illusory paradises, or disappearances into realms of spiritual phosphorescence and dissolution. During these transitions, the one great task of intelligent and truly individualized persons is to overcome the pull of the past and the bondage to memories of frustration and pain (substance of man's subconscious), or even to remembrances of ancient greatness and achievements. The one great task is to be "liberated" and to move on into the new. But liberation is a tragic process; in it, individual purpose is pitted against the inertia of collective tradition.

It is true that the Piscean type, just because it is normally burdened with recapitulations and balances of accounts, finds it easy or even natural to dwell upon the harvest of the ending cycle and to return again and again to the past. In some cases he is seeking understanding or atonement; in others, his backward glance betrays the inability to let go and to disentangle himself from the net of recollections of pleasure as well as of pain.

Seeds have come forth out of this past which hold within their pregnant core the mystery of tomorrows. And it is for the sake of these seeds and the life-to-be that the individual must wield the sword of severance -- the sword which Jesus brought to mankind. The sword is heavy; and the multitudinous ghosts swarming from the unconscious, or massed into the awesome appearance of the "Dweller on the Threshold", are cruel enemies. The Piscean temperament is a battlefield.

The Nazarene did not come to us with a bestowal of peace. He came to give us faith, a foundation for tomorrow, a path for victory over the unconscious -- its rituals, its automatisms and its disintegrations. He came from the very heart of the spirit to give us c o u r a g e; courage to destroy useless bodies and cultures, even while fulfilling the eonic Law that once brought forth these incorporations of spiritual vision; courage to assume the responsibility for the birth of the new civilization, even though it meant the sacrifice of the seed into the germ of the new life.

Such a sacrifice is no death. It is the ransom of immortality. The useless vesture -- the golden leaves of autumn and their glowing beauty -- is thrown away to feed, as humus, the growth of the germinating seed. Truly, there is pungency in the late autumnal woods; great beauty and peace can be found in the unconscious of him who has finished nobly his cyclic task. But what the spirit brings to man is more than beauty and peace. It brings Christmas -- and the sword that cuts away all obsolete, useless attachments and memories: the sword and the courage to wield it fearlessly.

The message of Pisces -- and of Christianity -- is a message of liberation. Liberation of the mind was the theme of Buddhism; liberation of the ego and the will, the message of Jesus, heir to the ancient lineage of the Zarathustras and the Hebraic seers. However, the spirit cannot offer to man liberation as a gift. Freedom must be won. The spiritual Teacher gives to his followers the sword; but the individual alone can use it and make himself free. He alone can transform his past into manure and seed, and use death to feed the renewal of life. He alone can assimilate the digested contents of his and the race's unconscious. He alone can win immortality, because he has had the courage to look for his immortal Self behind and through the menacing shadows of his earthliness.

The vision of the Self (and of the universal Being) demands of man courage -- as those who gave India the B h a g a v a t G i t a knew well! But to sit passively waiting for glimpses of the unknown, or emotionally to crave for escape into the blissful pseudo-nirvanas of transcendent states, does not require courage. Nevertheless the positive spiritual essence of the Piscean temperament is courage. Death must be destroyed before life can live. Without severance there can be no rebirth. Without the willingness to die to "Adam" there can be no incorporation of the "Christ" in the total person.

Indeed, the seed of the past must be retained, but only the seed, the quintessence, the spiritual harvest. All else must be cut away and surrendered. Spiritual living is a piercing t h r o u g h -- through nature's phantasms and to the core of the Self -- through "astral" disintegration and to the revelation of That which remains Itself, though cycles wax and wane as billowing waves of the ocean of mankind.

The great need of the Piscean temperament is the capability to endure. En-durance is the ability to remain one's self under the impact of the cyclic dissolution of all things; and no man (or nation) can endure through the disintegrative process attending the close of a cycle unless he has courage and faith. Courage toward the past -- faith in the future: these two virtues are interdependent, as man and woman are interdependent. The man cuts away the veils woven by the energies of the unconscious; the woman envisions the archetypal Image of the future day.

Without vision there can be no faith. Faith is the dynamic impact of vision on the human will, unified and mobilized by the poignant expectation of the envisioned goal. "Vision" may not be fully conscious -- the substance of a dream perhaps! The mind may not be able as yet lucidly to formulate the goal in words or patterns; nevertheless the inner happening -- the impregnation of the soul by the power of the new purpose -- must have occurred if faith drives on, oblivious to the perils and hardships of the way.

In his great book, "Flight to Arras", St. Exupery wrote: "We had lept over the whole defeat. We were above and beyond it, pilgrims stronger than the desert through which they toil because already in their hearts they have reached the holy city that is their destination." Indeed, the strength of the man of the "Last Day" consists in this, that in his heart, he has already reached his goal. Jesus was strong enough to chase the merchants from the Temple because, in his heart, he had already experienced the Father. The martyred Persian Prophet, the Bab, a century ago, had the strength to oppose the fanatic Moslem world and declare the era of Islam ended, because, in his heart, he had already envisioned the "Glory of God" whose incorporation in the person of his successor, Baha'u'llah, he came to herald.

Every great individual born at the end of an era becomes an agent of the creative spirit in proportion as he wields the sword of severance from the ghosts of the past with the power of a faith born of a vision of the new cyclic goal. Every divine Messenger is a revolutionist, because he starts the new cycle revolving. He lives in the end of things, yet not of it. His "heart", his goal, his purpose is established in the future. He strides over cycles. He closes a door by opening the one ahead. He does this at one stroke of his spiritual Sword, because that Sword fecundates even while it destroys. Such is the eternal way of the spirit.

To live according to the rhythm of the spirit is indeed to live every moment as if, in it, the end of a cycle was being metamorphosed into a birth of futurity; it is to live in a perperual act of germination. Alas! there are many spiritual "seeds" -- minds and egos of men -- that refuse to germinate, that seek at all costs to retain their external identity, to draw to themselves vast powers in a tense, self-centered effort to immobilize the past into an eternal enjoyment of their own being. There are powerful men on earth who cling to their mental structures, their prestige and their sensuous or intellectual possessions, who withstand, with a fanaticism born of fear, the great tides of on-moving life. These too display at times great courage; for it takes courage to stand against evolution and to oppose the will of God. But what a blind, what a desperate and tragic courage!

That courage which is a gift of the spirit can always be known in this that he who uses it is always willing to exchange the lesser for the greater, the pattern which excludes for that which includes more, yesterday for tomorrow. True courage is born of trust. It is a song of creative power and of unflinching belief in spring, even as the north wind's blasts bare all autumnal things for what may seem unavoidable death. But death is never inevitable. Death can contain birth in its agony, mother of new life. Death is merely change; and all changes are to men what men make them be -- either through their faith or through their fears. And faith is inseparable from courage.

It takes courage to brave the darkness and the horror of

battlefields, to refuse to be stopped by the dance of death, and through moans and wails to hear the small voice whose magic overtones rouse in the mind a vision of new goals. It takes as much courage not to forget the tone and the image once perceived, as the contest between confusing claims keeps raging through the days which follow the end of battles, and the feel of tomorrows seems lost beneath the anguish or the stubbornness of men incapable of faith, with petrified minds hammering against the fate they themselves have produced.

If there is courage, then the darkness recedes and great wings beat across skies washed clean with dawning light. They are wings of spirit. They are harbingers of spring. Man rises. Man is creative. His whole being is a harp vibrating under the rhythmic impact of the spirit. All needs are fulfilled, Man is whole. And in the harmony of plenary being Peace is known ... Not a peace beyond understanding; but that peace, born of understanding, in which all names and all powers, all gifts and all virtues find their place and their use.

Indeed, it is the Most Great Peace, whereof the Prophet spoke. In that Peace all conflicts are absorbed, all transitions are resolved into Christ-births; the divine potential in every man is raised to its highest pitch of glory and realization. To those who have no faith, this seems the "Millennium" -- and they smile, saying the word. For others, it is Reality: Reality to be made, to be won, to be sung -- to be lived.

THE GREATEST GIFT

THE GREATEST GIFT

Once we use the twelvefold zodiacal scheme of the seasonal cycle of the year as a basis for the classification of human types, we have also to state that the zodiac as a whole symbolizes that in which all men share: "human nature". Underneath all differences of type man's common humanity stands: a foundation, a vast structure of potential human energies and latent faculties.

No man or woman lacks such a foundation, unless perhaps critically injured in the process of birth. Much of this human potential may remain latent. It may be strongly activated only in some directions. Yet it is there, ready to be actualized under a variety of circumstances, favorable or seemingly unfavorable as the case may be.

What constitutes any one of the twelve types of human beings is the characteristic manner in which this particular group accentuates a definite quality of response to life and the source of life. This source, in zodiacal symbolism, is the Sun; for the spiritually inclined thinker or devotee, it is God. But, regardless of the interpretation, the essential fact is that each and all of these "qualities of response" are latent in every human being; they constitute his human inheritance.

The great danger inherent in all classifications of human types (physiological, psychological or astrological) is the all-too-frequent tendency to identify the person we meet with the established type that appears to fit them. We say: Look, how typical an "ectomorph extrovert" or it may be a "cerebrotonic", or a "Leo" type, or a Jew, a French artist, a Cockney, a hobo.

When we do this, we forget the two most essential factors: the common humanity in which we and all these persons share equally, and the uniqueness of the living individual who cannot be pigeon-holed by type, class or race -- who eludes all defining, simply because he is not only "indivisible" (i. e. an individual), but essentially single and un-duplicatable.

Actually these two extremities of every man's total being means the same thing, when we look at them in a practical and spiritual sense; because what makes a human being truly "human" is his potential capability to be a unique individual.

Every human being, it has been said, is a whole species of life. Billions of plants of wheat have identically the nature of "wheat-ness". But no two men are identically the same manifestation of "human-hood". I do not speak here of superficial differences of body-shape or environment; no two things in Nature are absolutely identical in shape. I speak of more basic characteristics, of the inherent potential of development in any one human being. Because that being is "human" there is within him the potentiality of his reaching an absolutely unique status, of fulfilling a unique function in the universe.

This uniqueness is his implied Soulhood. Every human being can find his or her singleness of being; provided his or her life takes a definite course in a direction which is his or her own by "spiritual birth-right". He can; yet he needs not do so! This twofold fact makes him "human".

What makes a being "human" is his ability as a particular person to choose; and therefore his ability to fail. No man would be "human" who would not be able to fail to become integrated with his divine essence, his uniqueness of function in the universe, his Soul. Man can be divine, eventually; but this potentiality may not be actualized by him. He may not even know that the potentiality exists; and not knowing it is latent in him, he cannot orient his consciousness and will toward the fulfillment of it.

The failure to use this latent inherent potency gives rise, sooner or later, to this peculiarly human phenomenon which we call "evil". The possibility of evil is simply the shadow -- or negative aspect -- of the possibility of becoming divine, and by so doing of fulfilling the essential meaning of the "human" status of existence.

What stands between the two opposite possibilities in man? Individual decision -- myriads of them, yet, in a sense, one great decision, made at some critical time, as the result of a long series of antecedent choices, which themselves are conditioned by a multitude of experiences of "awareness", positive or negative, of the basic potentialities in man.

Man can and, whether he likes it or not, eventually must make this essential decision. Yet, perhaps even then, it may not be absolutely irrevocable; or rather, it may not be utterly un-redeemable. In this resides the deep and awesome mystery of Divine Redemption. God "redeems" man as an individual, just because man alone of all living beings, has the capacity to be truly individual, and thus to make decisions singly and alone. Because man can and must decide singly and alone, God, Who is "the One", must react to man's great decision.

The cosmic "One" and the many single individual "ones" are indeed two polarities of one essential all-encompassing Harmony. Thus, the failures of the many human beings call forth a complementary, harmonizing response from God, the One -- just as the over-accentuated use by a certain type of person of a specific aspect of human nature calls forth, as we have seen, a complementary "gift of the spirit".

However, when we deal with consistent evil we are confronted with a situation in which the whole of human nature in a man is committed; it has turned wholly negative, anti-"human". The only act that could answer such a total perversion is an act of the One God, of God as a Person. Only a divine Person can fully "redeem" (i.e. neutralize or balance in the cosmic World-Process) the very negation of "human Potential" by an individualized human personality.

This act of redemption implies the "gift of Self"; it is symbolically the sacrifice, by the Deity Who is the origin of the World-Process, of His "Son" -- that is, of His personified power. The divine Universal "becomes", in relation to human individuals who have chosen to respond to the source-energies of their nature in a negative manner, a particular manifestation of life.

This particular manifestation can be said to have one evident purpose: to be a kind of "antidote" against the poison of evil. Yet, simply to say that does not go far enough. One does not understand very deeply the act of Redemption by considering it as a payment by God for man's sins! God does not "buy back" (the ordinary meaning of the term, redeem) man or his soul from a personified Devil. What is meant by this divine act of compassionate Love is that the One having projected Himself into a multitude of human centers -- of little "ones" -- must assume the responsibility of the negative results of human integration (i.e. of a man becoming an individualized, unique, single, non-duplicatable person). Evil is the generic term for all such negative results, for all the perversions of this process of individualization characteristic of "human" nature.

This process can and does backfire. This is the "exciting" fact about it! Man is God's excitement -- shall we say, half-humorously? But if we change the colloquial word, excitement, to more philosophical terms, dynamic out-reaching, we are getting at what is (at least in so far as we can understand at all cosmic ultimates!) the heart of the problem. We are approaching the "ineffable" core of the mystery revealed (i.e. "veiled again") in the mythos of the Redemption. This core of the mystery can, I believe, be formulated in a simple little word: more.

The meaning of any universe is to make forever more inclusive, more valid, more powerful the Harmony that is the substance of divinity. We may conceive this Harmony in any way we wish, or are able to; but no concept, in my opinion, can explain significantly human experience which does not give to the factor of "motion" an absolute character. There must be perpetual, eternal activity; and this activity must be toward m o r e than what is, toward an ever fuller actualization of an infinite potential of being.

This is the essential meaning of the term "creative". Man is creative in so far as he can become more-than-man. God is creative in as much as the manifestations of God's potentiality of existence are not only infinite, but always greater, always more inclusive, more encompassing. God is changelessly whole, but t h e Whole forever unfolds. To be compassionate (actually, if not etymologically) means to want to encompass always more.

But how could the "more" be reached except by the temporary experience of inadequacy and want? How could a greater realization of abundance and of the meaning of plenitude of being be attained save by periodically realizing oneself empty, so that the spirit might fill, more than ever before, the cup of consciousness? How could the fully distended lungs inhale more air, unless they first exhale? How could God reveal m o r e of His infinite potential of being unless there were evil to compel Him -- because of God's very nature of absolute Harmony -- to manifest in the act of Redemption?

To create is indeed to redeem. It is to answer a need for forms which will include more meaning, greater beauty, and thus a more inclusive and challenging sense of order and integration. God, the Creator, must be God the Redeemer. New universes emanate out of the Infinite Storehouse of Potentialities because old universes have ended, leaving a vast residuum of failures and waste-products; because God's nature cannot admit failure and therefore must create again.

For the Infinite Harmony no discord can be permanent. Discord, separativeness, evil can only be foot-stools to climb to a higher level of consciousness and inclusiveness. They are the servants of the greater, even in the very act of destroying the lesser. "Better" is forever the foe of "good". The Devil serves God, by opposing the old forms of the divine, in the world as well as in man. The function of evil is to compel a new "descent" of divine creativeness.

Indeed, the real original sin is that of self-satisfaction with things as they are, the refusal to accept change and the always offered gifts of the spirit, the refusal to be transformed and to become m o r e than one is now. The inability to receive steadily, and quietly to assimilate a new influx of spiritual power compensating for one-sided or tense activity, is the root from which all karma, bearing seeds of evil, eventually stems. Spirit knocks at the door of the soul, but the frightened mind rushes forth to bolt the door, impelled by the ego's obstinate clinging to its form and its privileges.

Yet even this fundamental inertia of the ego which forces the intrusion of evil into the evolutionary process on earth is made to serve the ultimate purpose of evolution. It releases, in due time, the greatest of all divine manifestations, the Redeemer of the self that has turned away, in hatred and violence, from the One Self. God must answer to the "lost" self by the gift of His essential power of Selfhood. This is "the greatest gift", the gift of divine Sonship. It is indeed the one essential gift, because it is the single gift of "the One".

We are judged by our response, as individuals, to each and all gifts of the spirit. We can refuse them; we can also take them for granted. In either case nothing is really gained. Indeed nothing is ever gained spiritually except the individual, having received the gifts in deep and vibrant gratitude, feels inescapably the responsibility of matching the spirit's bestowal with his own beneficence toward others.

Actually the principle operating in such matters is not: "Having received, give" -- but rather: "Give, that you may receive". Be empty, that spirit may fill you with more gifts.

with greater power. This is the paradox of the spiritual life, which Jesus stated with enigmatic yet challenging power, in the so much quoted and so little understood "Beatitudes".

The man who is full and satisfied with fulfillment, the good man basking in the light of his own virtue or achievement, the "aristocrat" who merely enjoys his superiority and his culture, with patronizing and stilted offerings to the less endowed: these men can perhaps be blessed only by humiliation, sin and destruction! They must learn first to become empty.

The rebel and the criminal will meet, some day, their Redeemer. They will know that there is no ultimate failure, and in that knowledge they will be "saved"; they will be healed of their previous incapacity to use power constructively by being given greater power wrapped in love -- in deeper, more-than-human, love; in that all-encompassing divine love that forever redeems, because it ceaselessly creates new solutions for the needs of the world, even for man's darkest evil.

Spirit is creative movement. It is the free flow of goods, of values, of meanings, of Images of ever wider perfection. It is incessant relatedness aiming at ever more inclusive wholeness. More volatile than air, subtler than perfume, it flows through all things. As it flows through, it transfigures. To hold the spirit within sealed vases, to cling to the divine Presence as it passes through the soul and through every moment lived in beauty and in personal abundance is blasphemy.

To be oneself a tide of gifts, to pour one's creative energy in incessant yet discriminate giving, wherever there is need and in terms of the need, is to live as the spirit. And to live as the spirit is to live by the spirit and for the spirit. It is indeed to be so identified with the rhythm and purpose of spirit that there is no longer any separateness from the need of every moment. It is to perform all necessary actions and only necessary actions. It is, indeed, to be God-in-Act -- oneself, a "gift of the spirit".

(1944-45)

THE WAY 'THROUGH'

Twelve Basic Challenges and
Tests of Individual Existence

To
VIRGINIA SEITH

in warm friendship and grateful
appreciation for years of devoted
cooperation.

D. R.

INTRODUCTION

The opposition between man and nature stressed in the first chapters of this book may disturb the reader who has been accustomed to think of man as a "natural" organism, a body-mind determined by biological heredity and social environment. It may also confuse at first the intellectual who has sought an antidote for the artificialities and anxieties of our modern living in certain Oriental ways of life, particularly Zen Buddhism, which has now become quite fashionable. To people who have been stamped since childhood with the great American ideals of success, achievement, wealth and popularity the Zen doctrine of relaxed, spontaneous, inconspicuous, goal-less, and "natural" activity may well seem indeed the solution to their conflicts and harassment.

Actually, the attitude to life which I am presenting here is also based on the thought-feeling that whatever exists can only be fulfilled in the realization and actualization of its own "nature". The question is, however, how one defines "nature". Confusion arises in many minds simply because this term, nature, is used with two distinct meanings. "One's own nature" (s v a b h a v a in Buddhistic terminology) should not be confused with "nature" used as a widely inclusive term to refer to the over-all activities and the instincts of living organisms of all kinds everywhere on earth. When capitalized, Nature means simply the outer conditions and phenomena generally prevailing in the realm of life on earth -- or, as it has been called, the "biosphere".

The belief that it is man's nature (first sense) to become victorious over nature (second sense) has been a widely accep-

ted religious and metaphysical belief. What man is to overcome, according to such a belief, is "earthly nature", or more
precisely the conditioning, pulls, desires, drives or ambi-
tions which are inherent in the "life-force"; that is, in the
instinctive, largely compulsive and unconscious manifestations of human, and indeed as well animal, existence.

Actually, Zen agrees essentially with this idea of "overcoming"; but strong controversies have arisen concerning the
method of overcoming, and, deeper still, the quality of consciousness -- the quality of feeling, thinking, and acting --
required in the process. To take only one aspect of the question: The typical Western way is to reason out, to pit a capitalized Reason against feelings -- the "higher Self" against
the "lower self" -- "pure" consciousness and light against
"dark" unconscious instincts -- "will", operating through the
cerebro-spinal nervous system, against "life-urges", operating through the "vegetative system" of the body.

On the other hand, Zen and the original doctrine of TAO
in China, ask of you to "flow with the stream"; not to oppose
anything; to become "empty"; to experience in simple awareness, and to act in unconcerned spontaneity after having let go
of all doctrines and social forms of bondage and devotionalism. But how can you reach such a state of absolutely free
spontaneity and unobstrusive "flowing-with" the stream of existence?

At this point we come across a paradoxical situation. Ef-
fortlessness is the ideal, but the Zen monasteries are places
of rigid discipline. Non-violence to, and harmony with, nature is the ideal; but the old Zen Masters were not adverse
to using physical violence on their disciples -- and we have the
famous story of Bodhi Dharma -- this great Hindu Patriarch
who, having come to China and becoming the father of Zen
proper, is said to have cut his eyelids because they would
wearily close in spite of his will during prolonged hours of
meditation. How different is this from parallel actions of
Christian ascetics as well as of Hindu yogis?

Bodhi Dharma, if the story is true, used will and violence

to sustain his strenuous efforts toward a spiritual goal. The
rigid discipline and frugal life in the Japanese Zen monasteries is a paradoxical method of attaining freedom through co-
ercion. In all teachings of the spiritual life, whether Eastern or Christian, paradoxes abound -- the most famous instance being Jesus' teachings called "the Beatitudes". India's
Bhagavat Gita is also actually a long paradox. Arjuna
is told to fight because it is his "nature", dharma, as a
man of the Warrior-Caste; but he is shown how to fight while
not becoming "involved" in the fight.

The idea of an effortless striving and an unconcerned ambition is a central idea as much in Jesus' Gospel as
in Hinduism or Japanese Zen. One must have purposefulness,
yet no ego-formulated goals. There must be ever-renewed
victories, but no sense of superiority or achievement in victory. Man is a natural being whose nature is to overcome the
nature which opposes him, yet is fulfilled in his victory. And
Man also is a social being whose one creative social function
is to overcome the conformism of a society which can only
grow in meaning through the acts of individuals who challenge
its power and its patterns.

Is this all non-sense? All spiritual paradoxes are significant non-sense. When you live them through, you become their meaning. Thus the traditional reply to the
question: What is Zen? -- "Walk on". You may stumble; and
if you do, neither nature nor society will have much pity.
You may stumble by being too eager, too strenuous, too concerned over results; or by being too weary, too lax, unres-
ponsive and insensitive. But you cannot stop. Nature will not
let you stop.

What, then, is nature? -- It is that which, overcome by
you, finds itself full of meaning in the very moment of your
overcoming. Realizing this, we may speak of "the Eternal
Feminine", and pass on. If we do not "pass on", we are caught.
Yet we cannot just pass on beside, for there is no space
for men on earth outside of nature. There is only one way to
pass on, and it is to go through.

THE WAY THROUGH

Everything is known through its opposite. The Full is known through the emptiness which it fills. God is known through the condensation of spirit He emanates into the expectant human person -- a vase shaped by the whirling pressure of the hand of experience.

What man experiences is always "nature". There are levels upon levels of nature; but always, at any level, the law of nature is the law of descent toward an eventual state of even diffusion and scatteredness. Whatever is born (n a t u s) must decay; must fall from a condition of high potential to one of low energy. This is "entropy" -- the running down of energy. Nature -- as we use the word here -- is all that in the experience of man flows down the stream; however high the source of the stream.

Nature is not "life"; it is not "consciousness". To nature belongs the organism through which life acts itself out, the mind through which consciousness reveals itself to itself. Nature is the collectivity of infinitely varied systems of organization, from nebulae to atoms, from conceptual theories to political states. It is everything that, having been brought to the condition of integrated existence, will become in time -- days or eons -- disintegrated. Nature is that which constantly reveals a trend toward the "less"; the present, ceaselessly becoming the past; the created, on its way to obsolescence.

Nature is man's field and object of experience. Man experiences himself man only through nature. In this experience of that which is becoming ever "less", ever "past",

man realizes and enacts his manhood by liberating the p l u s
factor which ever creates a "more", a "future". Man always
yearns to be m o r e than he is, if he is truly man. His increase in consciousness polarizes nature's entropy. Man answers the downflows of nature's energy with the rise of his
illumined consciousness which has received and assimilated
the spirit, emanated by God. The spirit: God's answer to
man's need, to man's essential emptiness.

God is the Full. Man is the Empty. Man's destiny is to
become filled -- t h r o u g h his experience of nature, through
contrast with an earth forever dying. Man is man through the
challenge of the earth; meeting which, he calls upon himself
the release of spirit from the heart of divine plenitude. Man
thus rises into the ever-unattainable fullness of God, Who,
being the absolute Whole, is forever identical, through the fall
of nature and the rise of man.

"Through" -- small, yet mighty word! Everything is what
it is t h r o u g h its opposite. Man experiences through nature. He rises through nature. Not against, but through. A
piercing through. An act which cuts from side to side the resistance of the opposite; thus which acknowledges it, which
feels it, with which it becomes interwoven in space, yet opposite in direction. As man moves in a direction which opposes nature's, while occupying for a while the same space,
man, the experiencer, e m e r g e s f r o m nature.

The hand passes through the water. It experiences the
water, the fluidity of it; and it emerges from it, still a hand
-- the integrity of a hand, p l u s consciousness from the experience. Consciousness is "through-ness". It is born of
thoroughness of experiencing; and to be thorough is to pierce
through and through the substance, the weight, the glamor,
the whirlpools of nature. Having experienced to the full, man
is "through" with this particular field of experience; because
he has gained consciousness of himself, the experiencer.

Nature, for us, human beings, is represented primarily
by the earth -- the mass of the earth, the challenges of the

earth. Nature is gravitation, the pull toward the dead level
of uniformity and undifferentiated substance. Nature is the
depths, the unconscious, the Mother-image, the universal collective, love that binds, glamor that bends radius into tangent
and waylays into the mesh of green trees arrows shot straight
to the heart of the sun. Nature is everything through which
man must gain consciousness, and through consciousness an
immortal form of emptiness, chalice for the downpour of the
Holy Spirit -- the light of the Whole. Nature is everything that
man must overcome in order to be more than only man.

Overcoming is a "passing through", not a dismissal. Nature is not to be dismissed before the experience; it is not to
be shunned and avoided in fear. It is to be met in contest
within the limited field of the life-experiencer. Nature and
man occupy the field. Each, by inherent destiny, is bound to
a goal. The two goals are opposite. Nature cannot be forced
back outside of the field. Man should not be forced back by
nature. Yet each of the contestants occupies the entire field.
The only solution of the contest is for man to enter the whole
of nature within the field of experience, to pierce through nature, and, emerging from nature and the field, to continue
his path toward an ever more total fullness of being -- toward
the absolute Full that is God.

Man's personality is the contest; his body -- the gross and
the subtle -- the field of experience; his soul, that which already has pierced through; spirit, the gift after the victory;
and God, the eternal bestower. There can be no victory if
man clings to any s u b s t a n t i a l trophy from nature. True
victory is victory that inflicts no defeat. The elements of nature are left to follow their gravitational course, the natural
entropy which they must obey eventually; which is their fate.
Man's defeat would only give them an illusory, temporary solidity, which the downward sweep of the universal cycle would
ultimately shatter. But man's victory does not merely mean
that the normal cycle of material transformations will not be
retarded; it means that nature, as a whole, will find in this

victory its eternal and ultimate significance.

As man knows himself through his contest with nature, so does nature realize itself whole by the light of man's victory. It is this light which alone illumines nature. This indeed is the destiny of all nature; that it can realize itself whole, and thus reach its own fulfillment, only if it is successfully overcome by the man whom it must oppose so that he might know himself by piercing it through; and knowing himself, illumine it by the light of that knowing.

Indeed, everything is realized through its opposite. Man realizes himself in consciousness through nature. Nature realizes itself through the light shed by the man who overcame its gravitation. And this light is the spirit gift of God, the Full, Who realizes His fullness timelessly through all the contests between the opposites, man and nature, in which man is the victor. As man, the positive, demonstrates his positiveness in successfully piercing through nature within the field of experience -- and thus allows nature, the negative, to reveal its negativeness in contrast to man's positiveness -- God's Wholeness is forever demonstrated to Himself through man.

In this process nature acts as challenger. It challenges man; yet, with the unconscious desire to be overcome by man. These challenges operate within the field of the earth -- the field of experience for humanity as a whole. They are circumscribed by the boundaries of the earth. To the individual human being, they are framed by the two great axes of consciousness, horizon and meridian -- the symbolical "cross of experience".

The Son of Man is nailed upon this cross. His organs of action -- hands, feet and the adrenal glands controlling muscular action -- are pierced by the soldiers of Rome, the symbol of an organized and dictatorial nature. His head, abode of consciousness, is crowned with thorns which are nature's weapons. Will the Son of Man gravitate to the earth with his dripping blood? Or will he gather to himself all his powers, and passing through the disintegration of nature, emerge in radiant glory?

"C o n s u m m a t u m   E s t" -- he said. He had gathered all of himself to his self; he had consummated the experience. His being now reached from hell to heaven. He had become indeed the Son of God -- the Victorious, the Perfect. The earth that challenged him was blessed by his victory. It realized itself whole, through the light of his overcoming.

Challenges of the earth; tests of men who meet nature within the field of human experience -- their bodies, their everyday living. Every man born of woman must meet these tests; must become crucified on the cross of horizon and meridian, which establish the framework of his world of experience; must emerge whole and illumined, or cling to natural elements, whose normal disintegration is thus stopped -- for a while; this "while", a hell or purgatory.

A multitude of tests. Every experience is a test, a note in the great symphony of man's victory. Yet this symphony has well-defined movements. One after the other, man's pattern of experience unfolds; revealing perhaps his ability to include the whole space that surrounds his birth, his ever-renewed emergence into the world of light, of spirit and of divine pleroma; or else, ending in his being scattered into the empty space of defeat and frustration.

The fullness of space is God's signature; empty space, the illusion produced by defeat and materiality. Victorious man conquers the fullness of space. And his path unfolds in counterpoint to that of the physical sun, from which streams forth the energies of nature, because man can only realize his selfhood in contrast to nature. Starting from the dawn-point of his selfhood, man must first reach depth; then he ascends counterclock-wise to zeniths ever more radiant with the realization of ever deeper depths experienced as shrines of the immanent God.

A cyclic symphony: a symphony in twelve great moments, twelve great tests, twelve avenues of victory -- or disintegration. Each type of test presents a negative as well as a positive solution; a fall and an emergence. To every individual belongs the power to choose. It is his divine birth-right.

Not to choose victory, is to decide for defeat; for both nature and man are moving on, in opposite directions. The field is limited. Each contestant fills it entirely. There is no way out for man save t h r o u g h a n d t h r o u g h -- or back. To pierce through nature and move God-ward; or to fall back, entangled in the fateful advance of natural energies toward chaos.

THE TEST OF ISOLATION

Birth is a process of isolation. What was universal being becomes a particular entity, with a space of its own, with a time of its own -- a particular kind of tuning in to the harmony of the universe. Every newborn punches the clock of nature at a particular time; this time begins the life-long contest between the individual and nature. Nature, in him, starts to unwind; this is nature's essential character. The moment a man is born, nature in him begins to die; it flows downward along the path of universal entropy -- first, at a slow pace, then with a progressively greater rate of acceleration.

Man, however, is not born all at once. He is born first as a particular body. He is born further as a particular ego, with individualizing reactions to his surroundings -- physical, social, and cultural. Some of these reactions we call "feelings", others "thoughts". In proportion as these make him different from other human beings, we see in him an individual. As he integrates these individualizing traits into a consistent all-around pattern of behavior, of feeling and thinking we invest him with the name "personality".

Man is born as a particular body from the womb of his mother and of mankind. He is born as an individual person through a process of individual differentiation and self-consolidation out of the matrix of society and civilization. In both cases, birth means isolation.

The trend toward isolation, through differentiation and individualization, meets at every step nature's trend toward uniformity and the levelling off of energy. Every human experience is a contest between the two trends; indeed between further birthing and further dying. Man always seeks to be more completely what he is. Nature forever flows downgrade under the law of deterioration of energy. If man, for the many years of his youth appears to gain in organic strength, it is because the momentum of his impulse toward isolation normally keeps on the increase until mid-life. He succeeds in steeling himself more effectively against nature's entropy -- and against the pressure of social traditions. He meets the challenge of earth-experience with great enthusiasm. If various conditions destroy this enthusiasm, neurosis sets in. If a sense of inferiority or fear confuses his will to individual self-assertion through all social or family experiences, he follows the path toward uniformity inherent in natural energies; he takes refuge in social anonymity or in subjective escapes. He dreams expressionistic or sur-realistic dreams, while the dynamic potential of his organism gradually deteriorates and his emotional responses become blurred into the indifference and weariness of psychasthenia.

Every experience is a potential birth. Every experience can increase the individual's isolation from the collective average. And it should -- if the individual is strong in manhood. Every experience can so be met that the experiencer realizes more deeply that which he is as an individual. There is such a realization if the experience is lived through and through; if the man emerges from it integral and whole with the added plus-value of consciousness; if, through the experience, he maintains his integrity even where he is most closely interwoven with the fabric of natural impulses and energies.

Every experience can be an experience of oneself experiencing. This leads to an increase in the intensity or sharpness of one's own characteristics -- thus of one's isolation and one's singleness. It makes personality more consistent and more significant, more distinct, even in its pliability and its seeming giving way to the impact of nature's energies. There is a "giving way" which is born of weakness; another, as in Judo and in the Taoist's way of life, which derives from intelligence -- the power to adjust to experience while retaining one's integrity, one's isolation.

Isolation has been given emotional connotations of loneliness by men weak in selfhood. Every man who is a self, an individual person, is necessarily isolated -- yet not alone. He needs not be lonely in isolation. Loneliness is an admission of defeatism in front of experience. It is born of fear. Lonely men are men who fear they might not emerge, whole and integral, from the contests with nature -- weary men, who lack enthusiasm to keep on forever being born. There are always new births ahead. Isolation can always become more total as selfhood becomes more encompassing. But the isolation of which we speak is not to be considered in relation to space and distance from other objects or entities. To be isolated is to acquire well-defined characteristics, a unique character. It is to be what one is in spite of, nay through, all the possible impacts of nature and life. It is to be a self, and to be more thoroughly, fully, consciously this self through every experience, however intense its whirling suction, however tenacious its hold upon the body and the psyche, however insistent the challenge of earth-existence.

The negative way to meet the test of isolation and of birth is to insist on being and remaining different from other human beings. The positive way is to insist on being ever more distinct. The integrity of the self is based on distinctness; the separativeness of the individualist, on an emphasis of differences. Distinction emphasizes form and character. Differences give rise to feelings of distance, of solitude, of fear, of incompatibility.

The test of isolation forces us to choose between becoming ever more distinct or more different, more single or more solitary. It creates the outstanding person, or the individual who feels "left out". It is the test of birth. Either the experiencer keeps being born, or he crystallizes into what he was before the experience, or he gives up "name and form" and slides wearily into the anonymous and formless -- which is spiritual death. Every experience constitutes such a test, because every experience is a challenge to self-awareness.

It produces a new horizon, a new "point of sunrise"...unless man refuses to be born again through the experience; to rise, with the sun, to his zenith; to shed the light of consciousness upon a new "day"; unless man seeks refuge into the collectiveness of the earth, and lies down on the couch of inertia to accept the embrace of fate. Fate is the refusal to be born again. Every man creates fate by refusing to become more distinctly a self.

Distinctiveness implies formulation; social distinction, a sense of form and cultural excellence. To be a self is to have a permanent form. The opposite is formlessness, "sloppiness". The "sloppy" individual refuses to meet his everyday experiences with distinction. He does not distinguish himself in the contest against nature. He lets "nature take its course"; and that course means always entropy -- the progressive erasing of distinctive features. In contrast to this, "personality" is revealed -- or displayed! -- by the man who meets every experience with distinctive response, whose reactions to life are stamped with the character of selfhood. His living is a series of "signatures". Every experience adds strength, recognizability, uniqueness, and impressiveness to the signature. He "makes his mark upon time and place". Wherever he goes, he is an origin. He is perpetual victory over uniformity and death. All he touches acquires character -- his own.

To this, there is a shadow. The individual who seeks forever to be different, craves to appear "original". He dilly-Dali-es through a life of sur-realistic gestures which increase only the emptiness around him. He isolates himself, not by achieving distinction, but by creating distance. The distance produces solitude; the originality, a vacuum which nothing will ever fill with living substance. The original individual lives in self-contaminated air, in the formalism which crystallizes living forms into mummies, in the artificiality of show-cases crowded with mannequins forever gesticulating under public gaze.

To seek originality is to seek the embalming of differences.

Everything vital is taken away save surfaces and make-up. To be an origin is to fecundate society with the consciousness drawn from experience. Consciousness, however, is a vase. What fecundates is the l i q u o r   v i t a e, the gift of the spirit that ever comes to fill the vase in answer to the need of the Empty. Every new dawn creates an emptiness for the spirit to fill. Every creator is a cup of consciousness overflowing with a downpour of spirit. The rising sun ascends from an ever new horizon; yet the Light is always the same. The containers are distinct; the contents are identical. Spirit is the eternal content. To be origin is to release spirit. To seek originality is to close one's door to the gifts of God, the eternal source of spirit.

Every challenge of earth-existence to man can produce three types of results. Man may refuse the challenge and fall, entangled in the shreds of the experience, toward the dead level of absolute indifference. And if, passing through the experience, he retains his integrity, he may do so either in openness to ever new horizons, or with the rigidity of automatic response -- as a rising sun, or as a mannequin freezing a sum-total of particular responses into a fictitious sense of permanence.

Permanence of this sort is not immortality. Immortality is not the overcoming of one experience of death -- and a repeat performance a d   i n f i n i t u m. Immortality is the overcoming of every possible kind of dying. It is the capacity to remain what one is while being forever born again. It is dynamic distinctiveness; not static difference.

Originality is a glorification of one's "complexes", of that which separates while differentiating. Creativeness is the quality of victorious emptiness that knows itself forever to be filled with spirit. It is the absolute certitude of ever-renascent fulfillment. It is the marriage with God. It is isolation, with the One and All filling one's self full. To know such a resplendent isolation is to be forever a rising sun.

THE TEST OF POSSESSIONS

Any organism being born is born out of something. It is present emerging from past; and this past constitutes always "nature". Human nature is the accumulated harvest of all that human beings have gone through, have built in their subconscious as habits and customs, have transmuted into the substance of civilization. It is, beyond this, the harvest which spiritual entities, builders of cosmic structures and of species, had produced out of their experiences during previous cycles. Every birth inherits the infinity of the past. Every new experience is lived on the unconscious background of all similar experiences that have ever been. Nature is this infinite all, in the past, brought to a selective focus by a particular type of birth in a particular type of species, of race, of family.

A selective focus. Each individual man is an essence, an expression of creative Intelligence, an "Idea" of the universal Mind. He is a particular attempt to use a particular section of the past of the universe in order to demonstrate a new present, a new power or "name" of God. He is this divine Idea facing a selected set of natural elements, for the purpose of integrating them into an organic whole, of extracting from them a seed of meaning. He is a potential solution to a problem as yet unsolved, a problem constituted by a particular arrangement of natural trends, of unharmonized forces, of left-over threads, of unfinished business.

The new-born individual at the threshold of the first breath -- at the threshold of any breath! -- is confronted by the elements of this problem, by a particular field of experience; also, by the tools he is to use, the powers and faculties he can call his own, the potential of cosmic, social, psychic, and organic energies he may tap while on his way to the solution of his problem of destiny.

These are his "possessions". Possessions can be wares, social privileges, and wealth; they can be muscular strength, healthy organs, mental gifts, psychic energies -- or the negative aspects of these things. In whatever condition he finds them at birth -- and in the beginning of every cycle of experience and rebirth -- they constitute the section of nature over which he is put in charge by right of birth. His attitude to these possessions becomes the substance of one of his most basic tests. A man's character is largely determined at the very first by the way in which he meets the test of ownership.

Man is in charge of some section of nature which he owns as a result of the very act of birth. He is put in charge; and this he must come to realize, and to understand. He must accept the responsibility it entails. To refuse it would mean that all the natural and psychic energies of his ancestral past, integrated for his use within the field of his total organism and of his congenital place in society, would be left to follow the course of all nature; which is, to disintegrate. These energies, however, were not integrated without a purpose. He cannot -- he must not -- leave them alone. This would be suicide; and there are a great many forms and degrees of committing suicide -- not the least of which is to refuse truly to be born as a manager of one's possessions.

Nor is the identification with these possessions and powers the positive approach to the test of ownership. The self is so that it can use possessions; not that it might be used by the play of their natural elements and energies. But "to use" means to use with reference to a goal, a purpose. And the great questions arise: What does the individual own his section of nature for; and, what is the quality of his sense of ownership? What is his relationship to the act of using that which, at any level, he owns by the very fact that he is a self experiencing through earth-nature? These are essential questions that every individualized self must answer before God, and before society. By his answers he makes or destroys his chances of fulfilling his innermost destiny.

The substance of an individual's immortality can be extracted only from the total substance of the man's possessions at all levels. He can only say fully and victoriously "I am", if he has known how to say according to the law of spirit, "I own". What is this law of the spirit? It is the law of fruitfulness, of consecrated use, and of non-identification -- three pillars of the spiritual life, the life of abundance, the life that creates values which do not bind the creator, but provide him with the substance of his immortality in God. God, the absolute Full.

To be fruitful and to multiply is God's one and only original command. It is so stated in the very first chapter of the Sacred Book of the Western world. Fruitfulness implies the subduing, taming, cultivating, and assimilating of natural energies. It refers to no "Garden of Eden" -- the secondary creation of a personal deity not to be confused with the creative God of the universal Whole. Man is not born to enjoy nature, to be the pampered son of a rich father and a bounteous mother catering to his every whim. Man is born to solve a problem. Nature is before him with its abundance, its inexhaustible dynamic potency, its infinite treasures of memories, for him to draw from. Nature -- psychic and physical -- surrounds man. Will it stifle man with goods and memories, or will man subdue and put to conscious, purposeful use its products?

This is man's essential dilemma. Man is not born to create energy; all conceivable energy is around him. He is born to release it, to use it. Using it, he produces wealth; he creates meaning. Using it, he solves his problem, the problem God delagated to him, that it might be solved through man's efforts.

Fruitfulness is the result of purposeful use. In nature --
thus, in the p a s t of the universe -- fruitfulness is unconscious, instinctual. The productive entity (be it plant, animal
or primitive man) is not aware of the purpose of its fecundity.
Man, in his glorious and tragic t o d a y, cannot evade the responsibility of a conscious purpose -- and remain truly human.
He has released from nature awesome powers; nuclear energy
from the atom, calculus and the engineer's vision from the
collective memory of mankind. These are his possessions.
Born with the potentiality thereof, he is using them -- to what
end?

To what end our civilization and our intellect? We cannot
answer this question as long as we identify ourselves with this
intellect and the products of our "scientific" civilization or our
"religious" tradition. If the rich boy identifies himself and his
destiny with his wealth, he lives in total poverty of the spirit.
Nature -- social nature -- lives him. He may add to the products of his inheritance; yet is it not rather this social inheritance which adds to itself through him, its willing servant or
slave? He is a tool for collectivity; and everything that is collective is "nature", because it represents the past -- that is,
every achievement of humanity, or of a group, u n t i l t o-
d a y.

Spirit deals only with today, not as a prolongation of endless yesterdays, but as the one and only stage upon which the
harvests of these yesterdays is to be given a new purpose, a
new meaning. Yesterday may bequeathe us great gifts, vast
possessions. These i n t h e m s e l v e s are of no value. They
are potentiality to be used. Unused, they oppress and stifle
the creative "I". No individual should ever be considered great
because of what he owns; only because of the use he makes of
whatever he owns.

An individual should identify himself with a purpose; not
with the elements of the problem which this purpose defines.
If I am born crown-prince of a kingdom, how can I serve the
purpose of this birth if I identify myself with the past achieve-

ments and traditions of dead kings? As potential king, I am the potential servant of the people. What purpose can I have, save to minister to the new needs of my people in their adjustment to new circumstances, new world-relationships, new challenges of destiny? The crown awaiting me is the challenge of potentiality. It is for me "nature"; nature, whose tendency it is -- if left alone -- ever to run down to a dead level. Kingdoms come to an end. Ancestral fortunes soon dissipate. They constitute nature; my opportunity, not my bondage. Following the past, I am bound. Using it for a new purpose, I am creative and spiritually "free".

This does not refer only to actually inherited possessions. All I own today is the inheritance of my past. As I rise every morning I am born again; all I own I inherit from yesterday. And every experience can be, should be a new birth. Every experience truly met releases a new potentiality of gifts, a new wealth of being. By living this experience to the full, I commune -- whether I know it or not -- with all men who before me have lived the same type of experience. Their harvest becomes potentially my harvest; their achievements, the pedestal for my achievement.

As I meet my God, I partake in the ecstasy of all men who have ever met their God. This is the true "communion of the Saints". And this experience establishes thus a new range of potentiality for myself. My "nature" has become enriched by all this past of human sanctity. Will I enjoy this past, or give it a new fruitfulness, a new purpose, a new meaning -- my own? Will I identify my "I" with this collective rapture that was, or will I use it as a new "Am" with which I may solve the problem whose solution "I am" in the expectancy of God -- and of Man?

Spirit-realized individuality is to be understood in terms of distinctness, not of difference. This we already saw. Likewise possessions have no spiritual value if they consolidate, fortify, make more virulent our pride-bearing differences; if they establish themselves as privileges. Ownership, to

the man of the spirit, is a means to make his destiny and purpose more distinct, more clear-cut, more effective. Possessions, to him, can only mean efficiency.

There is no sense in owning anything at any level unless
such an ownership increases our capacity for solving the div-
inely appointed problem our birth has been meant to solve.
Any society in which rank and authority depends upon privilege, and not upon acting efficiency, is spiritually dead.

THE TEST OF THOUGHT

Whoever considers man as a portion of nature fails utterly to grasp the significance of man. Man is born to solve a problem which nature poses; to solve it by emerging from nature, after having thoroughly experienced its energies, its whirlpools and its constant trend toward deterioration. Man experiences himself man "through" nature but in this interpenetration of man and nature the two protagonists move in opposite directions. Nature deteriorates; man, in as much as he emerges victorious in the contest, integrates. If defeated, if pulled downward by nature's entropy, man is not man. To be man is to be victorious over nature, thus fulfilling both himself and the purpose of nature. The star of man is the pentacle of victory.

The essence of this victory is the transmutation of nature into intelligence. It is this process which is called: thought. To think means for man to struggle with the multifarious, ever-changing problems which his experience of nature presents to him at every moment. It is to transform the legacy of the past -- body, memory, karma -- into an intimation of the future. To think is to release from all natural downflows the power to build with light a superordinate expression of universal Being. This implies the accentuation of this downflow into a man-made "waterfall" by the damming up of the natural energies. Not repression, still less suppression, but compression. A dam does not push back the flowing water -- a practical impossibility! It contains them. It forces the turbulent stream to develop depth and stillness. Thought can only be released out of stillness and of depth.

"Be still, O my heart! -- and know God". God is the absolute fullness of intelligence. God realizes Himself through the victories of "men" in countless universes. Each victory is an atom of intelligence. God is the perpetual and total transmutation of nature, everywhere, into intelligence. The substance of God is thought. In God all problems are solved; for God is the absolute victory. Man, the apprentice in victory, can only fulfill his destiny and purpose through thought -- through the transmutation into intelligence of that field of nature which is his own possession. He accomplishes his transmutation as he emerges from his contest with the energies of his nature by the power of thought. He emerges into intelligence by synthesizing intelligence out of the disintegrative energies of nature. So does the engineer "synthesize" light out of gravitation -- out of the weight of the river he has dammed.

Man may fail and become caught into the entropy of the universe in which he lives; the dam holding the deepened river may collapse, in part or completely, and the violently released waters may spread destruction. Thought may lead to destructive outbursts of the root-energies of human nature -- if man's thinking fails in its connective and synthesizing task; if the mental wholes built by thought cannot contain the essence of intelligence, which is, to unify all things and dissolve all problems by seeing them from the level of the universal Whole. Thought, the associative and integrative process, may collapse under the conflicting pulls and the load of all that it is to unify into a form of intelligence -- the great Idea, the redeeming Symbol, the dynamic reconciliation of cosmic opposites.

But thought does not belong to the realm of nature. Thought is not an expenditure of energy. It is not energy. The successful thought-process compresses energy into ideas and meaning. Organic energy may appear to be used in the act of thinking, but it is not actually spent; or very little of it is measurably expended. It is compressed and transmuted into intelligence. The dammed in waters of the river are not used out. They are given depth; their level-height is raised. They are transmuted into potentiality of electricity and light. But the water is not lost. Man does not lose; even though his natural organism misses that portion of energy that could normally have become "unwound" into some of the many functional activities of the human body and its psychic overtones.

What man loses in natural energy, he gains in intelligence. Man establishes by thought the foundations of his being in intelligence -- his being in God. These are foundations of immortality; because in intelligence there is no death. Intelligence, in its ultimate state, establishes a condition of complete correlatedness and integration with all there is -- with the victorious, because his victory makes him share in universal intelligence; with the defeated, because his defeat is the very next problem which the man of intelligence will have to solve in order to reach the more inclusive experience of more advanced stages of natural deterioration, and "through" it a greater victory -- whence a more divine state of intelligence.

Nature and man are opposites, but therefore complements. They need one another. If nature's trend were not to run down, man could not gain the power to transmute this down-flow into intelligence. The river must flow to the dead level of the sea, if the engineer is to gain the hydroelectric power he needs to light the civilization in the very fabric of which he will achieve social immortality.

It is the same with every man who dares to be man. He must experience nature, the very fullness of its energies, the very death it promises to all organisms and all substances. The more powerful the river's flow, the greater the light he may eventually release -- if his be the victory. Some men will be swept by the gravitational force of the stream. Others will build ambitious sky-thrust dams, only to see them crash into a cataclysm of destruction which may engulf perhaps many more men and lay waste fields of ripening crops.

Intelligence is the prize of a glorious gamble. Many are afraid. A few gain immortality. The energy they have condensed and repolarized into Ideas will create new worlds. Once more, in due time, they will be called upon to dam up the downflow of the energy of nature -- the nature of these very worlds that had come into being out of their Ideas. Once more, victory may be theirs. Cycle after cycle, the victorious performs again his renewed victory -- and each time a more profound, a more far-reaching victory. Cycle after cycle, the immortal Self re-establishes itself through victory in intelligence, ever closer to the absolute of intelligence that is God.

This is the challenge which the earth and its natural energies present to man. A similar challenge was made at a lower level of being when "life" was born on earth. Life, like intelligence, is an attempt to overcome the universal deterioration of energy. It is an attempt to transcend the mortality in nature through the immortality of the cyclically reborn seed.

Yet, this integration and self-perpetuation which occurs within the shrine of the seed is unconscious; the perpetuated selfhood is generic, not individual. The species immortalizes itself, not the particular organism in which there is life. The organism itself belongs to nature; it too has its entropy, which is death.

The seed, while it is in the organism, is not of the organism. It may break down and become a mere particle of nature -- we call this "decay"; just as any dam may collapse. But if the seed can survive the deliquescence of autumnal soils and the freezing of winter it wins its victory over death, and the vernal sun crowns it with the prize of victory: rebirth in the new cycle. Germination is not death for the seed. It is fulfillment in tomorrow. It is the achievement of the seed's destiny: to bridge the hiatus between two cycles -- to establish the continuity of life in a universe spasmodically rushing to chaos.

What the seed accomplishes for life in unconscious, generic instinct, the truly individualized self performs in terms
of intelligence. Life operates within set geographical and climateric limits; it is conditioned by space and bound by the
rhythm of time and seasons. Intelligence is not bound by space
or causality. Thought operates e v e r y w h e r e at o n c e
t h r o u g h o u t t h e W h o l e. For thought does not act as energy. It is the polar counterpart of natural energy in man.
Life, likewise, is actually not energy. It is the result of the
transmutation of energy into "desire", or sensitivity, toward
the re-establishment of the seed. The biological species releases the power that is life. Man, the individual self, releases intelligence.

Life is, truly, the foundation for the release of intelligence, yet man's purpose and cosmic destiny is to rise out of
the unconscious field of the "biosphere" -- the realm of life
-- into the conscious field of the "noosphere" -- the realm of
mind and intelligence. He must fecundate life by intelligence,
t r a n s f o r m i t s p o w e r i n t o l i g h t: the power of the
seed into the light of the thinking self.

Intelligence is commonly defined as the capacity of conscious adaptation to the requirements of man's environment.
But the environment of man is established by life, by the organisms through which the seed perpetuates the species' character, by the successes and the failures of these species in
the earth's past. The biosphere is the past which man must
transfigure into future. It is, in this sense, "human nature";
for all that is past represents "nature" to man.

Man should not be considered as a biological species. He
is that divine agent to whom it is given to "own" all that the
evolutionary effort toward life-integration has already produced. In his body-organism man meets and experiences the
sum-total and synthesis of all this vast effort of the biosphere.
It is for him to tune it up to the greater pattern of universal
integration; to transform the time which binds life-instincts
into that creative cyclic duration which is an ever-renewed

formulation of intelligence -- to release life's bondage to geography into the freedom of thought which is universal and instantaneously spread throughout space.

Intelligence has its shadow: intellectuality. During the binding process and the damming of nature man may feel frightened by the possibility of failure. He crystallizes the thought-process into a system; further still, into a dogma. Thereafter, intelligence emprisoned in systems begins to deteriorate; it too, like any physical organism, becomes caught into the cyclic death of all natural compounds. Intellectuality is intelligence running to dead level. All intellectual systems must disintegrate, and he who clings to them -- the intellectual -- must know the death of intelligence. For him, there can be no immortality in God.

Intelligence is re-established at every moment of universal time by the victory of "man" everywhere in the universe. This intelligence pervades a t o n c e the entire space of the world. Every mind can resonate to it. Every man partakes in the victory of every other man. He partakes also in the defeats, the fears, the crystallizations of all men who fail to achieve victory. Victory must be a daily performance, if man is not to freeze intelligence into intellectual systems and reduce thought-process into automatic cerebrations.

To be truly man is, every day, to win conscious and individual participation in the universal process of creation of intelligence which, every moment, counteracts the down-flow of energy. The performance is constant. Natural deterioration forever must be polarized by integrative thought. He who stops after a day's victory loses intelligence, retains but intellectuality. To be divine is forever to serve in the perpetual rebirth of intelligence.

THE TEST OF STABILITY

The fourth great test which man encounters in every cycle of individual experience depends essentially upon the fact that a time always comes when man must put a stop to his effort at compressing the energies of his nature in order to transform them into thought, intelligence and individual values. The engineer builds a dam to hold the waters of the stream so that he may transmute the power of gravitation -- the running down of all energy -- into electricity and light; but the dam cannot reach safely above a certain height, or else the pressure of the waters it contains would cause it to collapse. The individual, likewise, must not go on forever increasing the tension of his thinking processes. He must not seek to relate to his self an ever vaster aggregation of dynamic facts and to assimilate experiences wrenched from ever larger fields of nature, lest his mind may burst under the pressure of too much power and too many challenging discoveries.

Man must stop and gather within a solid structure of some kind the booty he has accumulated in his victory over nature. Before he can creatively use intelligence he has to incorporate it into a structure of selfhood -- a structure which can hold the mass of materials he has gained from experience. The engineer has to consolidate his mastery over nature. He has to anchor his structure of concrete and steel so firmly that he can meet the falling mass of waters with an equally moving mass able to use, under control and to the fullest extent possible, their impact. He must know how and when to stop the down-flow.

A time comes in all things when man must say: enough. He can say it too soon for ever attaining greatness of intelligence and of stature as an individual person. He can say it too late, and see his personality split and shattered by powers he could neither hold steady nor assimilate to his self. He can build his dam too low for illumining with thought a personality hardly able to rise above the collective average of mankind. But he can also get drunk with intelligence and power, and erect psychic "towers of Babel" which require countless workmen to be built, enormous expenditure of power, and a constant effort of management so great as to allow for no peace -- and to lead ultimately to crystallization, tyranny, and spiritual death.

Man has need of stability. Sooner or later, he must stop in his avid grasping of sensations and experiences, in his attempts to force nature into the expanding net of his intellectual avidity for knowledge and for powers -- sensational, spectacular powers above all. And this need to come to a stop becomes the substance of his greatest test.

The test of stability is the test of when, where and how to stop. Everything thereafter will depend upon this when, this where and this how. Where a man "stops", there will be his foundation: his personality, his home -- and ultimately the structure of his after-death condition of being. On these foundations, he builds. From these foundations, he goes forth in self-expression, in progeny, in spiritual rebirth. But whatever happens after man has accepted as a fact his having reached bottom will be conditioned by and derived from the depth, the solidity, the potential carrying strength, and the essential character of the foundations thus established. A man says: Enough! -- and at this very moment he has rooted his self and his destiny in one type of energy and substance or another. He has set the limits of his potential growth.

To ascend in height requires a foundation in depth. Thus, the problem of reaching towering peaks of intelligence and of being able to encompass, from the vantage point they offer, a vast panorama of consciousness is first of all a problem of how deep one is willing and ready to go. Depth, here means nearness to center. The substance of one of the great tests man must meet is his willingness, and readiness, to reach center. It is the test of the "midnight Sun" -- of which Masonry speaks. To reach this midnight Sun one must first pass through the center of the earth. Center is reached by seeking one's own nadir, one's own depth of being -- the core of one's own "emptiness". For as the Irish poet truly said: Where there is nothing, there is God.

At the center there is "no-thing". The entire world of nature is balanced around emptiness. Gravitation, at its maximum, ceases. Gravity of thought in its utmost depth is... laughter. Lazarus, who has known initiatic death and returned from this zero-point of existence to bring men his vision, can best formulate it in a song of laughter -- as O'Neill so vividly expresses in his great work, "Lazarus Laughed". Levitation is not reached by a stubborn fight against gravitation at the surface of the earth -- or at the superficial level of human experience and consciousness. Levitation is the proof that man has reached center; that man has accepted fully gravitation. Such acceptation leads the daring and strong soul to center. It leads the weak and the timorous to suffocation and decay.

The paradox is, as always, that man must oppose nature while accepting nature. He must know himself as the polar opposite of nature even while he embraces nature and pierces through its mass. He must use nature to overcome nature. He must use gravitation to reach the center where gravitation ceases. The engineer must go along with gravitation if he is to build foundations deep enough to erect a massive and towering dam. He does not deny or fight against the weight of the waters and their down-flow. He increases this weight, he condenses time -- the natural rate of down-flow ("entropy") -- into moments of accentuated release, once he has gained the power to control and to use that intensified release of water-weight.

Someday engineers will be born who will not be contented to build foundations deep into the rock-bottom of the earth. They will realize that, farther than the deepest shaft sunk into the surface of substances which have mass and weight, there is "center". For the engineer to reach center is to gain a foundation which dwarfs all now known engineering foundations. To reach center is to reach that core of emptiness round which all masses and all energies are balanced. It is to gain a leverage from which all nature can be moved and controlled.

' We have become accustomed now to the concept of atomic fission or fusion and to the frightening power these processes let loose. But this power is as nothing compared to that which may be used by the individual who, because he himself is established in being and consciousness at the center of his own nature, can act upon the centers of all things. With ease, with the least exertion, he can affect and rearrange the balance of all that surrounds these centers. For, at the center, all lines of pressure so neutralize each other that there is absolute ease and absolute freedom to move in any direction -- and that intelligence in which God speaks; for God is the ultimate center of all conceivable universes.

The test of stability! The question is not only upon how deep a foundation one's stability rests. It can be formulated in a more crucial and challenging manner. What kind of stability does one seek: that which consists in an extended base at the surface of things -- that which is rooted in a relative depth of foundations -- or the stability established at the center of nature where all gravitation ceases and God is known as supreme, universal "I"?

It is an awesome question. By his answer -- unconscious though he be of its character -- a man establishes, in his innermost self, his future. It may mean strength or futility, "liberation" or slavery to powers of the "under-world", the greatest victory or long cycles of tragic regathering of energies to the self that has met defeat. No one can make such an answer with his brain or his emotions alone, or on the basis of some traditional religion or philosophy. No one need formulate in words the answer, lest he arouse, too soon perhaps, the powers of the depths. Yet, at the very core of every human self, the answer is formed, conditioning the man's future, determining the individual's basic relationship to nature, his innermost "truth", his essential purpose.

There are men, even entire civilizations, who seek stability by spreading themselves over a wide surface of experience. By interconnecting a great number of superficial data into a network of relations, consciousness may thus feel secure enough to build skyward. The intellect is an agency for associating observed facts and social contacts at the surface of an experience from which have been discarded at the outset the things which do not fit, the things which reach down into the realms where the sun of rationality does not penetrate. Intellectual stability is "map stability": the surveyor goes about covering the widest surface of things and connecting peaks and valleys by lines of orientation. These, projected on paper, constitute a map -- an abstraction of surface-appearances.

Our modern civilization is built upon maps and a map-consciousness. It contents itself to associate sense-perceptions and the results of experiments in terms of measurements -- of yardsticks, compass, scales, and clocks. Its statistics deal entirely with the surface-being of groups and categories; its laws, with averages and map-expectancy. It seeks -- or claims to seek -- a global fulfillment. But the globe it envisions is essentially a shell. It has no living core; no center; no single originating focus.

All the observations of science depend upon what is observable at the surface of planets and of stars; and observability here means light, product of the surface of the sun. Because it deals with surfaces, the modern intellect cannot recognize the meaning of "emptiness" at the center of all there is. It prolongs the concept of mass and surface-gravitation to a theoretical, mathematical center. The substance of this postulated center is not different from that observed at the surface -- except that it is claimed to be "hotter"! It is ordinary substance that happens to be placed at a particular geometrical point called "center". But it is not the living center of reality.

The living center is a void to our intellect and our perceptions of mass and substance. Through this void, the creative power of the universe speaks. It is the innermost chamber, which is God's dwelling place. Not the "glory" of God projected upon the screen of the sky to illumine all surface-things and all devotees craving for pomp, radiance and miracles; but the "poverty" of God, of which a few great mystics spoke -- the still, silent voice that resounds through the most ultimate void -- God in the Empty, whence is born all power and all reality.

To reach this center where there is nothing -- this is the great Crusade; the taking on of the Cross that leads to the deepest hells, foundations for all Resurrections. And few indeed ever qualify for this crusade, which only steady individuals can pursue through the burning deserts and the frozen midnights of an un-spectacular quest. Many lose their way and are heard no longer. The dim presentiment of tragedy warns all but the most daring or the most desperate that there must come a time when it is good to stop -- before it is too late. To stop; to consolidate one's gains; to establish one's depth where one can still see the glow of noonday light.

Humanity thus, normally, builds between nadir and zenith -- roots for the nadir, flowers at the zenith, green branches spread to meet the horizon. The issue that differentiates men, spirit and reality, is: "How deep are your roots? How secure are your foundations?"

The average man does not even realize there is a center. All he "feels" for is solid ground, rock bottom security. He builds his home; he erects the structure of his personality. And he becomes bound to that which gives him security and structure, incrusted in a particular place, crystallized in a

way of life and in an intellectual, social, and moral system
which defines once and for all his horizon and his goal. Animal and plant; man can roam over the surface of things, reaching beyond animal-hood in that he remembers and measures
the course of his wandering and builds maps -- or man may
root himself into one geographical spot, grow roots, stem and
seed; then, beyond plant-hood he learns to multiply c o n s c-
i o u s l y his seed and to worship in it life -- the fatherhood or
motherhood of God, as he also says in his most reverent moods.

But he only is truly "man" who leaves behind the spaces
of the earth-surface or the security of the root; who dares dying to the noonday light, that he might reach at the ultimate
depth of his own individual being the midnight Sun, in the sublime darkness in which all men are one, all voices are silent,
all bondages total into freedom. At the center, gravitation
ceases. Weight is overcome, as the individual willingly accepts all weights to the last, bitter end.

From this acceptation, liberation is born. The bitterest
hour ends in joy beyond all imaginings. Suffocation gives birth
to the endless song of spirit. Unbearable pain slides away to
reveal peace -- the peace no pressure can ruffle, for there is
no pressure where all pressures are accepted and balanced.
From the center the individual can go forth in any direction
God chooses -- the God that he has become. He is free, because he has made himself into that emptiness through which
God forever answers all needs which rise, from the surface
of things, to the sky. The sky reflects to the center the needs
born of the surface. And from the center, through the void
and the stillness, the answer comes. Spirit answers as power. That power raises harvests, or stirs the earthquake.
Always and forever it answers all needs.

Men who have reached center channel forth these answers.
They create, they destroy. Through their eyes that know supreme emptiness, through their hands that can plough the surface of all things, the Eternal One makes Himself known. He
it is of whom the Bhagavat Gita speaks, saying: "There dwell-

eth in the heart of every creature, the Master, Ishwara who by his magic power causeth all things and creatures to revolve mounted upon the universal wheel of time. Take sanctuary with him alone, with all thy soul; by his grace thou shalt obtain supreme happiness, the eternal place..." *

---

* William Q. Judge's translation -- by far the best.

THE TEST OF PURITY

Man must act; to live is to act. All actions imply a movement away from a relatively stable basis or state of equilibrium, away from a center. Movement requires an expenditure of energy. Power is released, that had been wound up -- into star, seed or soul. The nature of the power, the rhythm and quality of the release, its motivation and its aim: these determine the character of the act.

To release power there must be something through which the release can occur: an instrumentality or mechanism of release -- an agent, an engine.

Where the release of power occurs in nature we speak of "agent". We consider the instrumentality for the release an entity, perhaps an organism. The agent, in the human kingdom, appears with the character of individual selfhood; he becomes a responsible agent, a free agent.

Where the release of power occurs through a man-made instrumentality we speak of an "engine". Every man-made object through which energy is set free in an act or motion is an engine; a watch, a turbine, a dynamo -- and also a symphony, a stage-play, a religious ceremony, a baseball game; yes, even the vast ritual of a nation's business, correlating factories, trains, trucks, office workers according to a complex pattern of unceasing activity -- or the tragic ritual of war, in its destructive use of energy and substance.

The sun is a natural agent through which power is released. So is the cell, the seed, the plant, the bird at the level of this type of release we call "life". When man thinks and projects his thoughts either directly in the world of mental activity or indirectly through physical instruments operated by tongue or hands, he sets free power at the level of human "personality" and society; thus, two levels of release, two modes of activity.

In sun and seed the release seems to us compulsive, automatic, controlled by inevitable cosmic laws or instinctual drives based on bio-chemistry. We say there is no consciousness in the agent. In man we witness the appearance, not only of conscious awareness, but of clear motivation, intent and deliberate purpose. A man "plans" his actions, as he controls the expenditure of his various energies by means of the inhibiting and releasing power of the will, servant of his conscious individualized ego. He uses these energies as he sees fit. Consciousness, in him, directs the release of power -- at least of s o m e aspects of the power for which man is a releasing agent.

Consciousness -- Power: the great, the tragic dualism of man. In all the kingdoms of nature some sort of awareness or instinctual consciousness results from the release of power, as an overtone, an after-act product. But man, when he comes to be truly man, un-identified with nature -- man as a "self", as a spark of divinity -- is not only a f t e r-a c t consciousness, but b e f o r e-a c t consciousness. Not only Epi-metheus, but Prometheus. Not only one who remembers, but one who prophesizes -- a Seer, an Engineer. One who sees ahead, and uses f u t u r e releases of power under control and according to plan.

To be an engineer is man's great and tragic burden -- God's Signature within him, his inevitable responsibility. It is greatness, because participation in the creative processes of the universe. It is potential tragedy, because, being able to control energy and the "gestures" of energy-become-act, man, the engineer, can also distort the rhythm of all releases of power. He may use them for an activation which v i o l a t e s the natural character of the power itself. He

can do this because he is a self -- a unit of creative consciousness -- as well as an agent through which the powers of the
universe can be released.

As a unit of conscious selfhood he can transform and alter
the natural instrumentality through which human power flows
out-ward: his organs. He can add to, or subtract from the ef-
ficacity of his body and his psyche. He can extend their capacity for power-release by means of man-made engines, or
bring upon them sickness and corruption. He can think individual thoughts, transform nature by them, or distort universal
Ideas, breed mental monsters to channel the perverted dynamism of his rebellious or demented ego. He may be a Son of
God, God-in-Act; or he may oppose the divine Creative Harmony by pitting his will against the vast current of evolution,
against the universal Plan of the Great Architect of the Universe.

The choice is his, in so far as he is a conscious self. As
a self, he stamps the release of his energies with his own inherent character and quality of being. He acts out what he is.
He acts in "purity" -- or in "sin".

To be pure is to be an agent through whom power is released according to the inherent character and rhythm of that
power and in answer to the human need which called for such
a release of power -- and to no other end and in
no other way. It is to use the natural instrumentalities
for the release of power according to their intrinsic nature
and their fittingness within the universal pattern of evolution.
It is to act in terms of inherent necessity.

Purity in action is adequacy to the character of the power
released. There can be purity in destructive acts as well as
constructive acts. Catabolic agencies can be just as pure as
anabolic ones. Poison can be as purely poisonous as clear
water, without the admixture of any elements foreign to its
molecular nature (H_2O), is pure in its cleansing and dissolv-
ing action.

Likewise, an engine is "pure" that releases a particular

kind of power without waste motion and at least with a minimum of residual substances. And a human personality is pure who releases its share of the power latent in humanity-as-a-whole without emotional waste of energy and mental confusion. Such a man is what he inherently is, and nothing but what he inherently is, as an individual self. He is thus a clear agent for the release of human power.

Yet, purity in an individual person implies more than adequacy to function and perfect attunement to the rhythm of the power used. Of man it is asked that he take his place consciously and significantly within the great performance of universal evolution. He must not only play perfectly his own instrument, and release beautiful and vibrant tones that stir; he must also perform his part in the orchestra of humanity -- his part as it exists in the universal score. Purity for man, thus implies the correct rendering of his characteristic melodic line, rhythm or chord in the vast symphony that is "Man" -- the fulfillment of his function, his destiny, and his "truth".

Truth, spiritual identity, d h a r m a: various words to define immortal selfhood in effective and adequate act. The truth of an individual consists in all the activities necessary for the complete and correct performance of his life-purpose as an incarnate self. All that is necessary; nothing that is not necessary. In purity and in truth, freedom and necessity become identical.

The individual is spiritually free as he fulfills his essential purpose, and in no other way. He is concretely free as he is allowed by society, and determined by his own will, to perform these acts which are inherent in the character and rhythm of the power for the release of which he was created an agent. For an individual to be free to do a n y t h i n g he might wish or conceive has no meaning in itself. The only freedom is that of performing all the acts that are necessary for one's inherent spiritual purpose.

This purpose is l a t e n t in the very character of the powers which are pressing for expression within the individual's own nature. As he understands in truth the character of his powers, he grasps at the same time the nature of his essential life-purpose -- what he should be free for -- unless in the excitement attendant to the use of the powers (and this is the great test!) the individual identifies himself with the tidal sweep of, first this power, then that other; thus becoming a helpless sounding-board for the confused ebbs and flows of any and all natural energies which circumstances may arouse in his body and psyche.

In the animal or the plant, purity and truth-in-action are compulsory for any one particular animal or vegetable specimen. The plant is rooted in the ground and reaches as deep into the soil as it possibly can in order to establish a foundation for the ascent of its leaves and blossoms toward the life-giving light. The animal, on the other hand, moves about within a set circumference of motion -- or along a set migratory course -- and thereby establishes an equally set rhythm for the release of its powers under the sway of instinctual and compulsively unconscious emotions -- its life-urges.

Man is both plant and animal. He may stretch his desires sunward to God and ground them in deep shafts wherein he probes the meaning and reality of power as power; he may spread his experience over a wide surface and orient himself in his world of "maps" in terms of extension and surface-born emotions, of sensations and concepts. But man is more. He is potentially a planet, established in center, secure in cosmic selfhood -- a planet chorded with companion-planets in a "harmonic series" of releases of power, the "fundamental tone" of which is the sun. Each planet is an agent for the release of one kind of power. As a solid globe the planet is "agent", but it is more; the real planet is the s p a c e o u t-l i n e d b y i t s o r b i t.

This orbit, being an ellipse, has two foci. One, common to all planets (the sun), is the source of the one universal power; the other, which differs for every planetary orbit, is the source of individual selfhood and consciousness. As the solid

globe of the planet performs its periodic circuits around these
two foci, it channels outward into expression their combined
forces. As the one wanes, the other waxes; this in turn, and
forever. To be p u r e is to be an agent for the one solar power. To be t r u e is to be an agent for the differentiating energy of the self. Purity, in reference to power; truth, in reference to the consciousness of self.

In the cyclically altered harmony of power and conscious
selfhood, the man whose life is a constant enactment of his inherent destiny moves on like a planet. In essence, in total
four-dimensional being, he is the orbital space of his destiny.
In act, he is the cyclically revolving globe that focuses this
total reality of being into creative expression, through an unceasing release of power.

He who lives on and from the surface of reality is only su-
per-plant and super-animal. Consciousness results from action, follows after action; and consciousness is swayed by the
ebbs and flows of power, by the changing slope of sunrays
throughout the year, by the lunar rhythm of watery substances
-- sea, sap, and blood -- by the magic of unsteady desires that
pulse at the beat of the seasons. His life may be "pure" as it
gives expression to the nature of the power and the powers of
nature. But purity is of little avail to the man who seeks to
be truly man except it be united with truth. And truth is known
only at the center; one's truth, one's self.

The things that crawl, blossom, or sing on the surface of
our globe know only the urge of power; and their lives are
moulded by power, scanned by the rhythm of power, enslaved
by the fatality of power. But for whom center is an eternal
abode, for whom solid earth has become transparent to orbital space -- for such a one there can be no lure in power, no
glamor in sunshine, no desire and no pain in the waxing and
waning of life's urges. In him, power and consciousness are
harmonized. If power ebbs away, he knows in his inner being
the flow of more intense selfhood. His acts are performed in
the name of both. Love merges with intelligence; purity, with

truth. Their child? Divinity in act. God is Space, focused and defined by forever moving globes. Man is globe: God-in-act. This is man's truth.

There is no test of purity for a tree, a bird, or a tiger. They are compelled to be pure; they are unconscious agents. They grow, they sing, they kill -- as they must. Power, the dictator, compels; operates their glands and muscles; measures the beats of their hearts. Theirs is the realm of life -- and life is the surface of divinity; the warmth, the glamor, the desires, the fear, the loveliness, the passion, the horror of all that is born and must die -- unaware.

But the man who is man in truth, because he is established at the center in the marriage of power and selfhood and in freedom from earthly gravitation, is impelled by an inherent necessity to be c o n s c i o u s l y what he is, to move on forever as definer of space, as orbit-describer, as child of power and consciousness, of love and intelligence. He acts out his phase of divinity as a planet acts out its part in the cosmic polyphony of the solar system.

The test of purity, for such a man, is to be not only pure, but true; not only to release power, but to act out meaning; not only to perform the surface-operations of life -- the birthing of new organisms, new cultural forms, new songs, and new glamor-intoxicated thrusts skyward -- but to act out the alchemies of center, the reduction of desires into necessities, or emotions into meaning.

It is a complex test; a drama in several acts. At first, man's soul -- feeling one with all nature -- cries out in yearning for light, sings glory-songs to the sun in the choir of trees and beasts. Then, man experiences himself separate; he loses touch with nature. He must stand on his own. The pulse of his desires maddens him. He must extend his field, his kingdom, his world. Power haunts him, taunts him; he must trail it down to its source, pierce the flesh, pierce the earth. Has power no lair; have roots no deeper to go than instincts tell?

Man loses his purity. He wrestles with power; twists it to his passion; lightens his depths with electric fire; sunders the core of atoms with the quest for power; falls perhaps into abysses his ego conjured; explodes with the things he fissioned and the loves he smashed. Or he reaches center -- and peace. And in this peace he knows truth; his truth. To know that truth consciously he had to lose purity; and regain it -- in the cosmic context of orbital space, in the union of power and self. . . where God acts Himself out through man, the free; in man, the true.

THE TEST OF SUFFERING

Because man is both a unit of consciousness and an agent for the release of power he must undergo the test of suffering. Because he may use the power inherent in his total organism for goals envisioned by his consciousness, goals which do often conflict with the ultimate and ineradicable purpose of human evolution; because he may use his energies in ways which violate the natural character of the power itself -- man must experience pain. Caught in the very wheels his engineering skill constructed, he mechanizes his life into disease. He splits, together with the atom, his mind quartered by the pulls of self-gratification, self-denial, self-aggrandizement and stultifying fear.

Suffering is the shadow of man's unlived life, the pressure of unactualized potentiality, the kick-back of unspent energy. Pain results from deviated or frustrated instinct where there is consciousness to assess the loss and to struggle toward self-restoration. Suffering is the ransom of freedom -- the freedom to be "man" against "nature". Pain is the tenaciousness of life fighting for survival against depredation.

All that lives is subject to pain. Man alone suffers. In him alone the consciousness of pain, of defeat and futility, gnaws at the core of his selfhood. Man alone suffers, because he alone can be beaten by earth-life. He may know defeat, because he alone can experience victory. All suffering is defeat. It may be direct defeat. It may be defeat shared with those that are loved, shared with humanity -- an inevitable sharing. No man is truly victorious whose prowess implies

the defeat of other men.   The only human victory is over the
entropy of nature -- the victory over death.

Christ said, according to the Gnostic hymnist: "If you had
known how to suffer, you would have had the power not to suffer. " The only way to overcome suffering is the way of the
Resurrection. He who uses his suffering as a foundation for
his Resurrection needs, in time, no longer experience suffering; for the Resurrection is the full living of life, the complete actualization of human potentiality, the total release of
natural energy, as man pierces through and emerges from
"nature". The Resurrection neutralizes suffering -- though
it may not obviate the inevitability of pain wherever there is
life and conflict.

To know how to suffer: this is the test. To make suffering s e r v e the purpose of the Resurrection: this is the
essence of spiritual living in individualzed man. To   u s e
frustration, fear and defeat as springboards to immortality:
this is the ancient and eternal technique which leads to eventual mastery. To do it, man requires a courageous attitude
toward failure, an objective evaluation of the causes of failure, and emotional detachment from the past -- any past.

First, c o u r a g e. He who is not willing to fail can never
truly know the Resurrection. To close one's consciousness
even to the suffering of the most distant human being is to
bargain with eternity -- and to fall back, empty handed, in
the lap of time. Every individual defeat is Man's failure. Ultimately it must mean pain for all. Every man is involved in
the suffering of all men. Yet, to experience victory one must
dare court defeat and assume one's part of the responsibility
of any suffering any man may experience as a result. What
such a responsibility might be, no one may know beforehand.
This is the test of courage, and of faith. Faith in God. Faith
in Grace: the vibrant sustainment of the spiritual Whole, which
no one lacks who has courage, who risks annihilation for immortality.

Courage. The spirit within the soul has courage. Where

the desire is strong or the despair unbearable enough, the daring word or deed goes forth easily enough, perhaps. But the living of that which follows; the everyday bearing of the darkness and the pain; the watching of the ripples which the stone of one's decision makes, larger and larger, in the pool of destiny -- how hard the suffering these summon, how poignant the unfathomable pain! Further testing comes; not only of the will, but of the mind. The causes of the failure must be confronted, met in almost blinding lucidity, and objectively evaluated.

Objective evaluation. This is the test of vision and understanding; one factor, then another, isolated, measured, and weighed against the whole of the values which life, culture, and society -- and the words of God-inspired men who spoke in centuries of long ago -- have presented to the individual since birth. To measure, one compares visually with a paragon of accepted value. But spiritually to weigh, one "stands under" and symbolically experiences the burden, in an act of understanding. To understand is to experience the fact to be understood as a symbol of essential reality -- sub species aeternitatis. But whether vision or understanding is at stake, the first requirement is the capacity to be objective to the factor one is to evaluate. This means to sever oneself from this factor; to stand alone and un-identified; to break one by one, or in one great gesture, the myriads of threads which bind the consciousness to the thing that has been born of one's living, as a child of one's womb. To stand naked; and to know it. To stand deprived; and to realize that one is father of the deprivation; yet to accept and to smile, as Buddha smiled when he understood the world, and was free.

Severance is not only of the consciousness; and still less only of the intellect. It must cut down to the roots of feelings, even to the deepest unconscious roots. It must reach indeed the feeling of feeling. It must still this strange throb of the inner life without which most men could not bear living, so great, so awesome the silence that follows the stilling. Christ told us He came not to bring peace, but a "sword". And the sword cut deep into the consciousness of men and let escape many bleeding ghosts; for man became afraid.

It was too still on Golgotha after the Consummatum Est -- when millenia of history reached their con-summation in the ultimate acceptation of suffering by one who had learned how to suffer, on his way to the Resurrection. And men -- not understanding, not able to "stand under" the Cross of suffering -- emotionally, indeed wildly, sought to glorify suffering, to exalt pain and sing strident paeans to death. But suffering is not to be glorified; it is to be used. Death is not to be glorified; it is to be smiled through. Pain must be understood as a protective gesture of life; not only the body's life, but far more the psyche's life.

Pain is the custodian of our undiscovered treasures. It shows that we are going away from the fullness of our potential nature, we are losing our inner substance of being, we are inefficient managers of our human riches. There is nothing great of itself in tragedy, unless we give it the meaning of self-discovery; unless we use it. Suffering is a sign of human greatness not yet fully realized, or wantonly wasted. It is a summons to our self, to our most glorious victory...yet to be. And the sharing of suffering with other men and with the corporate wholeness of humanity makes little sense, unless it be on the path which leads from one's limited self to the greater reality of Man, in whom all individual selves are chorded into a vast resonance sounding out throughout the world the many names that, heard together, sum up into "God".

Suffering can never be a goal or have value in itself. It is a training in objective understanding and emotional severance; a test in endurance of our will and our faith. It is the shadow necessary to make the white form of our self known, the mounting required to frame and define clearly the color of the powers that are our jewelled inheritance. Suffering is a process of conscious realization of value: a transition. Man suffers because he is more than he knows himself to be. Suffering is the condition for breaking man's identification with the "less", as he climbs on his way to the "more". It is the pressure of his greater destiny upon his attachment to his lesser goals. Unless through suffering man learns utterly to sever his consciousness and his feelings from his past and the past of humanity, suffering has no meaning. Whoever looks exclusively forward does not suffer. Yet this lack of suffering means also the failure to evaluate objectively the past.

The past must be understood. From it, the essence of "meaning" must be extricated. Everything else must be forgotten, dismissed -- with a blessing. The man who never looks back has yet to understand the significance of cyclic time. He grows like a tree; not like a man. But to look back with longing, with regret or remorse is not to grow at all. It is to fall back in spiritual exhaustion to the roots, under the weight of useless suffering.

The criterion of all spiritual living is the u s e we make of our experiences; and the experience of suffering is a magic key, if only it is truly used. It is the key to the right use of power. Power must be used, or we suffer. It must be used "right", according to its natural character; or else we experience pain. And because man is spirit and spirit means consciousness, power and the mechanisms for its release must be understood in clear objective consciousness. We "understand" power only as we are subject to the pressure of its possible effects. And this is the great lesson of total war and atomic power.

The establishment of constant global interrelationships between all men generates an enormous amount of collective human power, which so far had been only latent in mankind. This power can be given adequate mechanisms for its release by the modern intellect -- by scientists, technicians, specialized managers and administrators. We can learn to organize a Normandy Invasion and its incredibly complex and accurate patterning of group-activities spread over months of preparation and culminating in one great individual decision and one great mass-effort. We can also correlate the skill and inventiveness of men of all races, and through months of research and application learn to release atom power -- the foundation required for world-integration at the level of economic production and distribution. But this is not enough.

The scientist does not understand atom-power simply by means of his involved equations and his test-tubes. The Commander-in-Chief does not understand the collective power of a fully activated and interrelated humanity simply by reading news about China or hearing the sound of an exploding atom bomb. Really and significantly to u n d e r s t a n d these things man must be subjected to their weight in his personal or group experience. He must "bear" their pressure, the fears and doubts as well as the expectations they arouse, the sight of the horror their misuse produces. The ancient patterns of his life must be disrupted by the new powers. He must be temporarily stunned by the blinding light they release. He must accept full responsibility for this release. All of which means suffering and pain, disease and intemperate death.

Then only can man understand. He understands in his soul, symbolically, if he is wise and mature enough to evoke the full essence and reality of the powers he released; otherwise he can only understand through suffering and pain in concrete physical experience. Understanding, he can learn objectively and incontrovertibly the nature of the power, the character of its constructive application in the furthering of human evolution, the danger of its uncontrolled expression.

Then, comes the test of suffering. Will man, dismayed by the monstrous death he brought forth, shrink in adolescent anguish from sailing on the unfathomed sea of the new power, and seek irrationally to return to the charm, culture and peace of an era which the new release of power put violently to an end? Will he mourn the past and give himself up to its ghosts, so beautiful on its death-bed? Or will he, after a last look of supreme awareness, sever with a sword of courage the

cable that makes firm the vessel of his soul and venture upon
the vast expanse of an unknown world of energies?

Here, the great and subtle lure which distracts many a
soul is: self-pity. "Why has this to happen to me?" To this,
there are varied metaphysical answers. The one practical
reply, however, is: "Because you do not know yet what your
full power and your essential goal are. "

Not yet. Not yet. These two little words contain the essence of all human tragedy. All suffering, all pain are their
progeny. Not yet. Men are not quite yet "Man". They are
moving toward the Mastery -- the right use of "human" power; whether in their own bodies, or in those projected fragments of consciousness which they are taught intellectually to
externalize under the convenient name, "atom".

All power man can ever use is human. The whole world
man lives in is human. Even rocks are fragments of our human perception. We see them rock-like because we need
them rock-like to give support to our static sense of selfhood.
We sunder now the rock's core and release the fire caged in
the mysterious atom's den. And men die horrible death, and
cities are burned alive...in our souls that had built them for
love, pleasure -- and greed.

Why? Because we fail to see that atomic fission and fusion make no sense except as they give power to the transition
from narrowness of self to the greater selfhood of Man in
whom all men live, chorded in response to the purpose of God
for us all. Suffering, pain and death -- because this is a transition. The substance of them all is pain; and in man, the
conscious and the understander, suffering.

Suffering is the footstool of our divinity. We may stumble
over it and fall back into the womb of time to renew once more
our tragic attempt at metamorphosis. Or we may step upon
it, raise our countenance by damming the very stream of our
tears, and use suffering to reach the extended hands of Him
Who is our resurrected Self. Suffering can only cease with
the Resurrection, in any man who is truly human. For to be

man is to be ceaselessly more what one is. Until humanity merges into divinity. Until the individual becomes Man. Until all victorious men, having learnt to use rightly in its fullness the power that is theirs in God, no longer need suffering.

In God, there dwells eonic peace. He who includes all things and uses all power adequately for the need of all men -- in Him, there is perfect Harmony. He is risen; through suffering, unto victory; through fire, unto light.

THE TEST OF MUTUALITY

More than nineteen centuries ago, Jesus gave men two
fundamental precepts: "Love one another"; "Do unto others as
you would have them do unto you". The second of these great
statements explains and gives to the first its most essential
meaning.

So many things, strange and wonderful, have been meant
ever since by the word "love"! It has glowed with tender and
mystic light; it also struck here and there tones of frenzy and
even depravation. Who does not claim to love? But love,
throughout our Christian culture that strove toward other-
worldly goals and sought to deny the "good earth", this love
has assumed the ideal character of transcendental feeling,
rather than that of productivity and radiant activity.

Yet Jesus did not come to teach man to despise the earth
and the activity of the earth. He did not come to exalt feeling
and sentiment over productive and creative action. He came
to show a new way of activity: the way of conscious
mutuality. As he took birth at the dawn of an age which, he
well knew, was to stress above all the principle of individualism and ego-separateness, he offered to humanity as a gift
the antidote of the sickness of isolation in self: "mutuality"
-- which means interchange, reciprocity, the "one another"
in all deeds.

The first great test of the spiritual life is "isolation".
Birth is isolation. All great things begin in isolation. But
they can only mature through mutuality. Selfhood is singleness; love is cooperative sharing. These are the two polar-

ities of human growth. That which begins in self must understand and realize itself in mutuality and in love. Love is not
primarily a feeling; it is the seed of mutuality. It is the vision of the "one another" to the "one", the annunciation of activity performed in common.

Not merely "in common", however -- rather, in mutual
interchange. Where there is no interchange, no interplay,
no reciprocity, there can be but the shadow of love. One-
sided love is no love. Love is mutual action; and the mature
"feeling" of love, this wondrous essence of fire and light, is
born of mutuality in sharing, of the "one another".

The word "mutual" comes from the Latin muto, which
means "to change". The etymology, here as in so many instances, reveals the core of the mystery. The realm of self,
where the I stands in singleness out of God, is established in
eternity. The "I am" is the invariant tone; the permanent
foundation in spirit; the seed which at the end of time is that
which it was at the beginning and which it ever remains throughout all birthing and dying. But in the realm of relatedness
there is constant change. There is change because there is
inevitable mutuality. Each acts upon the other, as he re-acts
to the other. This is "Karma"; action that is caught in the
web of response woven by the universe resounding to the act.

In child-like man this mutuality is unrealized, because he
does not know yet that he, out of his singleness of self, can
be an origin; that he can give birth to a new chain of action
and throw the weight of creative decision into the pond of the
surrounding life. As the child becomes adolescent, his sense
of individual freedom intoxicates him. Wildly he catapults his
decisions through the space of, to him, an empty universe,
just for the joy of throwing away seed and feeling himself un-
burdened of self. And great is his dismay when the universal
womb responds to his sowings with a progeny, for him to father in responsibility.

Through pain and weariness, he comes to learn the lesson
of mutuality -- the balancing of action and reaction in res-

ponsible productivity, in efficient management, in this love that is not self-projected alone, but the love of one another; love that is rhythm, interplay, interchange; love that is the one changing into the other in the mysterious antiphony of the sharing of each other's gifts and each other's burdens, as melodies of individual being weave themselves into garlands of deeds, from the one to the all, from the all to the one.

Mutuality is change that returns to its source after having partaken of the universal life; not only the interchange of lovers immersed in relationships and tossed about by waves of passionate blendings, but the great play of universal change in which each becomes all, so that the whole might become focused into every one.

This mutuality is a universal fact; none can escape the return tide, who ventured forth into the sea of action. But the horizon of most men is so narrow that the wave which throws them stunned upon the rock of their separate existence seems a thrust from nowhere. Could they but see, far in the abysmal distance, its recoiling from an originally opposite direction, they would know that the blow that fells their proud singleness is the child of the unlived relatedness of gestures they themselves threw into a space which they thought but passively receptive.

Space is not a hollow receptivity, a bottomless vase. Space is mutuality. It is indeed the substance of universal and total relatedness. Everything cast away into space returns with the whole world added to it, as a sounding board adds overtones to any original sound. Every note that ever sounds forth resounds enriched with myriads of overtones. Each string of the universal harp calls forth a resonance from every other string. To the bound ego, this is karma. To the wise, it is love. Jesus' mission was to transfigure karma into love. It is always the task of the Christ-being to transfigure karma into love, unconscious interdependence into conscious mutuality, unwilling reciprocity into deliberate sharing -- nay more, into joyous participation.

Conscious mutuality becomes joyous and creative participation as the related selves transfigure the walls, which bind
and isolate them as particular egos, into living membranes
through which flow the osmotic currents of love; for love is an
osmosis of life, of light and of truth. Walls are forever to be
shattered; cell-membranes forever to be enjoyed. There can
only be pain out of fortified boundaries; there should always
be joy as skins that touch one another become thresholds for
the life of man's common humanity to pass through, in the
flow of companionship and common participation.

Conscious and joyous participation makes of universal space
not a mere web of related "world-lines", but instead an organism of love. Love is space become full with creative joy; it
is the song of birth of a universal Whole in whom all related
selves have incorporated the fragrance of feeling released by
the flowering of communal deeds. It is mutuality made significant by men and women who overcame unconscious fate
through the magic of conscious love; mutuality not only accepted, but given meaning -- not only purified of passion-heavied
dross, but transfigured as the light of a birth of spiritual living.

Mutuality is change. All life is constant change. A Buddha
overcomes change by encompassing the Whole in intelligence
and in perfect peace. A Christ makes change significant, fe-
cund, and warm with conscious mutuality. He w a l k s upon
the sea of change. He calls unto Him those who are not afraid.
Most men, alas, like Peter, are afraid; they sink heavily into the world of change, because they are not at peace with
themselves and the world. They have not bound themselves
joyously into the companionship of the Whole, where every
life would support them, in as much as they would then be fit-
ted into the magnetic pattern of the love that encompasses all
-- the pattern of the universal Harmony, that is God.

Harmony is the effulgence of love; the substance of mutuality. Harmony is the "becoming one" within the act of participation in the Whole. To experience truly Harmony, is to

become consciously implied in the wholeness of the Whole. The Whole implies you; your activity implies the Whole. This is real sharing, boundless sharing -- a current which stops nowhere, as it returns everywhere. The Whole flows into the part; the part "loves", as it focuses the Whole-in-act in the name of, and together with, all other parts sharing in the act and in the love. Every part is united with all other parts through that which makes it distinct from all other parts.

Distinct; not different. No one becomes greater by becoming different from all other men. Greatness comes from distinctness. What one has to say, that must be said distinctly, clearly, forcefully -- in purity and in truth. And the word that left the firm and vibrant lips speeds forth among all other distinct words. They are l o g o s and they are truth. And as they interact in mutuality of response, in participation of meanings, the vast resonance of the Whole organizes all truths and all tones into that all-encompassing Harmony which men who are wise in wonder and in awe understand to be God.

God is substantiated in love, even as He is expressed forth in selfhood. Love and Self are the two polarities of God, the two wings of the Bird of Eternity. Through Self that is changeless, the Divine Essence becomes substance and power in the infinite polyphony of a love in which unity demonstrates itself as mutuality, and the Whole is "made flesh" in change forever revealing in the total relatedness of space That which, in the wholeness of any and all cycles, IS.

To love is to bless change with the realization of inclusive eternity. It is to participate joyously in the Harmony wherein all selves become what they are by resounding to what everything is, while demonstrating in utmost distinctness that truth, that identity and that flame which constitute their share of responsibility within the universal Whole. Love establishes the sharing; God, the responsibility. Man becomes truly man as he understands both and fulfills both in that reciprocity of being which constantly renews and proclaims the common foundation of all activity and all consciousness.

To share, while remaining distinct; to be harmony, while retaining the indivisibility of self; to act out power, while losing none of objective wisdom; to swim rhythmically with the tides of change, while secure in the inalienability of that identity which is God's Presence in man; to love, yet to be at peace; to give all, yet forever increase the substance of one's external being -- these are some of the many phases the test of mutuality includes. It is man's most poignant yearning, the yearning to love.

...And Jesus said: "Love one another". His eyes must have glowed with great light as he said the words. His hands perhaps swayed, a little extended, as if to gather the vastness and the mystery of space. Yet, there must have been in the taut smile that glided over his lips a strange and subtle poignancy; for he knew -- oh, how he must have known! -- that the love he summoned into the midst of men would often be dark and heavy with the presence of death; that there would be pain and despair in hearts seeking in vain to grasp within themselves a space they could not contain -- and not containing, would be lost. For "love" without "one another" is a sea haunted by ghosts of ships that found no harbor, and love without sharing is a deep fog -- as self without love, a desertic waste.

But Jesus said: "Love one another". And his words rose to the stars. And the stars sang with joy; they, that forever move throughout spaces and times without end; they, that circle in the companionship and the mutuality of light, single but at peace, in that Harmony of the Spheres which men, who love greatly, in wonder and joy experience as God.

THE TEST OF RESPONSIBILITY

As birth establishes a field of natural and social owner-ship for the individualized spirit, so does human relationship establish a field of responsibility for those who participate in this relationship. Mutuality in relationship produces new en-ergies and new facts. The new energies must be used -- and lack of use is still a negative type of use! The new facts must be met -- and shrinking away from them, through fear or in-attention, is a negative way of facing what must always be faced, however delayed the acceptation of the challenge of re-lationship.

All energy is born of relationship. It is produced or re-leased by the interaction of currents of desire or of compas-sion flowing from the polarities of the universal Whole, as well as from those within human bodies or personalities. En-ergy is relationship in act. It is the productive "fact" of re-lationship. Man's attitude towards this fact -- the use he makes of it -- establishes the character and quality of his participa-tion in society and in the universe. Society is what the use it makes of the energy born of human relationship forces it to be. In the problem of personal o w n e r s h i p the two poles of the energy-producing relationship are the individual human spirit and the collective wealth of nature and society. In problems of r e s p o n s i b i l i t y the two polarities involved are two hu-man persons, or two groups assuming the legal role of per-sons.

At the limit, responsibility links man, the individual per-son, to God, the cosmic person; it links them in an intimacy of relationship which the great mystics alone truly experience, who boldly declare in an ecstasy of transcendent mutuality that God has need for man, as man for God. But in any case, responsibility implies actually three factors. It implies two parties to a bi-polar relationship considered within the frame of reference of some whole in which the two persons participate, be this whole a business firm, a church, a nation, or the entire universe.

Both parties to the relationship are "responsible", withal in different ways. The manager of the corporation is responsible to the owner or the executive board; but the responsibility of the owner to the manager is just as real. Both types of responsibility have ultimate meaning, moreover, only with reference to the corporation as a whole or to the social community which includes all the participants in the business.

Responsibility is an expression of mutuality in relationship; it is the unavoidable outcome of it. To meet one's responsibility is to see the mutual relationship completely through. And this is the great test which all men must meet in various degrees, who enter into any kind of relationship. There is no complete, or even no vital experience of relationship if the responsibility for its products is not assumed and discharged; just as there can be no complete individual life without a full use of natural and social possessions. In both cases, objectivity is needed. The individual ego must be objective to his own innate gifts or powers and to the traditional wealth of knowledge or attitudes he acquires during his youth, if they are to be used discriminately and with intelligence. Likewise the partners in any relationship must gain a real perspective on their relationship, if the fruits thereof are to be made to serve significant ends.

The first tests in the two basic fields of the personal and the social life deal respectively with the primary experiences of independent existence (or self) and of relationship (love or partnership); but these original experiences and trials of earth-life mark only the beginning of two complementary processes.

They lead to two subsequent steps, dealing with the u s e to which what has bee.1 revealed in experience has to be put.

To be, to use, then to understand: these are the three primary phases of human living. Each phase summons forth a basic challenge to the individual human spirit. It leads to tests of strength and creativeness in activity, or of thoroughness and effectiveness of productivity, or of skill and purity in understanding.

Because all types of activity in our world of concrete manifestation are inherently four-fold, being, use and understanding operate in four basic directions. No man can truly "be" unless he be a creative origin, a stable organism whole, a polarity in various kinds of mutual responsibilities, and a functional participant in a larger whole. "Being" must forever be p r o v e n through use, and d e f i n e d through limits and characteristic meaning. Then only can come the C o n s u m- m a t u m   E s t which crowns any complete human victory. Only then is man ready for the Resurrection -- man emerging, t h r o u g h nature overcome and illumined, as Son of God.

At the core of any relationship is the principle of polarization. Wherever two elements enter into relationship one kind or another of polarization is established. It may be the electrical type of polarization expressed in atomic particles such as protons and electrons, or the biological type manifesting in sexual factors, or the social type found wherever leader and led, manager and workmen are related in productive work or in economic-political strife. Even where apparently unpolarized factors are discerned, as the neutron in the atom's nucleus, these can still be said to polarize space itself or unorganized substance. All these types of polarization have one common character; they make change, transformation and progression possible.

Sex, for instance, is the variant-producing factor in all that lives. Reproduction through division and multiplication of one single cell is a static kind of process. But as two here-

ditary lines blend in bi-polar sexual fecundation, each with an
infinitely complex and inclusive past, a "mystery" is set into
dynamic operation. The creative newness of the "moment" is
expressed in form. God, who is eternal and constant creativity, utters Himself in a new gesture and tone of life.

The Eternal Creative performs t h r o u g h sex, and in varying degrees through any polarized relationship, because polar union opens the door to the new variation -- to the mystery. God is substantiated in renewal, not in sameness: in
"adventure", not in conservative acts. There is no divinity,
no human genius, no real greatness anywhere, except through
that which releases the new, the yet-to-become, the yet-to-
be-known. God is always the yet-to-be-known; for, as Oliver
Reiser said, "When God is known He becomes man".

The secret core of this challenge of the earth to man and
woman, to the genius and his community, to the leader and
his people, is the command to make God a man. It is the challenge of Incarnation; and it is the challenge to assume the responsibility for this incorporation of divinity into a new human
fact -- a grave, solemn, often tragic responsibility. And the
challenge is to b o t h participants in the relationship; to the
"woman" pole, that there should be in her a vibrant, calling-
forth expectancy of the new man, the yet-unknown God -- to
the "man" polarity, that there should be in him positiveness,
definiteness, purity, vision, courage, and the indomitable will
to be of God in the very midst of chaos.

To be responsible is to assume the burden of a new birth,
of a new venture, of a new fact. Responsibility rests upon
both parents of a child; upon the inventors of a new process
and the discoverers of a new truth, but also upon the society
which conditioned and defined their opportunity to invent and
discover by its needs, its desires, its expectations, its vices
as well as its virtues. Responsibility for the atomic bomb is
upon the scientists who produced it, but as much upon the American society and the whole Western world that sought after
it for destruction. And no man can "wash his hands" of res-

ponsibility by refusing to face it, or by forcing it -- cleverly or crudely -- upon others who, in blindness, may willingly accept it.

Every human situation implies responsibility; it reveals or conceals a relationship between individuals or groups, and no one can evade it who is implied in the relationship -- which means, ultimately, every human being that has been, that is or ever will be. Every human situation is an inescapable challenge to human renewal and human creativeness. Every act of living among men, or even in the universe, involves responsibility for whoever acts; and to refuse to act is only acting negatively.

For the spirit destined to be human, to refuse to be born was (at the beginning of man's evolution) to let evil enter the earth through the spiritually unguided (thus meaningless) proliferations of material animal organisms. To refuse to create when the call rises from the waters of chaos is, at any time, to accept the responsibility for decay and death. This is the ultimate as well as the truly original "sin". Evil is born of the refusal of responsibility. This refusal compels those who made it to assume, in tragedy, the responsibility for evil. Every man is responsible for evil who fails to assume the responsibility of any situation and any relationship in which he was and is a participant.

Thus is "karma" born. Every man bears the karma of himself and his community. Every man bears the sins of all humanity, for he is always and forever a partner to everything human and he is implicated in all births and in all abortions. Karma is not produced so much by a wrong kind of action as by the type of action which derives from a refusal to perform creative acts, when the need for them had come. Karma is caused by a denial -- conscious or unconscious -- of the creative potentiality of the moment by those who live that moment.

As a moment of time is left un-expressed by the living spirit in man, this spirit must become a slave of more time.

Every spiritual monad must reincarnate as long as it fails to incorporate in creative acts the creative power of every moment it is incarnate. To create is the incessant responsibility of the spirit in and through embodied man, because creation is simply the fulfillment, by the spirit, of the potentiality inherent in every moment of time. Time is God's compassion for chaos; and man is the agency through which this compassion must operate in terms of creative acts.

Creation is the fruition of relationship; and "In the beginning" -- that is, the birth of time out of eternity -- the one relationship is that of spirit to matter. Matter is the unredeemed past, the manure of the universe that was, the chaos of disassociated elements which could not reach integration and fulfillment. Spirit is the potential of all conceivable futures. This potential of futurity alone can redeem matter. It alone can cause matter in chaos to be gathered once more through a world process creative of cosmos, toward the goal of integration. This process of ingathering and eventual integration of material elements is evolution.

Evolution predicates form; that is, structures within which the process of integration, refinement and transmutation can operate. And, metaphysically speaking, "Man" in any universe is the basic as well as ultimate Form. He is the universal Paradigm, the operative Logos, in and through whom spirit relates itself to material elements ready for this union. To prepare the way for this fulfillment of relationship is the cosmic task of man.

It is a cosmic task, and it is also an everyday task to be performed in the humblest way, in the lowliest circumstances. Indeed, it is performed most intimately and most effectively where material elements need it most, where there is the greatest darkness and the most disintegrating conflicts. Thus Jesus, the Christ, was born in a manger, in the town of Beth (the feminine principle), in a land rigid with formalism, in a race that extolled the ego in the blood, the Saturnian Jehovah.

Upon Jesus was the responsibility of Christhood: the responsibility of wedding the spirit of creative newness to the egocentric, race-worshipping, passionate type of personality which the Jewish culture bred under conditions of rigid dogmatism. But not upon him alone. It had to be shared by the Jews, the negative pole of the relationship; as later Rome and the Caesars had to share the responsibility of Christianity.

But the Jewish culture could only produce a Paul, who permeated the Gospel of eternal creative newness through simple, God-illumined, personal acts with the emotionalism of the old Jewish atonement and the heavy sense of sinfulness and death. And Rome made Christianity Roman and imperialistic, Catholic and stultified by legalistic formulas and dogmas. Matter had pulled spirit to its heaving, matriarchal bosom; and spirit shone no longer, except through a few great mystics and through the stones and liturgies of sky-flung cathedrals which made of the simple light of Christhood a tragic chiaroscuro of sin and redemption by blood.

Upon every man is the responsibility of Christhood; upon every woman the responsibility of being one of the Marys -- each according to her own temperament and inner virtue. But also upon every community and every nation is the responsibility of summoning forth in collective consciousness and faith Christs and Marys. The responsibility is not the individual's alone; neither is it the collectivity's alone. All responsibility is born of relationship -- is the fulfillment of relationship within the larger whole of life in which those that are related participate.

For this reason, the love of man and woman does not only blend their energies and their souls. It relates them to the community and to the universe. For this reason, no corporation that weaves the activities of managers and workers into a pattern of production can remain alone and self-sufficient in society, but is responsible to and with society. Always and everywhere mutuality is the keynote. And mutuality proves itself in jointly assumed and joyously discharged responsibility. It blossoms out in significance.

THE TEST OF SIGNIFICANCE

As individuality grows into thinking, so mutuality blossoms out in meaning. To think is for man to struggle with the multifarious, ever-changing problems which his experience of nature presents to him at every moment. It is to transform the legacy of the past -- body, memory, karma -- into an intimation of the future; to be victorious over the downward pull of natural energies, to compress natural energy so that it may release the light of thought. The successful thought-process transforms energy into ideas. It overcomes the disintegrative tendency of natural compounds by giving birth to the typical substance of "human" integration: intelligence.

Intelligence is released as natural powers are used in a human way by the individualized human being in his effort to achieve victory over his life-environment. When, at a later stage of his growth, man has faced the tests of mutuality and responsibility, the integrative power of thought gives birth to a new phase of intelligence, to "meaning". Meaning is an expression of the sense of mutuality when confronted with the solution of problems and conflicts caused by the assuming and the discharge of responsibility.

Individual being must always prove itself through the use it makes of natural energies or social wealth. Relationship likewise must prove its worth by the results of cooperative activity. Love acquires value and significance through the utilization of its fruits, be they psychological or physiological. Human society demonstrates its greatness in the civilization that is founded upon the characteristic type of human relation-

ships which constitute its warp and woof. Relationships of
love or business partnerships must be productive if they are
not to be destructive. Abundance of fruits, however, is not
enough. The value of any fruition depends upon the significance with which men endow it. The factors of worth and
meaning are essential correlates to the actual fact of productive mutuality.

Where being and individuality are concerned there is no
question of value or significance. "To be" is a primordial
fact which requires no valuation or justification. There is no
problem as to the meaning of "I am". It is; this "is-ness"
is to itself an absolute. The famous query of Hamlet, father
of modern neurotics, "to be or not to be" is a senseless question, if taken at its essential value. What Hamlet actually
meant to say was: "To be related to this world, or not to be
related -- that is the question". His doubt was as to the significance of his relationship to his relatives, his traditional
morality, his familiar world. Falsely, he identified himself
with this world. All doubts and neuroses are born of such an
identification.

The "I am" is -- this is all that need be said; and no "I"
can obliterate itself, though it can feel its relationship to its
world so meaningless as to want to destroy this relationship.
It can destroy the process of integration which binds it to the
world of men and of nature; it can destroy "life" and "intelligence". It cannot destroy itself. It cannot, with any sense,
give significance or no significance to itself; for the self is
entirely out of the realm of significance. Self is; but relationship has meaning, or fails to have meaning.

Likewise, the self does not "produce". It uses and controls natural energies, or it does not. It imprints itself upon,
and integrates through intelligence, these energies; or it fails
to do so. But any relationship can and must be productive.
The purpose of the productivity, the character of the products,
the use to which they are put, the way problems of production are handled and their consequences met, the manner in

which they fill or fail to fill the needs of the producers and of
the society in which they participate -- all these factors have
to be considered. They give significance and value to the relationship, or condemn it as senseless and worthless.

No relationship can be considered as an absolute. "I am"
is an absolute; relationship is of the realm of relativity. Relativity is the characteristic substance of all relationships,
and the result of relationship. Value, sense, significance,
are expressions of the need there is for any human being to
integrate in his experiences selfhood and relatedness.

This integration results from the individual giving a valid
meaning to the products of each and all relationships in which
he is a partner. If he cannot give a valid meaning to any relationship he has entered into, it becomes destructive. All
unproductive relationships are more or less destructive of the
integrity of the selves related through them. And some relationships are productive of positively destructive factors.

Yet the "I" must relate itself to other selves. While the
"I" is an absolute to itself, selfhood is not an absolute w i t h-
i n the universal whole. It must become polarized to
relationships. Through this polarization, the element of value enters the realm of i n c o r p o r a t e d selfhood; that is, of
personality. All selves a r e -- outside of the realm of value;
but a personality potentially has value in terms of its capacity to participate in constructively productive and significant
relationships.

This capacity is not inherent. It is never to be taken for
granted. It is determined by the use which the self makes of
the energies of nature over which he holds sway by right of
birth in mankind and in a particular race, society and family. It is determined by the character of the "intelligence"
the self generates by compressing natural energies into ideas,
as the engineer deepens and increases the weight of the waters
of the dammed-in river in order to generate electricity and
light.

Intelligence in the personality is a promise of value and

meaning in the relationships which this person will weave on the warp and woof of social-cultural living; but only a promise! Meaning as such can only be born out of the actual experience of relationship -- relationship, not only with another self, but also with objects and social entities of one kind or another.

To be; to use; to define -- a basic trinity of human existence. Individual being is demonstrated by the individual use of available natural powers; yet complete incorporation as personality requires not only individual use, but also an individual focus of intelligence through which individuality finds its particular character d e f i n e d by the process of thought.

In the sphere of the individual self, intelligence is the defining of the boundaries of the individuality and of the thinking that seeks to exteriorize and to give form to the innate realization of "I am" by providing particular and relatively unique characteristics for the ego. In the sphere of the concrete personality, intelligence manifests as technical skill, as the adequacy of the means to the end. In the sphere of relationship in mutuality, intelligence is reborn as u n d e r s t a n d i n g.

To understand is to become aware of meaning. There is no need for understanding one's self, that is, one's essential "I am"-ness; the need is for self-realization through characteristic acts within the limits of one's ability to use power in terms of one's own individual nature. The injunction "know thyself" requires the perception of individual limits, powers and character. For modern psychology, what is meant by "understanding oneself" is mostly the understanding of what the experiences born of personal relationship have brought to the concrete personality; whether it be fulfillment, power, personal fruitions, or frustrations, inhibitions and complexes. It does not refer to the essential individuality, the spiritual identity; but rather to the personality a f t e r it has grown out of the varied and complex relationships of years of living in a family and in society.

To understand a situation or an idea is to "com-prehend"

all factors brought to a condition of operative and productive (or inoperative and sterile) relationship in the situation or the idea. These factors may be images and concepts, or personalities and their words. "Com-prehension" is literally "taking together" these many factors and defining the character, quality, purpose and eventual results of their togetherness.

A concept, a scientific law, a juridical principle have the one function of establishing significant and valid forms of relationship between perceptions, images, experiences and entitles of one kind or another. A religion likewise gives meaning to the relationship between men and one or several transcendent or cosmic Persons; and as the basis of sanctions for ethical conduct, it gives significance and value to specific patterns of mutuality. In either case, religion sets limits to the relationships it believes to be within its field; and logic sets limits to the associability of statements and concepts.

To define is to set limits. In some cases, limits can be set a priori by an authority external to the relationship being defined. This leads to formalism, artificiality, political or religious tyranny, Fascism. In other cases, limits are set in terms of the inherent capacity, purpose and function of all the factors in the relationship considered as a whole. This alone is the way to understanding.

To comprehend is to take all factors together and to define thus the character of their relatedness; but to understand is literally to "stand under" this gathering of elements, and to bear their weight. Not only to see and evaluate objectively as if from a distance; but to experience by actual feeling and by direct pressure. Understanding is an internal process; comprehension may remain an external process. Intellectual judgment on the basis of a priori formulas of significance and value is the negative shadow of understanding, just as intellectuality is the shadow of intelligence.

Understanding alone is a true foundation for meaning; and there can be no "second-hand" or vicarious understanding, without it ceasing to have any right to be called "understanding". Yet understanding need not always require direct personal experience. It can be reached also through actual identification of feeling and being with the experiencer or understander. Understanding can be based on the memory of past experiences -- even perhaps of experiences of past personalities with which the consciousness is transcendentally linked beyond the hiatus of physical death. Understanding can be attained through the experience of a collectivity, group or nation, in the life of which one vitally and totally participates in root-identification of feeling and blood.

In any case, real understanding cannot be merely an intellectual, formalistic and indifferently objective operation. It is conditioned by actual relationship and identification with the relationship as a whole. Yet identification can only be temporary. The self that understands must pass through this stage of identification and emerge victorious. Meaning is the prize of victory.

It is the "pearl of great price" found hidden in the seadepths, within a hard shell that hides pain, irritation, suffering. The test of significance is the testing of a man's determination not to be contented with externals and mirages, but instead to search the very core of all relationships -- personal and social, collective and universal -- until he has reached the essential meaning. Only in essential meaning is selfhood integrated with relationship, and the Great Work of human living is accomplished. "God" is the perpetual emergence of meaning out of the antiphony of selfhood and relationship. Self, Love and Meaning constitute the trinity of the perfected consciousness of man.

Meaning is the "Spirit of truth and understanding" that descended like "tongues of fire" upon the men who, all of one mind, formed the Apostolic Brotherhood of the Christ. The spirit of significance is the Holy Spirit; and holiness is a correlate of wholeness perceived and transformed into an expression of meaning and value. Likewise, law should be considered as an expression of significant and all-inclusive relationship, if law is to belong to the realm of meaning and understanding, rather than to that of formalism and intellectual convention, or of arbitrary rule by an ego who failed to meet the challenge of mutuality.

The concept of law is indeed tragically in need of revaluation, for by being identified in our society either with the dictates of an autocratic law-giver (be it man or God) or with the decisions of a formal and usually unrepresentative majority-vote procedure in an elected legislature, law is seen as unrelated or opposed to the harmony of the whole people, and often to meaning. Law can only be an expression of mere convenience or opportunism whenever it is actually an easy substitute to the realization of harmony and to the expression of meaning experienceable by all the selves affected by the power of this law over the relationships in which they participate. The spiritual function of social law is to define the sphere of any and all human relationships -- not to dominate and control their arising and their character. Likewise, the true function of intelligence is to define the character of the individual self and its ability to use natural energies.

Law deals with relationships; and true relationship can exist only on the basis of mutuality. Where there is mutuality, law manifests as harmony -- as the "joining together" of selves in terms of creative participation in the activities of a greater whole, a social or cosmic organism. And where there is no harmony, no understanding, no awareness of significance, law can only be a mask for personal or group rule, with or without the formalities of so-called democracy.

The test of significance is the challenge to any man and any association -- whether in marriage or in business, in politics or in cultural fields -- to accept no participation that cannot be significantly defined as to its character, procedure and purposes. To be significant is the requirement of any relationship. And significance is the crowning and soul of mutuality; creative harmony, the formulation of effective and productive love.

THE TEST OF POSITION

Every complete cycle of individual experience begins in an assertion of selfhood: "I am I" (phase 1). Through the use of the energies of nature which, by biological, social and spiritual birthright, fall within its field of operation (phase 2), then through the associative processes of thought (phase 3), the I that was "In the beginning" only I -- a rhythm, a quality of being -- becomes a person, a concrete organized whole (phase 4). Having experienced the great "test of stability" and chosen a type of foundation -- in surface-extension, in earth-rootedness, or in the realization of center, victorious over gravitation -- the individual person seeks to express outwardly in a characteristic manner the energies of his personality (phase 5).

There are correct and incorrect ways of using the power rising from a concrete organism. They lead to increasing proficiency in action, or to pain and waste (phase 6). Through self-discipline and suffering man learns the lessons of objectivity and respect; failing to learn, his sense of individual isolation or frustration turns into physical and psychological invalidism, rebelliousness or rancor.

No individual can experience completeness and fruitfulness of being while alone. To be is to enter into relationship (phase 7). Relationship lived in a spirit of mutuality produces great fruitions (phase 8). As the constantly arising responsibilities for the management of the harvest of partnership and love are shared by all the participants in the relationship, understanding is born in illumined minds; physically useful joint activities take on meaning and value (phase 9). They become integrated within the field of a culture, a religion, a society of significantly interdependent personalities wise in the ways of relationships -- of relationships which "make sense" because they are consistently and intelligently referred to a harmonic whole-in-the-making (phase 10).

Human society is forever in the making. Even where a particular society or culture is outwardly disintegrating, as a plant in the fall, "seeds" are being matured and sown in the very midst of decay. Social living implies a participation in a constant process of integration or of disintegration. The participation of the individual man or woman in the social process may be positive or negative. It may build or maintain, transform or destroy v a l u e s. It may mean, for the individual, joy and success in the discharge of the responsibilities born of relationships -- or quasi-slavery to an alien and unwholesome rhythm of work, from which the individual gains no value save the bare fact of existence in relative comfort and to which he brings no creative vision or dynamic intensity.

The individual's contribution to social processes -- whether in the household or in the factory, in the fields or at sea -- establishes his place and function in society. The character of the relationship between the individual "I" and this factor of place-and-function is one of the four basic constituents of every human personality -- a "cardinal" factor, one which determines (together with the other three) the total and fourfold "approach to life" of any particular person.

This fourfold approach is symbolized most significantly by the four directions of the space marked by the daily motion of the sun -- by the east (or dawn-point), the noon-point, the west (or sunset-point), the "midnight sun". But as the individuality of man develops in counterpoint, or contrast, to the flow of the life-energies of nature, the order is reversed. Man is "born" an individual at the symbolic east, builds the foundations of his concrete personality at the nadir (or midnight-point), experiences relationship in mutuality at the sunset-point, then finds his place, and fulfills his function in the larger organism of society at the noon or zenith-point.

As a particular person lives in a particular locality and in terms of the particular characteristics of his race, class, family, religion, cultural-economic and spiritual level, his "place" is thereby determined -- and, if he accepts the social responsibilities associated with this place, his "function" also. In some societies the place-function factor is almost entirely predetermined by birth and inheritance. In the more modern democratic countries every individual may choose, at least theoretically, his place and function within the economy of his society.

Actually racial, economic and educational discrimination limits greatly the field of opportunity for many minority-groups almost everywhere. In many instances the work is in waiting for the man, who must take it, whether he likes it or not, in order to exist, or subsist, and to fulfill the responsibilities accruing from the personal relationships which he has entered deliberately, or which have been imposed upon him by circumstances beyond his control.

Any person who functions actively according to his place in society has a "position". In this word, position, we find combined many social and psychological elements which make it most adequate to characterize the tenth of the basic tests which individual existence on earth presents to every active person in any kind of social grouping. Position implies the factor of place; but more than this it refers to the fact that every man in any "position" should assume in full the responsibilities of this position and may wield, to however small a degree, influence and authority of a sort. Position, socially speaking, is place with reference to an operative and organized whole. It includes thus functional activity and, whenever the function is successfully filled, prestige.

Any society in which "position" gives prestige to an individual e v e n if he does not live up actively and successfully to its responsibilities is to some extent an unhealthy or spiritually degenerate society. A man's position in society should always be the fruition of his individual selfhood; it should be the proof and consecration of his achievement as an individual. The "proof of works" is demanded, by the spirit, of any person seeking to experience the fullness of individual living. It should likewise be required by society, which, only after the proof is given, has any right to bestow upon a man prestige and authority. This bestowal is what is meant by "con-secration": the Whole endowing an individual participating in its life with authority and delegated power, by entrusting him with an "office". The union of the right person with the significant office is the consummation of all human existence, at whatever level of social or spiritual being this union becomes effective.

The test of position is therefore the crowning test of a man's life-experience. The attitude of an individual toward a position is the factor by which he will be judged socially and spiritually. By it he will stand or fall as an individual person. And "position" means here any kind of effective participation in the life of society and humanity in terms of the "organic" requirements of the collectivity in which the individual actually realizes himself as a component part, and to which he feels, with the whole of himself, that he "belongs".

No position is less noble than any other. The street-sweeper keeping a city clean, the housewife fulfilling family and home duties, the mine-worker, the clerk or politician, the artist and the religious reformer leading their followers to a new path of social-ethical and spiritual-creative transformation -- all these persons occupy "offices" and perform functional tasks in their community. The manner in which they perform these works determines their social, and as well spiritual, status as individuals.

The quality of the performance, in turn, is determined by the character of the progressive approach which the workers have taken to this culmination -- this "zenith" -- of personal living; by the manner in which they have gradually prepared themselves, and have been prepared by their education, for this crucial test of "performance". No person can put into an actual performance more than what he has put into the process of preparing himself for it.

In the broadest sense, a person fulfills his office according to: 1) what he has r e a l i z e d himself essentially to be as an individual -- 2) what he has m a d e himself actually as a concrete personality -- 3) what he has c r e a t e d out of human relationship. Indeed, by the very pressure of his own previous attitudes, he finds himself compelled to meet the tests of power and authority according to whether this power and authority have come to him as the result of relationships made fruitful in intelligence and understanding, or whether he has sought relentlessly to acquire them by cornering the energy born of relationship in order to feed his ambition.

Understanding and ambition are the two roads to "position"; and each is based on one type of approach to human relationship and to the use of the fruits of human relationship -- a positive or a negative approach. In turn, any man meets the problems of human relationship according to the way in which he has faced his own self and has built himself as a particular personality. The whole of the personal life is consummated in the use one makes of "social power" -- power, not generated by the individual as a single organism, but instead by the interdependence and cooperation (conscious or unconscious) of a group of individuals. Will this power of position or office be considered as a "trust", or as a "booty"? It is for every individual to choose -- within the framework of his particular culture and tradition, of the education and the opportunities which his society has allowed him to have.

The tragedy of our individualistic type of so-called democracy is that the entire trend of society, subtly or brutally, urges the individual to consider whatever power or authority he acquires in the fulfilling of his social position as strictly and without moral reservations "his own". This power and authority are presented as if they were for him alone to use, as he pleases and with no reference to the welfare of society as a whole. Yet power and authority of this kind are actually generated by the individual in so far as he is a participant in the life of his entire community and not in his capacity as a single individual person. They do not constitute a "private", but instead a "public" factor.

For instance, real estate profits caused by a neighborhood boom, wealth due to the fact that someone invented a new chemical method of treating some mineral ore, deposits of which one owns, and even more all stock market gains, are products of c o l l e c t i v e activity. Wherever the individual acquires power because of position, this power should be considered as a trust -- as is likewise (and more specifically) a trust the power of the policeman, of the judge, of the army general and of all public officials. It is power of office, power born of social function in terms of relatedness; and all participants in the relationships involved in the production of this power should theoretically share in it, indirectly if not directly.

It is true that all members of a community do share in the advantages and comforts insured by communal living. Society gives to every one of its component individuals a participating interest in the benefits of civilization and cultured behavior; it takes also in the form of taxes a portion of all gains which the individual makes as a social person. Yet, the underlying individualistic attitude of most human beings stamps so deeply with the quality of greed whatever gain an individual makes out of his work as a member of society that the social-cultural heritage -- the hidden collaboration of all men to the social achievements of any one man -- are taken for granted or ignored. The rugged individualist rapes nature and society, enslaves the weak and the congenitally oppressed, in order to nurture his ambition; he uses what he can get out of the collective life of his people to swell his egoism, or he wastes it to tickle his bored fancy and his jagged nerves.

In the process, all sense of personal consecration to a

task is lost; the essence of individual selfhood deteriorates along with the decay of all natural things and the entropy of all energies. The spiritual value of "position" is denied. For, in position, individual selfhood and relationship should become integrated in the act of self-dedication and social consecration. If any relationship and its fruits are made to feed the ego of a person, then, to this extent, the person cannot reach a spiritual status. Conversely, if the individual selfhood of a man is made the slave of social production at all costs, the society which makes such a demand upon the individual -- except in the case of a defensive war -- can never, however powerful it may become externally, give birth to a spirit-realizing and spirit-emanating civilization.

Selfhood and relationship are to be integrated in consecrated works; they can be integrated in nothing else. Whenever one factor uses the other to its exclusive advantage human values are perverted; "Man" suffers a perpetual abortion. Each time an individual usurps the power invested in his office and function -- be it even that of a nurse or a factory foreman -- in order to expand his ego and his wealth at the expense of the social activity which it is his responsibility to perform, Man suffers. Each time a society -- through its central nucleus of power and authority, the Government -- makes individuals subservient or slave to its craving for collective expansion and greed for power, Man is brutalized.

There is never any question, spiritually speaking, of the supremacy of individual persons over society, or of society over individuals. A strict individualism is, ultimately, as much a destroyer of spiritual values, as a strict collectivism. The rugged individualism of days of frontier expansion, historically useful as it may appear, is as opposed to the total fulfillment of Man as is a totalitarian collectivism imbued with the vitality of creative goals. There can be, in the last analysis, no truly spiritual value except out of the harmonization of the two polarities.

This means that the individual must learn self-dedication;

and his society must "consecrate" every individual in his function. The individual dedicates his self to his position or office; society gives to position or office a sacred character by dedicating it to the creative energy of the individual fulfilling his responsibilities. In this factor of "position" individual and society meet. The man and the office become one -- and sacred. For the man to consider the power and authority of the office as his own, for him to use as his emotions or ego moves him -- this is the greatest of all crimes. But as great is the crime of a society which enslaves the man to the office, so that society and the controlling mechanisms of the state may wax bigger and more powerful.

Our modern world is today disrupted and brutalized by the wholesale occurrence of both types of crime. World Wars are the symptoms, not the causes of the deteriorization of Man. Individuals starve and die in torture; nations crumble, while bureaucracies wax tyrannical. Why? -- They have failed to understand that individual selfhood and group-relationship are the two pillars of civilization, the two supporting limbs of Man. They have failed to respect the sacredness of both the office and the individual person who officiates.

As this occurs, all performances of work become senseless and uncreative, because the individual and society do not unite in them, polarizing the descent of the Holy Spirit of understanding and of truth, of constant self-renewal in group-creativity. Individuals become mechanized into automatons; communities turn into graveyards for the creative spirit. Civilization becomes the "Shadow" of Man, a nightmare filled with the catabolic activities of men that are destroyers in mind and helpless neurotics in their emotional lives. Such is, indeed our modern Western civilization!

Yet, behind and beyond the Shadow stands the Illumined Personage. The Crucifixion in our solid world of bodies and egos, must always be the shadow of the Transfiguration. As Jesus is transfigured into the Christ, he hears the tidings of his death from the mouths of those who have preceded him and represent the past -- Moses and Elijah, the "Law and the Prophets", fixity of rule and passivity to the divine Voice. Jesus is "christed", as every man may be, in spiritual creativeness. He is not only "illumined", but light-bestowing. He who has "stood under" and thus understood all that is human can now become a sun. And to become a sun is to have a star become you.

To be a sun is to give light to a group of dark bodies gravitating, in desire for light, around the radiant core of one's giving. To be a star is to "belong" to the "Companionship of the Sky" -- to a constellation of spiritual Intelligences and "Sons of God". Every zenith is a potential noon-point; but before the coincidence is perfect, the individual must be poised and grounded in his own equator: a profound symbol indeed! The star of the true zenith becomes the "position" of the noonday sun only at the equator. The self-dedicated individual fulfills his office in society -- as he radiates the "solar" power of his selfhood through his social performance, his "office" -- only as he is balanced in equatorial splendor, as North and South are equally active in his fulfilled and "global" personality.

This is the state of human plenitude; and toward it humanity, having seen itself commingling in death and devastation, is slowly -- oh! so slowly! -- veering its course, however distant the ultimate goal. Yet even plenitude may cast a shadow, the densest of all! Fullness of materiality means maximum of weight and opacity, and total emptiness of spirit. It may be named success, yet be the death of all that is real and creative in man. To many, alas, nothing fails like success! There is blindness in all noon-day suns, murderous heat in all equators.

Spiritual fullness dwells only where the stars join in the translucent wholeness of the sky, symbol of Deity. He who can experience the midnight sun at noon; he whose zenith star at midnight can be like a sun illumining all men -- this man, indeed, is an incarnate god. He is the universal spirit incorporated in an office. In this incorporation, and in it alone, the individual reaches fulfillment of the spirit, by the spirit, and for all men.

THE TEST OF DISCONTENT

Social position and participation as a productive person in the "work of the world" constitute the zenith of the cycle of individual experience. All zeniths are symbols of consummation and achievement; the past experiences of the individual are con-summated, and as this summing up becomes a creative synthesis, there is achievement -- the individual becomes, to however small a degree, a "chief" and leader.

"Chief" means etymologically head (caput). In the achievements of a n y human person the whole of humanity and of its social processes comes indeed to a head. For every man's success is predicated upon, even while adding to, the achievements of his civilization; and every individual is thrust to his life-zenith by the power of all the relationships in which, consciously or not, he has participated, even while giving by his very attainment a new meaning to those relationships and to society as a whole.

Attainment is no end in itself. Yet, for society and for men completely bound by social horizons, the effective discharge of the responsibility of office by the official (or officiant) usually appears as a satisfactory conclusion to a cycle of individual experience. From the collectivist's point of view, the individual, having reached the position in which he can best serve his community, becomes thereafter completely identified with this position. Absorbed in and by his work, the fully socialized person should have no concern save to bring society, through his daily performance, to a condition of ever greater fulfillment and happiness. He becomes literally a "cell" in a vaster organism, and is lost as a characteristic individual. As a perfectly efficient productive unit -- a unit of work -- he is collectively fulfilled in the communal happiness of his society.

In this collectivistic paradise the value of the individual self is dissolved into the vast tide of human evolution. One pole of human existence has seen its activity reduced to a minimum; just as the other pole -- man's collective being -- is almost entirely repudiated or forgotten in the individualistic paradise of the successful millionaire who lives in splendid and self-contented isolation while thousands of men slave to pay his dividends. Both extremes lead to automatism and to crystallization of all values; and at long last, to rebellion.

Among the many over-socialized persons, some arise who challenge the set social order and its empty forms -- even though the challenge may mean a martyr's death. In the other instance, among the children of the wealthy individualists, men are born whose feelings revolt at the sight of the oppressed masses. They lead the slaves against their individualistic tyrants whose selfhood has become an egocentric vacuum sucking in all social values toward senseless waste and destruction.

Creative progress for humanity and for every man means the constant expansion of values; not the expansion of either social mechanisms or individualistic egos. Values and meanings must grow in scope, extension, depth and height. They it is that must forever increase in inclusiveness, if life is to repeat again and again its triumph over death, and spirit to renew itself cyclically through ever vaster integrations of being. And the growth of value and meaning requires the gradual transformation of all the forms which held the sense of value and the search for significance focused within set patterns of thought, feeling, and behavior.

What is the transforming power? Who is it that makes little of social happiness or individual comfort, and starts with feverish heart on the quest for beyonds that spell pain, anguish and revolution?

He is the individual in whom have surged new forces, a new vision, a new goal which collective forms and social traditions could not contain; and, not being able to contain, had repressed or insulated themselves against. He is the individual whose openness to the unceasing creative flow of life made it impossible for him to be insulated against anything that is living and surging; made it impossible for him to be satisfied with the acknowledged and collectively authorized contents of a respectable social personality. He is he who would rather be eternally empty and searching, than bounded by rigid recipes for plenitude and contentment.

That which is absolutely full can contain no more. He who is satisfied has enough (satis). Happiness will refuse risks. The Good cannot realize the Better until life has smitten it with the fire of unexpressed depths and unenvisioned heights. All marching forward is based on a denial -- the denial that a particular place contains all space. All growth is energized by dis-content.

There must come at the very zenith of an era individuals who refuse to be bounded by the social limits of a standardized attainment and to be satisfied with the official contents of the human type bred by his society and its culture. In them burns the fire of "divine discontent". From discontent to rebellion, these great iconoclasts -- breakers of rules and destroyers of idols -- pursue relentlessly, or perhaps subtly, their crusades against a stultified sense of plenitude and surface social harmony. They shatter the crust of respectability. They pierce all fortified walls and tear through the smug contentment of souls that contain nothing but dying or dead memories. They are bursts of emotional disgust or passionate fervor. They make themselves tragically empty, that a new sense of fulness might rise from psychic and mental depths wide open to the great drives that impel souls to endless adventures, be it toward gold or toward God.

These men are eternally dissatisfied. They officiate in

the revolutionary ritual whose god is Discontent, and whose sacred host is the reformer's death. They are the Luciferian Spirits; literally, the Bringers of Light. They are the enemies of paternalistic gods whose commands fill with content the souls of contented men. Churches and Parties persecute them who refuse to conform. For them, there can be no fulfillment where so many must live empty lives in the shadow-side of society and culture. How can they know satisfaction where millions hunger?

They too hunger with terrible, unappeasable hunger -- hunger for love, perhaps, beyond the niceties of socialized emotions; hunger for God, beyond religions self-satisfied in their all too conscious virtues and their patented Revelations; hunger for "Man" -- the ever-receding goal of civilization ever stumbling under the weight of "good" men that hate the "better" far more than evil.

To these individuals who have felt the pangs of essential discontent, there comes also a great test: To what use can they put this discontent? They have achieved, and in achievement found emptiness. They have proven their social worth as individuals; yet it has seemed to them worthless, because fictitious -- dead, because insulated against all new life. What then? Shall they dramatize their dissatisfaction and relentlessly poison all and sundry with their hunger? Shall they gesticulate and shout their revolt, hammer away all restraint and, like Romantic poets and "accursed souls", force their society to behold in them the very shadow of its respectability, the festering sores it masks with morals and with cosmetics? -- or else, shall they use the power and authority or whatever social position is theirs to push outward ever so little the vicious circles of tradition, that these circles ever-repeated in dull automatism by good men, may become spirals, gradually more open to creative spirit?

In many cases, there appears to be no choice for the born revel. Because of family, class or temperament -- because of dire experiences in youth and perhaps of thwarting sickness

-- the individual may fight, from his very adolescence, against a conventional participation in society. He senses himself, as he faces the earliest stage of maturity, an outcast. Has he, therefore, any choice, except to conform to what he hates and live a miserable and senseless life within stifling frames of social respectability, or to make of his very pain, his hunger, his iconoclasm a pedestal from which to harangue the people and to draw to himself those that, more mildly, feel unsatisfied?

He might, however, make a determined attempt to conform, put on a mask, learn stubbornly all the tricks of culture and society, and sooner or later reach attainment, perhaps fame. Then -- he might think -- he could use the prestige his performance brought to him in order to lead his community away from traditional ruts and toward creative freedom. But, having thus "played the game" and attained, will he be able to lead others toward freedom of the spirit? Or will he not rather have carried his mask so well, that underneath it his own discontent will have died and he too will conform and bask in respectability, even though he might occasionally utter grand words about spiritual values and individual creativeness in order to soothe his numbly aching soul and hide the tragic, perhaps unconscious, emptiness of "success"!

How often history has dramatized such a pattern of life! How many potentially creative persons, who might have become guiding lights to a renewal of civilization, have been enclosed into rigidity by their attempts to reach fame first, then...! But there is often no "then". Success is a greedy and jealous mistress. The successful personage remains a "producer"; he may cease to be as "transformer". And real creativeness is based upon the power to transform -- oneself, as well as the materials of culture and society.

To produce successfully what society is accustomed to accept, with enough original variations to stimulate interest and meet competition, gives a man friends, honors and all the overtones of social comfort and contentment. To transform and regenerate the patterns of custom and tradition is a thankless task, even for the most able and most careful. And to renew oneself through the performance of a life of social responsibility and leadership is a work that requires the utmost watchfulness and the most unflinching determination, as well as resilient strength of character and mind.

For these reasons the youthful and uncompromising rebel finds it, in many cases, far easier to dramatize his rebelliousness and his dissatisfaction. He takes on a pose. He glories in his emptiness and his hunger, as in his "openness to the universe" which often is little more than passivity to spiritual dreams still in the limbo of subjective feelings. Either he drapes himself in the dark robes of the poëte maudit -- the over-tragic hero cursed by fate and birth in an alien culture -- or he exacerbates his sufferings and his loneliness in masochistic self-indulgence. He keeps his wounds bleeding dreadfully, that all men may witness the tortures a heartless and rigid society inflicts upon the halcyon soul filled with great dreams.

In this tragic spectacle and in the sympathy it arouses in a few, the rebel's ego can also find some sustainment, however somber. Does it, however, assist human growth in the individual or in society? It does so only in the sense that discontent can be contagious, that the smugness of the bourgeois type or the self-righteousness of the religious devotee must be somehow dissolved, that there can be no transformation and self-renewal without the denial of the sanctity of traditional form and of the "complex"-bound ego.

The essential problem, however, must be met at another level. To transform a circle into a spiral a constant centrifugal force must be applied. The inertia of momentum will ever pull any activity back to its source, unless there is a power that constantly bends the "karmic" sequence of cause and effect away from center and toward all-inclusive space. This is the great principle of transformation, the law of spir-

itual performance. Cause-and-effect must be overcome unceasingly by creativeness; karma, by compassion. At every
point, space must overcome center; the pull of the
Galaxy (the Companionship of the stars) must ever so little
triumph over the gravitational power of the sun; the will to inclusiveness must bring new (and at first unwelcome) contents
into the set structures of society and personality.

These structures must let go of that which is obsolete in
order to admit the disturbing and frightening newness of ex-
centric spaces. Letting go of old contents is literally to experience discontent. To open oneself to new substance in an
act of inclusive creativeness and positive openness to space
is to experience joy. Joy is born of discontent; happiness is
the essence of fulfillment within form.

Here again the correct balance between space and center,
between discontent that fathers forth creativeness and stab-
ility-in-form that gives birth to happiness, is the only key to
harmonious growth. An emphasis upon individualism leads to
increasing discontent among men; the rigid, collective stability of a planned society, such as that most perfectly exemplified by Brahminical India before the sixth century B.C., leads
to greater social happiness, but as well to spiritual stagna-
tion. Centripetal collectivism and formalistic classicism must
be constantly challenged and bent outward by the centrifugal
energy of the individualist, the non-conformist, the rebel --
if human evolution is to proceed. Wherever there is actually
growth, in a personality or in a society, this creative challenge has been effective. Without it, there can only be ossi-
fication, automatism -- the vicious circle of habit.

There are, nevertheless, two alternatives. The circle of
social performance may, out of its inherent vitality, bend outward into a spiral without losing form and harmonious proportion; or it may zigzag in distorted jerks, as explosive individuals or group-revolutions overcome violently the momentum of a life encased in unyielding patterns and frightened
formalism. In the first case, the element of meaning is kept

alive throughout periodical renewals; in the second, frozen meanings and oppressive symbols or social categories having become brittle with the automatic worship of an enslaved people, have lost all capacity for internal transformation. They must be shattered, or at least, ruthlessly renovated.

Wherever form remains, there can be meaning. The destruction or temporary obliteration of form results unavoidably in the loss of meaning. But form is not formalism; consistency does not imply rigidity; communal harmony does not necessarily require the denial of individual freedom and the suppression of the rebel spirits that incorporate the will to vaster spaces and greater inclusiveness. The spiral is the perfect form, not the circle; and a spiral results from the integration of an outward release of spirit and a circular motion. This integration is Life, in universal evolution and in cosmic meaning.

In man, the integration of happiness and of discontent, of one's "social circle" and of one's ideals which impel ever onward and beyond, can and should be conscious, purposeful and significant. Elsewhere, in the various life-kingdoms, one sees only an unconscious effort of the species to adjust its individual specimen to changing surroundings while retaining the unquestionable rule of instincts. These adjustments, when deep enough to alter constructively the structural characteristics of the species, are known to us as "mutations". Every valid mutation is a triumph of the creative life over the automatism of instincts. They are the successful revolutions, the great crises of spiritual transformation, which give to generic and as yet unindividualized mankind the proof of its growth.

In the human kingdom individuals bear the conscious responsibility for such changes. Though most men reap with society the harvest of productive social processes, a very few, impelled by an inner discontent, are forever ready to set aflame any harvest that power be released for new adventures. Their lives are perpetual Advents; their minds, funeral pyres whence surges anew the Phoenix, symbol of immortality. They are

the "shakers and movers" of human destiny, the Promethean
Spirits who bring "fire" to men enamoured of "seed" and solely bent upon the cultivation of seeds.   Theirs is the rhythm
of fire, the flame's eternal hunger. Society chains them, tortures them, as the vulture of greed ceaselessly feasts upon
the powers they released, the wealth they created -- leaves
them empty and bleeding.

Yet, they are the Victorious. New generations, illumined
by their light, grow wider minds. New societies are born.
Dreaming of them, young men go forth toward the great spaces
filled with stars.

THE TEST OF CLOTURE

No man can grow to his fully human stature except by developing his sense of value and his ability to bestow meaning upon all his life-experiences, be they dark or light, oppressive or exalting. True progress for humanity does not consist in building bigger and better social mechanisms, prouder egos and more efficient gadgets, however necessary social, psychological, or industrial structures must be said to be in the course of human evolution. Creative progress for man is accomplished through the constant expansion, refinement and expression of values. Only as values and meanings consistently increase in scope and inclusiveness can life repeat over and again its triumph over death, and man emerge, through the experiencing of nature, victorious over all challenges of earthly existence and ready for ever new cyclic rebirths.

Every cycle of human activity and experience should reach its consummation in a "seed". It does not reach it at the zenith of the cycle in terms of collective social achievement, but instead at the very close of the cycle in terms of the consciousness of value and meaning. The individual person does not reach fulfillment by "doing" alone, but by the illumined realization of the meaning and the value of what he has done, especially during the high moments of the cycle about to end. This realization is indeed the "seed" of eventual rebirth.

The character of achievement and success demonstrated during the climactic performance of one's basic function in the social and universal Whole depends upon the effective use of form -- the structure of one's personality, the pattern of

one's intimate relationships, the technical devices of which
one has become master.   Mastery consists in the perfect use
of completely adequate forms to fulfill entirely one's precise
purpose, with the purest motive and at the exactly required
moment.

Yet, forms bind even him who used them perfectly; for
they are the products of a set of activities and of a purpose
bounded by the limits of a cycle.   Forms -- as abstract patterns -- will remain forever what they are, unless they be
transformed by a new creative act.   The substantial body disintegrates; but the pattern of it is not changed thereby.   Death
destroys organisms, but not the idea or blueprint thereof.
The only recourse against the crystallization of forms is the
creative modification that renews them from within.   Only one
thing can effect this creative renewal: a new value.   Even
mastery is no end in itself; for mastery is bound to the particular set of values of which it gives a supreme and perfect
demonstration.

The mastery at whose core does not burn the fire of discontent and the spiral's will for ever-greater inclusiveness
through always new cycles -- is only a temporary and illusory perfection.   The master of any technique, any work, any
achievement, is the slave of the forms of his activity, unless
he uses these forms as mere tools in the service of a value
which he realizes to be in the process of constant renewal and
expansion; a value forever becoming more than what it is.

To know clearly, in the light of the universal spirit, the
value of all that one has achieved and the meaning of all successes and failures on the way to this achievement; then to
feel, in one's consciousness, this value expand and be reborn
within the framework of a new cycle and in terms of a higher,
more inclusive level of activity -- these are the steps of spiritual growth at the close of any cycle, however brief or vast
the cycle.   The unfoldment of value is the substance of the
spiritual life of man.   And there can be no unfoldment of value save through the transformation and renewal of those forms

which focused the lesser or less mature value.

Transformation and self-renewal require the overcoming of ancient habits -- of thinking, feeling, and acting. More precisely, it demands of every man, and of society as a whole, the repudiation of memories and images that bind to the past the consciousness and the will. He who clings to ghosts (whether cherished, feared or hated) barricades, with the torn fragments of experiences made heavy and dark, the path on which the future comes to greet his living soul. Ghosts must be released from the living with the sword of severance. Only the value, which past encounters had once sought to demonstrate, need be retained; not as a thing in itself, but as a fully understood and appreciated component in the substance of the new purpose. There can be no valid function for the forms-that-were save to be building stones of what is yet to be -- or else, sign posts to dangers that may repeat themselves in the future. Any past that does not enter the service of the future turns into poison. It must be purged away from the sacred circle of the new birth.

Yet, much as one must throw off the toxic substances accumulated throughout the ending cycle and renew or transfigure the forms, techniques and attitudes which have served to focus the purpose of that cycle of living experience, one should never repudiate whatever has been an incorporation of the spirit. Spirit is timeless; it dwells at the core of all cycles. A spirit-born realization within a man's experience is not merely one separate little stone that could easily be missed from the walls of the cathedral of the individual Soul's immortality. It is one in essence and identity with all other manifestations -- not only in that Soul's essential being, but within the total spiritual being of humanity as a whole. The substance and the form can be repudiated and left to disintegrate but the spirit cannot. No one can ever really dismiss that which cannot die. Re-embodied it must be, however remote the cycle which will witness this reincorporation of the spiritual factor long deprived of form and substance.

This distinction between what is of the spirit and what belongs to the closely associated realms of form and substance is an essential one. It is never more imperative than at the close of a cycle -- be it a personal or a social-cultural cycle. The "art of dying", which was cultivated diligently in many ancient civilizations, especially in Tibet, is the art of repudiating the substance of earthly existence and of transfiguring the form of individual selfhood, while holding fast to the spirit-revealing experiences of the ending life. It is indeed a supremely important art, for the substance of all new birthing is conditioned by the realizations reached with the experience of death.

Every birth is a solution to problems projected by a previous death. The key to every new embodiment -- be it that of a man, a civilization, a solar system or a universe -- is always to be found in two simple words: u n f i n i s h e d b u s-i n e s s. Simple words they are, but they rule all worlds and all cycles. They are stamped within the heart of every living person; to be taken as a challenge by the wise, as a curse by the weary or the ignorant.

To die is to bring to a close a definite and measured attempt to deal with unfinished business. And there is but one way for man of dealing with his unfinished business; which is to bring forth, as the concluding consummation of embodied existence, g r e a t e r v a l u e s. A successful death is thus a death in terms of the fullest possible realization of value. This does not mean in a spirit of proud accomplishment and self-glorification in all the things that have been done; but in a realization, as inclusive and as complete as possible, of the value of life and of the meaning of the self, of humanity and of God.

It is said in ancient books that the last thought held in death conditions the future birth. What is meant by "thought" here is far more than what we are used to consider as an act of thinking or cognition. It is instead an e x p e r i e n c e o f

v a l u e. It has been stated also that immediately after physical death the individual's good and bad, spiritual and material
deeds, thoughts and feelings are balanced on the divine scales,
and that the result determines the subsequent fate of the Soul.
But the "balancing" is not a matter of quantity, of plus and
minus; for nothing of the spirit is ever expressed by numbers
or quantities. What is at stake is the qualitative realization
of value. Value -- as we use this term here -- is a quality of
being, an expression of the inherent relationship between oneself and all there is. What is revealed at the close of any cycle is this relationship. It is the quality of one's relationship
to all forms of life, to humanity and to God.

The dramatist writing the last scene of his play, the com-
poser bringing the melodies, harmonies and rhythms of his
symphony to a concluding cadence, the orator impregnating
his audience's collective mind with a final utterance which
should remain as a determining factor in their lives -- these
men face consciously and deliberately the "test of cloture".
An entire development of human situations, of emotions, powers and thoughts, has to be brought to a conclusion. The
significant element in this conclusion is the effect which will
be left with the public; that is, the manner in which the relationship of the dramatist, musician or speaker to his audience
will have been finally established, and, having been so established, will remain as a value -- whether consciously re-
membered or unconsciously held as a determining factor in
future actions or thoughts.

To make an end which will bring all that has been uttered
to an unforgettable final situation, tone-quality or statement,
is indeed the mark of supreme artistry. A great artist is one
who charges the moment which immediately follows his last
utterance with an inexpressible and ineradicable quality of
emotion or mental vision.

What is most significant in the musical development of a
symphonic work is not the formal sequence of its many and
varied tones, but the silence after the last tone, the overtones

which keep resonating in the souls of men. These overtones, this silence after all speech, the quality of the moment after the heart throbs no longer -- this is "value". To end in value is to leave, as a transcendent seed in the soul of the universe, a silence so meaningful that God will forever remember it. This divine remembrance is the substance of immortality.

There can hardly be such a quality of silence where the main emphasis throughout the speech -- all living is a speech and a debate between life and death! -- has been placed upon either substance or form elements, appealing primarily to the senses or the intellect. If these elements are the ones which remain in the mind of the people who listen to the utterances, the spiritual factor of value is brought down to the level of sensationalism and of technical skill or mere virtuosity.

In the truly spiritual expression of value the elements of substance and form, however strongly developed they may be, are transfigured by the illumination of meaning and the dynamic realization of purpose. Indeed they remain only as frameworks for the value and meaning which are retained as an active essence creative of greater tomorrows. All that, in the process of building up such frameworks for immortal value, served only as temporary scaffolding, or represented side-issues and perhaps relative failures, must be repudiated.

Immortality is based upon repudiation of the unfit as well as upon the transfiguration of the fit, upon severance from yesterday as well as inclusion of tomorrow. This is why there are always more cycles, always new births of time and universe, new unfoldments of absolute space -- the point -- into the extended trinity of space-energy-substance; for, that which is repudiated eventually will have to be met again and integrated once more into living organisms.

As we began this series of meditations on the basic tests of earth-experience for the individualized consciousness, we stressed the dualism of "man" and "nature". We pictured man passing through a nature unceasingly compelled downward along the line of universal entropy; man, emerging from this embrace of nature and pursuing his ascent toward a state of always greater integration and ever more perfect illumination under the down pour of the spirit. But as man becomes increasingly pervaded by the spirit and made into the more complete likeness of God he reaches likewise a state of ever more total inclusiveness and encompassment, a state of fuller relatedness with all there is, was, and ever will be.

In this state, the dualism of man and nature, of self and not-self, while still existing as a fact of objective being, becomes literally transformed. In this state, the necessary act of severance and isolation, which is the essence of birth and rebirth, becomes the realization of the necessity for contrast and proper spacing -- a necessity which leads us to realizations that today we can only dimly experience in the realm of art.

The painter intent upon portraying a sunrise scene, or its emotional equivalent in terms of more purely psychological symbols, does not flood his entire canvass with golden yellow light; or, if the light is focused upon one section of the painting, he does not cut out and thus totally "repudiate" from his and the onlooker's consciousness whatever space is shielded from this light. He establishes instead significant contrasts between lighter and darker surfaces. He relates them in an all-encompassing perception within which they both have significance.

Likewise, the quasi-divine personage is able to include in his consciousness -- which then has reached a stage beyond mere ego-consciousness -- both the rise of "man" and the entropy of "nature". He includes them, yet keeps them in their proper relationship, at the proper distance. He establishes within his total being their contrast and their necessary spacing; he does not mix them into a meaningless gray. He uses strong and clear colors; yet so places the colored surfaces that what would be normally considered as harsh conflict between them is seen as significant contrast within the all-inclusive harmony of the whole. Even black surfaces fill their purpose in this harmony, and dark lines emphasize the characteristics of form and structure by defining, rather than merely limiting, the colored zones.

Indeed, he for whom living and dying are actually as one, while being utterly opposite, has reached the threshold of divinity. He is the most distant when the closest; the nearest, when the most isolated. He experiences ever-repeated deaths while most creatively engaged in the business of living and arousing in all he meets life more abundant. His dying moments are paeans to immortal living. He is all things and all trends in separate integrity and purity of being; yet he is also the harmony of their forever contrasting splendors and the silence that follows the ultimate resonance in which all discords are resolved into a "dissonant harmony" which leaves one speechless with the nearness of ecstasy.

Such a person has learned the art of bringing every cycle to a close which is no end, but rather the threshold of an immortal beginning. And "every cycle" ultimately must mean every year, every day, every fleeting moment of time. He who can experience eternity and totality in one ticking of a clock and maintain consistently such a quality of experience is indeed quasi-divine. He is able to meet at once all the tests of human existence. He answers, in one single logos or utterance of living, all the challenges of the earthly existence.

For us, however, who are still quartered upon the cross of time and must meet one by one the confrontations of a nature which still opposes and weighs upon our efforts toward the full realization of our manhood and our selfhood, the end of every cycle comes as the closing of a long and wearying road. On this road our feet and our understanding have stumbled many a time. Grievious have been our missteps; harsh, the reactions of life, love and society to our faltering speech. And when we come to the finish of the long debate and we seek to enunciate forcefully and convincingly the last utterance which would sum up all that has been said and felt, we find our minds confused by many and varied reactions that have struck at our uncertain or over-aggressive ego. We find our consciousness filled with fears of the ultimate response of life and of God after all is ended. We shrink from reaching the fateful end, while our speech grows dull and confused, dragging repetitively toward an inconclusive cadence.

It is then that we have to summon the courage to cut short the vacillating speech, the courage of repudiation and of severance, the courage to bring the cycle to a conclusion, whatever might be the type of balance we will have to face. We have to do this final gesture in the knowledge that this cloture is but a prelude to a future birth of cycle; that the ghosts which we dismissed, the memories which the surgeon within us has cut in order to free the spiritward striving life in us, will have to be met in days yet to come. We have to allow the cycle to reach its necessary conclusion for the sake of other cycles yet to come, other opportunities and other challenges. Our will must be clearly set upon the one great task of s e l f - r e - n e w a l.

Self-renewal is the one great task for men still bound by the circumference of an individualistic self unable to die into immortality. Wherever there is an ego that excludes that which it dares not meet and contain there must be deaths which repudiate unassimilated ghosts and eventual rebirths to confront once more these revived remains of an unresolved past. No one can completely overcome the pull of death and division who has not fulfilled life in spiritual victory.

Where death is necessary and near -- the death of any cycle, brief or vast -- one great challenge nevertheless is left to the individual to meet: that of preparation for rebirth. The challenge is consciously to summon tomorrows which will make more probable, nay, which will make certain, the fullness of man's victory over nature; to die with one's face turned to the light of a new and more glorious dawn aglow with the promise of immortality; to die in the consciousness of that new birth which can also be the last.

This is the final summons. Into it, the whole of man's power to will and image forth the immortal essence of his being can be poured. Every man, before the closing moment of the cycle, can call forth the image of the day-to-come. And this calling forth is a creative act. It introduces into the seemingly closed sequence of birth, death and more birthing and dying, a new factor, a new will. It is man's answer to karma, man's challenge.

This challenge is the substance of greater tomorrows, the promise of immortality. Though seemingly defeated by nature, man asserts his power of victory. He becomes victory ... in seed.

THE ILLUMINED ROAD

Planetary Stations
on the Way to the Star

To ARYEL DARMA
and B. P. WADIA

who inspired my first
steps on the Path—
in memoriam.

D. R.

THE WAY OF TRANSCENDENCE

Life begins in a release of energy radiating from the nucleus of a complex cell. Where there is life -- and presumably any kind of existence -- there is an original center of radiation but there must also be, implied or inherent in this dynamic release of energy, a principle of "form"; and first of all there must be boundaries, which outline the field of biological activity and functional interaction. The boundaries separate the within from the without. In the well-known drawing by Blake, God the Creator is seen describing with a compass the circle within which the universe will develop. Likewise in ancient societies the building of a city -- or even of a temporary military camp -- always began with the establishment of a circular trench marking the boundaries within which men were to proceed with all the functions of their collective life; and the drawing of circular boundaries implied the recognition of a center.

Power radiates from the center outward; then, as the vibratory energy reaches the boundaries of the field, it rebounds, and returns to its source, only to spread again outward. A circulatory rhythm of energy (a basic life-pulsation) is established, which becomes the very foundation of the primary life-activities. The outward phase of this pulsation sends energy throughout the field; the inward (or centripetal) motion deals essentially with the development of some kind (rudimentary as it be) of c o n s c i o u s n e s s, or (in the most abstract sense of the term) of "in-formation".

These two movements, centrifugal and centripetal, are

found everywhere in operation. Everywhere we meet and are dealing with "wholes" -- complex units of existence. These wholes are organized fields of activity, and as their component parts become functionally interrelated and constantly interacting within the boundaries of the fields, consciousness takes form.

Any whole of existence exists within a greater whole, and it contains a myriad of functional parts which are also, at their level of activity, little wholes. A living cell functions, together with many other cells, within a larger whole, a body; but within each of these cells a large number of molecules are at work which are also complex units of existence; i. e. existential wholes containing likewise component entities. The living body of an animal or a man exists within the earth's biosphere (the realm of life, extending thinly above and below the surface of the soil); and we know now, especially since the first Geophysical Year (1957), that this biosphere is an organized field of activities within which all life-species are interrelated and constantly, rhythmically interacting; what disturbs one species affects, in varying degrees yet noticeably, all others. The interaction between the mineral, the vegetable, the animal and the human "kingdoms" are well-known; and we can now have a vivid image of the entire planet, at least in its physical aspect, from the central core to the ionosphere and magnetosphere, and perhaps including still farther regions up to the Moon (the "sublunar sphere" of the Ancients). It is the image of an organic whole, even if we have to extend somewhat the concept of "organism" to make it fit this planetary -- and eventually a similar cosmic -- picture.

What one generally calls "evolution" is the vast process according to which wholes of ever greater scope and complexity are being produced -- a process so beautifully outlined in Ian Smuts book HOLISM AND EVOLUTION and also in Teilhard de Chardin's THE PHENOMENON OF MAN. There is, thus, latent in every existential whole, a tendency to strive toward the realization of, and participation in a greater whole.

Such a tendency is unconscious during the lower phases of the world-process, if we use the term consciousness in a strictly human sense. But when the human stage is reached, this movement assumes a definitely conscious aspect; and it may be thwarted as well as assented to and assisted by the mind and the feelings of the human individual.

We speak then of the conscious human drive toward ever larger modes and forms of association, toward the integration of different personalities, of groups and races -- toward the synthesis of cultural attitudes and conceptual systems. The small tribe expands into kingdoms, which in various ways, after periods of crises, merge into multi-racial modern nations; and we are now becoming aware of a deep-rooted trend toward a global synthesis, toward the integration of humanity within the vast field of the whole Earth -- the Earth which we can now feel is the one home of mankind, and also of all the other forms of earthly existence. The trend seems inescapable, however much individuals and nations may still oppose it, perhaps because it seems still premature and so difficult. Yet there can ultimately be no other constructive solution to humanity's always more insistent problems. The only question is how to bring the inevitable end to concrete actualizations; that is, on what basis and by what means.

The biosphere and the planet Earth are facts which cannot be denied. The interrelatedness of all sections of mankind has become this century an equally undeniable fact, thanks to modern technology, and historians now are beginning to realize that the development of the various cultures, when active and creative on this or that continent, has followed somewhat parallel paths through the centuries and millennia of the past (cf. "Les Metamorphoses de L'Humanite", Editions PLANETE, Paris, France).

This process of all-human integration, however, runs inevitably into many obstacles. Any living form -- and at the human level, any social or religious institution -- develops a resistance to change. Inertia -- which is actually the prin-

ciple of resistance to change -- is a basic fact of existence.
This fact is powerful in the development of human consciousness; it manifests in the clinging to privileges and to the security of familiar values, concepts and feeling-responses. It
is this inertia which gives to a person's ego (using the term
in its psychological sense) its obstinate repugnance to modify
its controlling attitude and to reorient its behavior and its
sense of value.

Until the egos of a significant number of human beings --
especially of individuals able to assume social and ideological authority -- have been able, willing and ready to accept all
the implications of the pull of evolution toward the stage of
all-human, global integration, the process will always risk
running into catastrophic crises which would delay vastly its
wholesome completion. The drive toward synthesis and toward a condition of quasi-organic participation in the activity
of a greater whole succeeds in proportion as men f e e l   i n-
t e n s e l y a sense of underlying human unity -- in proportion
as they are vividly aware of "Man's common humanity" underneath and through all superficial differences between individual persons, groups and races.

What we call religion -- especially the recent "great religions" -- constitutes an attempt to make this sense of Man's
common humanity vivid and compelling by projecting it, as
it were, upon the broad screen of the heavens as a supreme
Being named God. Religion tells us that we are, either mul-
tiple aspects of one all-inclusive transcendent Reality, or sons
of one Father-God -- or, in tribal days, descendants from a
common Great Ancestor. In this way the ideal of the Brotherhood of Man is held with emotional vividness before the mind
of millions of individuals who otherwise would only be aware
of the ego-differences and the conflicts of interest between
them.

The great ideal of "unity" has thus been given a religious,
transcendent power; and everywhere groups of men and women
"fascinated" by this deified ideal of Unity have been led to take

what is called "the Path of Return" -- the return to the One-that-was-in-the-beginning and whose unity will be reconstituted as all men's consciousness become synthesized and in some way merge at the end of the human cycle. It is to this final consummation that Teilhard de Chardin refers when he speaks of the Point Omega, an incandescent state of spiritual Christ-consciousness. In a similar way, Sri Aurobindo speaks of a Gnostic society of men transfigured by the descent and incorporation of the Supermind (cf. the last chapters of THE LIFE DIVINE).

The religious projection of the ideal of all-human unity upon the screen of the heavens ruled by an all-powerful and all-loving God, pictured in the shape of the Ideal Man, has taken many forms during historical ages. One of the oldest forms was the foundation of astrology. Astrology was based originally on the realization that the sky presented a magical picture of order and infinite peace. This picture instilled in primitive man, harassed by violence and fear in tropical jungles or in dark and dank northern forests, the faith that he was nevertheless living in an ordered universe where seasonal changes were predictable and the return of spring and fruits could be relied upon. Agriculture was born of that faith.

Then men began to people the sky with gods and creative Hierarchies. Constellations of stars were pictured with profound symbolic meaning revealing to the initiated the cyclic processes of growth, affecting all human beings because they referred to "Man's common humanity" -- all men being "brothers in the stars" and multifarious expressions of the Sky-god, the Great Man in Heaven, the Macroprosopus or Great Countenance.

Today this picture of the Zodiacal Man appears archaic and quite meaningless to the majority of educated men and women, for a new picture of the universe has been presented by modern astronomers and we worship a science which has been able to discover and utilize basic laws of the universe.

We see the earth as a small planet revolving around the sun, a not too impressive star among millions gathered within the immensely vast Galaxy. And this Galaxy appears to be separated by incredibly great distances from millions of more or less similar spiral nebulae, not to mention even more remote and mysterious celestial objects.

The picture of the sky has changed, but it is still a picture of immense power operating in an ordered way. The urge to explore interplanetary, and perhaps someday interstellar galactic spaces, has seized humanity; and this at the very time a global society, relating in some definitely and vitally organized manner all human beings, has been made possible. We are becoming "Terrans", whose home is the Earth (in Latin, Terra). As Terrans -- for our effort spaceward implies a cooperation of scientists from all nations of our globe -- we feel the need of relating ourselves to the whole solar system; and this need takes the perhaps fanciful or rather the as yet unproven, form of communication with beings from other planets, just as it arouses in the fertile imagination of science-fiction writers the image of a "Galactic Federation".

Imagination is a powerful force; but, alas, today it is too often used in the pursuit of commercial (or military) goals. It tries to make stories or to gain advantage over other men; it seems to have lost the power to create symbols, that is, to focus the collective energies of multitudes of men upon an "Image" able to arouse intense, enduring faith and hope, and the will required to make actual the "great dream". The collective emotions of national groups of men, when aroused in recent times, have basically been directed by short-sighted leaders toward some sort of quasi-religious "Crusade" against an enemy pictured in monstrous terms. The much publicized "Cold War" has been given, by both sides the cruel intensity displayed by the Wars of Religions of the past. It is indeed a Civil War of Man, for today mankind is factually a whole. What happens in a remote corner of the globe affects at once the lives and the jobs of men everywhere; and the press, radio and television make it impossible for us to forget this fact unless we desperately hide our ostrich-heads in the sands of our comfortable suburban existence.

We should look again to the sky for some great faith; and indeed our yearning to move in gravitation-free spaces -- underneath the utilitarian and military aspects of these costly ventures -- is a subconscious attempt to forget the earth's warring dualities and to participate in the ordered grandeur of the pageant of planets and stars. Soon we may feel that if the Earth, Terra, is our home, the solar system is our village-community. Then some more adventurous minds will begin to dream -- they are already doing so! -- of the unknown paths that will lead from our solar system to some other cosmic community and eventually to the great metropolis, the White City at the core of the Galaxy.

We are now able to think of such an adventure in terms of p h y s i c a l displacement, depending on the controlled technological use of energies powering some sort of concrete vehicle; but in the past there have been men here and there who have dreamt of such spaceward journeys in terms of a Soul-quest powered by psycho-mental energies in vehicles of consciousness not made by human hands, but built by spiritual faith, daring courage and unflinching will. We may call such men mystics, occultists, initiates; names matter little here, for we are not concerned with techniques as such and receipes, but rather with the understanding of what these men have ventured after, of the way they have followed, of the symbolic utterances they have left us so as to stimulate our own endeavors. They did not speak, these men, of galactic center; but they told of the Light and Love that pulsates throughout the universe, of the mystic Way, of ineffable glory or absolute stillness, to describe which they could only use this so much abused little word, God.

Now, in the new scientific picture of the universe, many men can find no room for an actual and concrete God; yet we can give to this ancient symbol, God, a new form, a galactic frame of reference. We still can think of a Path of Return; and now we see this Path reaching toward the core of the Galaxy -- and, as conscious men who have succeeded in producing the tremendous heat of the fire that burns in the "heart of the Sun", we can travel on this Path along with solar rays; for we too have become miniature suns. We have the power; we need only the imagination, the faith, and the daring to leave behind altogether our now obsolete vehicles of coarse matter and to set our minds firmly upon the course that our spiritual telescopes and radars enable us to map.

Symbols, of course; but is not the word God a symbol? Is not space a human word measured by our brain's responses to changes of awareness? Men are forever building new goals and ways seeking to lead our imagination and feelings to these ideal goals. Men create their universes; each man, in some respect, his own. We start from the near, the sensed, the felt; and we venture forth, dreaming -- and in dreaming we trace pathways to the stars which others will follow, more cautiously perhaps, yet, if too cautiously, perhaps too late to catch the dewdrops of light upon the vast meadows of galactic space.

The will to tread this pathway to the stars which leads to the very core of the Galaxy is the motivating power of a third movement which we must see as existing beyond the twofold rhythmic oscillations of "life". We can no longer refer to it as the involution of solar energy into forms, or as the evolution of consciousness from activity in forms. I have spoken of it as "transvolution". The path that this movement follows is the Illumined Road. It reaches symbolically from the Heart of the Sun to the very core of the Milky Way.

The First Phase: Reorientation

THE MOON STATION

The first thing to do is to leave: this is the basic fact in all adventures. The next thing is to find our direction. It must lead us away from what we are, from our customary all-too-familiar occupations. We have therefore to r e-o r i e n t o u r-s e l v e s.

The symbol of this initial step in our new adventure is the Moon. We have to reach the "hidden face of the Moon", as a platform from which we can survey the whole solar system. Then we can observe this system from a point of view no long-er geocentric (Earth-centered), but heliocentric (Sun-center-ed); this, because the Moon, our satellite, marks the ultimate boundaries of the Earth as a planetary whole.

In ancient cosmologies the space between the Earth-at-mosphere and the Moon was called the sub-lunar sphere -- or the astral realm: and the Moon was related to Saturn, the pla-net whose revolutions were said to mark the boundaries of the solar system as a well-defined cosmic field. The Moon re-presents thus, in the deeper type of astrological symbolism, the primordial awareness -- i.e. the "feeling" -- of being a person facing a complex environment and reacting to this en-vironment in a characteristic, spontaneous and organic man-ner. It is the original basis of the ego sense; but the ego it-self is developed as a real psychological structure only in re-lation to the family and social pressures of the environment, and Saturn -- the ringed planet -- symbolizes this ego as a structural pattern of responses to life's everyday contacts and challenges.

It is at this lunar level of basic awareness of oneself-as-a person that an individual must start his pilgrimage to the stars. This awareness has to be questioned. Its modes of operation have to be examined critically. The crystallized forms it has acquired under Saturn's influence (i. e. as a result of the pressures of a particular environment, culture, language, religion, etc.) must be challenged. This does not mean that the ego-sense will then vanish -- far from it. It simply implies a consideration of its origin and of the manner in which it has become set into a rigid and controlling frame of reference.

"Con-sideration" etymologically means "with the stars" (c o n-s i d e r a), a most revealing etymology indeed! To consider a fact is to try to discover the place and meaning it has in relation to the universe-as-a-whole. It is not to look at it as an isolated entity, but to integrate it into a vaster Whole in which it operates significantly. The change from an Earth-centered to a Sun-centered picture of the universe was the result of "considering" the Earth -- and thus of seeing it as an integral part of the solar system. A further change -- a reconsideration of the meaning of human existence on this Earth -- comes when the solar system as a whole is seen as a small unit in a vast Galaxy, the Milky Way.

The first step on what I call here the Illumined Road is to reorient one's consciousness and one's ego-sense; it is to recognize and irrevocably to accept one's position within the solar system. This means symbolically that the tie between the Moon and Saturn -- to which we shall return when dealing with Saturn -- has to be transformed. It has to be superseded, at least partially and ideally, by a deep, flaming realization of the essential relationship between the Moon and the Sun -- the Moon becoming, as a result, a Sun-oriented gateway to the solar system as a whole.

In primitive man close to Nature the Moon and the Sun are seen as two polarities of life; but this awareness of the bi-

polar character of life exists almost entirely at the unconscious level of animal (or at least "tribal") existence. The
Sun and the Moon are the two "Lights" related to the basic
rhythms of day and night. Man responds passively to these
rhythms as a component part of the Earth's biosphere. He
worships the Sun; but is not aware of the solar system
as a cosmic field of activity. He is totally and compulsively
life-centered as well as earth-centered. Later on, as his ego
becomes more set and his sense of being a separate individual
person increases under the symbolical influence of Saturn,
man remains earth-centered, but "ego-centricity" largely supersedes in him his earlier "biocentricity".

At this preliminary Moon-stage of the Illumined Road the
individual person, now relatively free from Saturn's egocentric stranglehold and consciously turned toward the Sun, is
ready to start on his long, arduous and dangerous journey
starward. He is beginning to "feel" -- very dimly and in-
securely at this stage -- that there is an Illumined Road, and
to sense the relation it has to the earlier primordial movements of life, i.e. the centrifugal and centripetal motions of
energy of which I have already spoken. He realizes that there
is a third movement which reaches from the "Heart of the
Sun"* to the very center of the Galaxy. This is the Illumined
Road, of which mystic philosophers often have spoken as the

---

* This term "the Heart of the Sun" is, of course, purely
symbolical. It refers to the Unknown Reality hidden, as it
were, behind or within the intense atomic activity of the outer
layers of the Sun, the photosphere. It refers to the Sun as a
star among stars, rather than the Sun as a sun, i.e. as the
center and origin of a system of planets. This distinction between the two ways of considering the Sun -- as an individual
star in the galaxy, and as the "father-mother" of a family of
planets -- is very important in terms of the type of symbolism used in this work.

Path of Return.

If we look from the heliocentric point of view at the two great movements of life-energy we see in the first instance life radiating as f o r m a t i v e   a c t i v i t y from the solar center to the Saturnian boundaries of the solar system, the trans-Saturnian planets not strictly belonging to that system, * then this outward formative tide of energy bounces back, as it were as r e f l e c t i v e   c o n s c i o u s n e s s. The life-energy, in a transformed condition, resonates back to the Sun, building structures of "mind" and group-relatedness. This two-directional oscillatory and circulatory rhythm goes on and on, outward activity and inward consciousness acting upon each other, until the life-force exhausts its innate potential and the cycle of organic existence ends. This is the "Wheel of life and death" of Buddhistic philosophy, S a m s a r a.

However, the possibility of a third movement exists in Man; and individuals here and there respond to such a possibility. They "break through" the circulatory rhythm of normal human existence at the symbolical Moon level; and, reorienting their "feeling-nature", they see the Saturnian power of egocentricity slowly wane as the Solar power of heliocentricity waxes in strength. They begin to feel, think and act as if the center of their being was established in the Heart of the Sun. And from this Heart of the Sun, which is "light" responsive to the vaster rhythms of the galactic "greater Whole", they become identified in an increasingly and irrevocable manner with the "solar Ray" reaching out, far beyond Saturn, to the galactic center. It is, I repeat, this center which, for a humanity whose consciousness is able to scan immense fields of space measured by "light-years", represents in concrete expression that cosmic Power hidden by the word, God -- o u r God.

---

* cf. THE PRACTICE OF ASTROLOGY as an Integral Approach to Human Understanding, by Dane Rudhyar (1967).

The Illumined Road is the path of the solar Ray -- the Ray that links the single star-sun to the center of its Galaxy -- but no one can tread this Road who has not reoriented his basic feeling of self away from the Saturnian patterns of the ego and toward the Sun -- which then (and only then) can truly stand for the individual Soul of the self-dedicated person. This path is of the substance of light; but on it any obstacle and any unredeemed ghost from the geocentric and egocentric past cast a crucially dark shadow. The fate of the traveller on the Illumined Road rests essentially upon his faith, his courage and his ability to withstand, without deviating from the guiding solar Ray, the torturing power of fear and seeming isolation.

Indeed, on this road every Soul travels alone, even through the sense of isolation is the great illusion. Every Sun must feel alone, until the Saturnian gate is crossed by the solar Ray. Every individual person must find for himself and by himself his path to that Star which symbolizes his place and function in the galactic Whole, his spiritual-cosmic Identity.

The presence of this Star can only be seen as the individual faces the clear, cold sky of the hidden side of the Full Moon with a consciousness reoriented and renewed. On one side is the Sun, on the other the Star. Yet no one can reach directly this Star except in a state of identification with the solar Ray, which is light and "love" -- a love transfigured by the light that streams from the Heart of the Sun.

Thus the individual facing the dark star-studded lunar sky is confronted by a basic paradox; for him, the path that will lead to the Star takes him at first in the opposite direction. He must forget the Star and seek the solar Ray, the only Guide he can trust. He can reach the Star only if he is one with a solar Ray. The Star-Self can only be reached in self-forgetfulness and self-surrender to the solar Ray -- that is, to the radiant power of the Sun-Soul.

All along the Illumined Road man's mind is confronted by paradoxes. As the solar Ray speeds starward from the Heart of the Sun it passes through the same stages which the life-energy experienced during the form-building and conscious-ness-reflecting movements -- stages that are identifiable as the planets of the solar system. But now these planets stand for a basically different aspect of reality. They are stations on the Illumined Road.

Seen with the heavily egocentric sight of ordinary men these stations may well appear as "Stations of the Cross", with Golgotha as an inevitable conclusion; and the Illumined Road takes on the aspect of a Via Dolorosa. But to him whose feelings and faith have been totally reoriented, and who himself has become in inner Soul-fact the Illumined Road, the path upon which he moves is indeed a Via Ardens -- a path of fire radiating light (a mysterious, troubling light) upon all he touches, while his eyes are riveted to the Star.

The Second Phase: Repolarization
THE MERCURY STATION

In the evolutionary process by which the unitarian and un-differentiated solar energy gradually becomes differentiated on its way toward the Saturnian boundaries of the system the first and most basic type of differentiation refers to that stage of energy which we call e l e c t r i c i t y. It is symbolized by Mercury, the planet closest to the Sun. However, the word, electricity, is quite confusing because electrical phenomena can be most varied in character, intensity and appearance. The spectacular lightning reveals electricity in its most awe-inspiring form; but if we study biology and man's nervous system we become acquainted with electrical phenomena of a very subtle nature, the operation of which we certainly do not fully understand. The amount of electrical energy in a cell and in the activities of the billions of cells interrelated within a man's brain is very small indeed; but how far-reaching the effect of these nerve-currents!

In any case, however, the essential characteristic of electrical phenomena is their bi-polarity. Electricity in operation is either positive or negative. The realm of electrical action is the realm of duality. Under the symbolism of Mercury we see the unitarian force of the Sun becoming a polarized energy: the One becomes the Two. As dualism enters the world of activity every mode of action is confronted with, but a l s o c o m p l e m e n t e d b y, an opposite mode. This is the great Law of Polarity, of which modern physics discover always more complex and fascinating manifestations;

for instance, atomic particles and anti-particles, matter and anti-matter, etc. But there are also particles which carry no electrical charge (neutrons, neutrinos), or perhaps in which electricity exists in a condition beyond polarity, for this neutral condition may also be polarized in another way in relation to some other form which may elude our power of observation -- perhaps in the sense in which fullness is the polar opposite of emptiness?

These last words may well contain a very valuable and significant key to the understanding of the process symbolized here as the Illumined Road. Might not this process occur when that which has become "full" in terms of solar-system values and power is able to make himself "empty" in relation to galactic values and powers?

After the evolutionary Sun-ward tide has passed through the Mercury level of the conceptual mind -- the mind filled with a transferable harvest of values gathered through significant personal experiences -- the individual Soul approaches the Sun. Will it dare step through the fiery threshhold of the flaming photosphere and seek the Heart of the Sun, the Holy of Holies? The Sun is a "devouring Presence", occultists of the past have said. At its center, man finds the Void -- Sunya in Buddhism; "God's Poverty" in Christian mysticism. He becomes totally denuded and empty. He becomes the Void.

It is in this quasi-timeless moment of utter denudation and deprivation that the individual Soul may sense the immensely peaceful and steady beats of the Heart of the Sun. It experiences the Sun as a star, as a vibrant unit in the "Companionship of the Stars" -- as a component part of the vast Galaxy. In this experience the individual Soul both loses itself and rediscovers itself; it rediscovers itself as a Pilgrim ready, willing and able to tread the Illumined Road, carried on by a "solar Ray" -- an effulgent "horse" in Vedic symbology; Pegasus, the winged stallion of Greek mythology.

The Soul enters upon the Path of Return; and its first realization is that it is now facing all facts of existence in terms of a new polarity of consciousness -- that is, in relation to that which as yet it can but dimly envision as the galactic level of consciousness. The Soul is again like a "little child" seeking to learn by polarizing himself toward the parental example -- and this is what the phrases so often misunderstood, "The Imitation of Christ" and "The Practice of the Presence of God" mean. The Galaxy is now a felt presence; a deep power of attraction. The solar Ray is moved by this power of galactic gravitation, and the individual Soul -- fascinated, yet still uncertain and insecure -- tries to steady itself and not to lose the direction revealed by a beacon light which attracts mysteriously and almost poignantly. Yet, all around this light of the galactic core, a multitude of radiant shapes present confusing and often seductive images, following which the Soul would lose its way in interstellar spaces; and occultists speak of the dangerous possibility of being spiritually seduced by some great "Star Archangels" seeking a base of operation among men.

Consciousness should be, at any level, the manifestation of the wholeness of an organic whole; but an organism has a number of organs and billions of cells, each of which has a degree of independence and functions in its own field also as a whole. There are thus various types of consciousness. Mercury, as the last stage of the evolutionary process of development of consciousness before the life-wave returns to its solar source, is a power of ingathering, of classification, of generalization and synthesis. It produces symbols (words, images, series of actions) which help us to understand the "holistic" meaning and purpose of our experiences. It creates philosophical, ethical and logical systems. It builds the great theories of science from which emerge what men see as the "laws of Nature" -- laws which may nevertheless apply only to our universe or perhaps only to the stage of the cosmic process in which we now live.

Mercury at this ideo-syncretic stage makes use also of

the principle of Polarity, which is seen then as that of logical exclusion -- the "either-or" and "true-or-false" principle of Aristotelian logic and of many of our modern psychological "tests". Such a principle is at the level of intellectual systems, a transformation of the Saturnian antagonism between the ins and the outs, between the people who belong to the tribe or the little group and the foreigners, the aliens. When "form" is seen as that which separates the outside from an inside, we have the principle of duality at work. Yet it can mean also that which links the outside to the inside, constituting therefore the threshold of mutual communication.

The whole process of life-evolution, which symbolically is the return tide of energies from the Saturn-defined boundaries to the Sun, is conditioned by the power of Saturn. Where there is organic living there must be form according to this Saturnian principle of exclusion; the inside must remain essentially separated from the outside. There must be a defining and thus limiting and structuring "frame of reference", the ego; and this ego functions in terms of at least relative isolation. Only a limited number and variety of data should reach the brain through the senses if the brain's power of associating such data of experiences is to operate effectively, and if chaos or confusion is to be avoided.

Moreover added safety devices are built-in by the culture and religion of one's group or people, and by the individual's own fears and insecurity, so that only that which would be acceptable and not shock-producing to the consciousness is allowed to pass by the "censor". This censor (popularized by Freud) is always busy rejecting, casting out and pushing into the subconscious what might cause a destructive shock or evoke images dangerous to the normal rhythm of the person's feelings.

When the fiery furnace of the Sun has been reached and passed through, the situation changes radically, though not at first completely; but most human beings, when they reach the proximity of the Sun, recoil in awe; they keep repeating the centrifugal-centripetal cycle of s a m s a r a, the wheel of life-and-death. Only a very few dare to go through the ordeal of fire; and perhaps but a few of these reach the Heart of the Sun, the Void and its awe-inspiring Silence.

Then the daring ones start on the Illumined Road; and the first realization that inevitably comes to them -- though with a more or less acute and upsetting intensity, depending on their past experiences -- is that their mental attitude toward practically everything they encounter in their surroundings has basically changed. Even their memories of the past have taken a different coloring. Something in them, though certainly not the whole of their personality still greatly affected by old habits, is re-interpreting their experiences in terms of a new sense of inclusion. But now inclusion is not conditioned by a rigid form or logical principle; nevertheless it does not bring a feeling of chaos.

Every fact of experience or memory-knowledge somehow seems to be consistently related to every other fact. The sharp differences between in and out are not only attenuated, but they are seen harmonized into an ever vaster and more inclusive complex of activities. Nothing now seems to be absolutely true; nothing absolutely false. Everything b e l o n g s; there are no longer any real outsiders, no fact that is "damned", no idea that seems totally unacceptable. No behavior is rigidly un-understandable or absolutely abhorent, because any action is seen inevitably bound to its opposite, and every light shines brightly in significant contrast to its shadow.

Yet he who travels on the Illumined Road k n o w s, in an undefinable manner and without doubt, the reality of the path he follows -- of the solar Ray that carries him onward -- the reality of the fact that somewhere in the vastness of the galaxy there is a star which is his galactic Self, his "place" and function in that immense, organism of radiant consciousness and power. He knows that he will increasingly become aware of his own stellar Truth -- his d h a r m a; that his capacity to understand the processes at work throughout the galactic organization of stars will gradually develop -- a new and wider kind of understanding that leaves nothing out as irrelevant and without significance. And as he moves along the path outlined by the solar Ray, he comes to identify himself totally with this Ray. As it is told in ancient books, he who follows that Illumined Path becomes in some incomprehensible manner that Path itself. He and the Ray become one; unless -- and the possibility is always there -- he becomes afraid; unless he becomes fascinated by some powerful Star-being whose intense gravitational pull may already throw him off his "solar horse" and draw him irresistibly to an ex-centric embrace in which he may lose forever his stellar Identity.

At this first stage of the pilgrimage upon the Illumined Road the individual Soul is still a novice in spiritual things. He has to learn how to learn in a new way, how to repolarize thoroughly and permanently his mental processes -- also how to face new and old responsibilities in a new way. New modes of perceptions may already arise at this stage. "Astral" colors, symbols, eerie sounds may be experienced; but these often are more confusing than helpful to the process of understanding, more illusory than real in terms of reaching the essential goal, the galactic core, God. At best they are but special manifestations of the process of repolarization of the mind and modes of "holistic" perception; and if they develop prematurely they tend to produce a glamor which makes the traveler forget that any such power increases his spiritual responsibility. What is more essential is that he should develop the capacity to see t h r o u g h all the facts of his existence, to understand their meaning in terms of his now much enlarged sense of being part of a cosmic whole in which all parts are interrelated and interdependent, yet in which also each unit has its own place and function, its own identity.

The little word, through, acquires here an unusual importance and significance. The Illumined Road does not stretch into some new and mysterious dimension of space; it does not cross fields of space totally unfamiliar to the traveler.

What is unfamiliar is his own reaction to what he encounters, his response to the meetings; the landscape is often exactly the one he has known before, the people he meets are those he met before along the evolutionary road from Saturn to the Sun; he may well travel the very same road -- yet everything is different, because he is different now.

I have spoken of the two great life-tides, involution and evolution -- the release and differentiation of energy into space and the building of forms of consciousness as energy rebounds inward after being stopped by the Saturnian boundaries of the field of individual existence. The pilgrimage of the Soul on the Illumined Road constitutes a third movement to which we might give the name of "transvolution", just because it is the way through all that had happened before -- not, however, in the sense that it is a "recapitulation" of past experiences, but a "trans-cending" of these experiences. Transcending means literally: to step through. But the adverb "through" has here a very potent meaning which implies also that of "beyond" and that of transformation -- a piercing through -- and, in the process of piercing through, a repolarization of awareness.

The French author and motion-picture director, Jean Cocteau, used at various times the symbolism of jumping through a mirror. The mirror reflects one's image; to the normal senses, it seems solid glass. But if the beholder dares to jump with all his power through the mirror -- and thus through his own image -- he discovers himself moving through a fluidic world in which everything encountered reveals new meanings.

This is pure symbolism, of course; yet it may be very stimulating to the imagination and very significant; because our normal ego-consciousness is a kind of reflection of ourselves as active organisms of living cells. Man has to dare to pierce through this consciousness -- not necessarily in one spectacular effort that challenges his rationality and common sense (i. e. crashing through solid glass), but according to a process of "transvolution" based on a radical repolarization of consciousness.

Mercury, on the Illumined Road, represents this phase of repolarization. In Greek mythology Mercury was the servant of Zeus-Jupiter, ruler of the visible sky and maintainer of the traditional order; Mercury was constantly running errands for his master -- and indeed the evolutionary Mercury-mind is normally the servant of the established order of the society and culture to which one belongs by birthright. But in terms of the movement of the Soul-consciousness speeding toward the galactic center along the solar Ray, Mercury is the mind having become identified with this solar Ray. Mercury is then the transvolutionary drive toward an ever more inclusive, cosmically consistent and significant realization of all the aspects of existence, regardless of appearances and tradition-ruled concepts or feeling-responses. It is the Star-oriented mind, the mind resonant to the integral and harmonious vibrations of the galaxy.

It is the mind of understanding; and understanding implies responsibility. He who truly understands "stands-under" the manifestations of existence with which his path of destiny relates him; and therefore, even if only in a subtle and transcendent manner, he bears the weight of such manifestations. Mere knowledge may leave the knower separate from, because external to the things known. But true understanding is only possible through a process of relationship which, even though it may not mean (strictly speaking) "identification", nevertheless implies responsibility of a spiritual order. It means an acceptation of the interconnection between all forms of existence, and an at least relative subservience of the part to the whole.

The mind which insists on separating itself from the things it knows, and which refuses responsibility, has led the thinker already past the threshold that marks the entrance to the path of the Shadow, which is the dark counterpart of the Illumined Road. There must be such a counterpart for in this realm of Mercury polarity conditions all possibilities of

existence. Mercury represents discrimination; and on the Illumined Road discrimination can indeed take on a very subtle
and elusive aspect. This is the phase of the spiritual process
which has been popularized in quasi-mystical literature by
the razor's edge. The choice between darkness and light lies
but too often upon a distinction between what appears as two
degrees of light.

The ordinary man's mind cannot make this distinction unless it has become repolarized by a descent of spiritual power and, in many cases, by the compassionate action of a Great
One who stands at his side, as Krishna stood at Arjuna's side
when the latter faced in utter despondency a poignant decision
which was to destroy his relatives and friends ready to fight
on both sides of the field.

At the entrance of "the Path" it is indeed often quite difficult to distinguish between true comrades and foes, for the
individual, though he has definitely resolved to walk on the
Illumined Road to the Star, finds himself not only attached to
human beings of all kinds, but attached also, at least in some
degree, to traditional judgments as to the meaning of categories of facts. He has to gain a new point of view, a new
frame of reference for truth. He needs a new Image of reality; and this is why, again like Arjuna in the Bhagavat Gita,
he begs Krishna, his charioteer and his guru, to reveal to
him in a vision the all-encompassing Countenance of the Supreme Being.

It is an awesome vision; and Arjuna's mind can hardly
stand looking at it. He begs his Teacher and divine Master
to take again His limited form as a human being. He is not
yet ready to face what, in our astrological symbolism, would
be the real Form which would be seen if we could use the
whole lens-shaped Galaxy as a lens to see beyond the core of
our universe. Such a "failure of nerves" is common indeed.
The Gospels tell us that the disciples on the Mount of Transfiguration could neither stand nor understand what was happening to their Master. Eugene O'Neill's remarkable tragedy

"Lazarus Laughed" ends with these poignant words: Men forget. They forget because, even in the best among them, that which understands is but a fraction of their mind -- a mind not yet established securely on the Illumined Road and divided against itself.

New experiences of seeing, hearing, sensing are needed. There must be "vision" -- clear, undimmed, perceptive, free from hallucinations and seductive shapes or from mere moods of unity misunderstood for "cosmic consciousness". At this stage on the Road, the disciple may think of God as the universal Eye -- the Eye not only that does not close, but that cannot close, the lidless Eye of all-encompassing consciousness. Every individual that has come to hold fast to the light of his solar Ray, which alone can lead him to the Star that is his celestial Identity, must never let go of consciousness. He must face all things and all men, all loves and all decisions, with open eyes that gradually become incapable of closing.

This requires indomitable strength -- a strength and a courage quite incomprehensible to the man whose eyes but uncertainly register, and whose inner being does not fully respond, insulated as it is by the Saturnian structure of his egocentricity. To see utter darkness and desperate anguish and yet to respond in understanding and in love, while holding fast to the Ray of spirit and not being swerved from the Illumined Road; this indeed means strength. He who arises filled with that strength has passed through the Mercury portals. He has successfully met the ordeals of repolarization of consciousness. He is moving on with centered gaze through new experiences of reality.

The Third Phase: Revaluation
THE VENUS STATION

The two first phases of the process of inner metamorphosis, the reorientation of the power of attention and of the will of the ego, then the repolarization of consciousness, lead to a third phase, symbolized by Venus. Just as we saw that the Mercury period (or function) in the complete cycle of life can be interpreted, first, in terms of the involutionary process of differentiation of primordial spirit-energy into the various forces animating all organic life, then, in terms of the evolutionary development of human faculties and consciousness, and finally in relation to a third process ("transvolution") represented by the Illumined Road, likewise Venus can be understood in three basic ways. Mythological symbolism already represented the planet under two aspects: as Venus-Lucifer, the Morning Star, and Venus-Hesperus, the Evening Star; as herald of light and harvester of the experiences of the day.

Venus within the frame of reference of involutionary differentiation (the Morning Star) represents what we call today "magnetism". As Mercury is the symbol of bi-polar electrical activity, these two planets -- the only two inside of the Earth's orbit we actually know -- should be considered as being closely related; because electricity and magnetism are almost inseparable expressions of energy. They constitute, at least from the point of view of astrological symbolism, the first two stages of differentiation of that Solar potential which is the undifferentiated source of all the energies operating within a living organism. Electricity operating through, or at the core of a "field" gives rise to various electro-magnetic processes. These, seen in their entirety, constitute the dynamic foundation of organic living, the electro-magnetic, or "auric field" surrounding as well as pervading the physical body.

Occult traditions, Western as well as Eastern, speak of the "astral body" of a man. Unfortunately this term has been given several different meanings in theosophical or pseudo-theosophical writings. Essentially one should conceive the "astral world" as the realm of "p u r e" f o r c e s in contra-distinction to the physical realm in which all we can observe are material changes -- changes which affect the behavior of particles of matter within and to-and-from organized wholes (atoms, molecules, cells, organs, bodies, societies, etc.)

When we speak of "pure" forces, we mean forces considered in themselves without the limiting concept of material substance. Thus, when modern physics interprets light as wave-motion, it speaks of pure force. What is considered, is not the substance in motion, but the rhythm of the force in motion.

Indeed the concept of substance vanishes almost entirely from the world-picture presented by some contemporary physicists. This picture is nearly identical with that to which the occultist of today or the Alchemist-Rosicrucian of the Middle Ages and early Renaissance alluded when speaking of the "astral" realm -- the realm of N a t u r a n a t u r a n s, the world of formative energies.

This realm must not be confused, however, with what is popularly meant by the term "astral"; that is, the realm of illusory perceptions, emotional cravings and disintegrating by-products of consciousness -- the Freudian subconscious, Jung's personal unconscious, and the "sub-lunar realm" of medieval occultists. The Venus function, in its involutionary aspect, is a creative and formative power. It produces, on the basis of the electrical activity of the Mercury function, "electro-magnetic fields". The diffuse and incoherent materials scattered in universal space are drawn within these fields. They are made to assume definite patterns; as iron filings are likewise brought into more or less symmetrical arrangement within the electro-magnetic field of a magnet.

These patterns, assumed by substantial elements of any and all types, make visible what are called the lines of force of the magnetic field. The Venus power deals with the organization of lines of force, but not with the substances drawn to and precipitating along them. Magnetic lines of force are the results of more or less steady and permanent combinations of wave-motions. They are expressions of "pure forces" in action. From the strictly limited point of view of the Venus function considered in itself, these dynamic patterns in electro-magnetic fields exist without reference to whatever precipitates and condenses along their lines of flow. They constitute reality at the true "astral" level: the level of an involutionary Venus function.

The process of condensation of particles of substance beside these lines of force refers to a particular aspect of the Moon function -- i.e. to the building of material organisms within the Lunar matrix. But Venus-Lucifer (literally "Bearer of Light") deals with patterns of light; with the archetypal Form of Man.

If now we consider Venus with reference to the evolutionary development of actual earthly organisms and of human personalities, we find this planet symbolizing essentially the factor of "value". The Venusian function, at the level of the individual consciousness, enables man to discriminate between that which has value for his individual growth and that which is valueless or potentially destructive. "Feelings" are the immediate manifestations of judgments of value -- not mental judgments, but instinctual, organic, emotional and inbred cultural-social-ethical judgments. Love and hatred, attraction and repulsion, happiness and unhappiness, the emotional sense of what is beautiful and what is ugly -- all such oppositions result from judgments of value, in relation to the vital requirements of our body, our soul, our cultural and moral sense of participation in society, etc. These judgments establish the foundations of man's emotional-personal life; they largely control in most cases, or at least influence and guide, the Mercury-phase of our inner life; thus, the development of generalized images, abstractions, concepts and systems.

However, when the individual man begins to tread the Illumined Road the Venus function undergoes a deep metamorphosis. The magnetism of the ego must be renewed by a process of identification with the quality and purpose of the Solar entity, the soul. Every habit of personal behavior and every motive of the ego, all the values of the emotional life and all the cultural and moral standards, gradually acquire a new significance and a new purpose. And this radical revaluation of all values has been expressed by the Christian mystics as they said: It is no longer I who live; G o d l i v e s m e.

Through the Venus phase of "revaluation" the emphasis is not placed, however, upon outer activity -- for this belongs to the next phase symbolized by Mars. The stress is upon a change in values; and this is what is meant figuratively by the expression, "a change of heart" -- or, in religious terminology, the core of the true process of "conversion". A man is what the values he puts on his inner and outer experiences are. Change these evaluations, and the man is no longer as he was; his activities change -- or, if outwardly the same, they begin to acquire a new quality of radiation and a new potency.

It was Nietzsche who popularized the phrase: the revaluation of all values. But the German philosopher and poet functioned as a destroyer of cultural and religious images. There need be such destroyers, but their fate and their responsibility are tragic. They are like the bomb whose explosion freed the energy locked within the electro-magnetic field of atoms of uranium and plutonium. They release power; but to what end? Liberation from obsolete values itself must be given value. It is worth what its ultimate purpose is. Whosoever destroys now useless cultural, ethical, religious values, except by the power of new and greater values, becomes caught into the destruction, as Samson under the ruins of the temple.

The "Solar" individual -- the christed Jesus -- does not destroy the temple; he instead cleanses it. He does not destroy the edifice of human values, but he floods men's souls with a new magnetism; he gives men to drink of the "living water" which supersedes and renders obsolete the water of tradition.

What is this new magnetism? Whence the "living water" of which Jesus speaks? From the symbolical Heart of the Sun these "waters" emanate unceasingly as Rays of the spirit. And these Rays are the electro-magnetic "lines of force" of the Solar "field". The change from the old to the new values is indeed represented by the change from a geocentric to a heliocentric field of values. Just as the Moon function has to be "reoriented" away from Saturn and toward the Sun before the ego can travel on the Illumined Road, carried on by the power of the Solar Ray, so the Venus function has to be remagnetized by the purpose and the quality of this Ray. The consciousness of the individual has been "repolarized" during the Mercury phase of the Illumined Road; it has become redirected Starward. But a new direction is not enough. New values are needed; a repatterning of the very aim and meaning of mental activities. It is not enough that the thoughts and concepts renewed by changed sense-perceptions be different. The very purpose and quality of thinking must be revalued.

The value of mental activity is not to be taken for granted. Why do men think? Why be conscious? To what end the association of images and concepts? These are not senseless questions. The usual modern answer to them is that thought is produced as a tool to insure survival, a better adaptation-to-environment, a more complex development of the human person -- body and psyche. But this is a "geocentric" answer to the problem of value. The Illumined Road now requires a "heliocentric" answer. Mind and consciousness are no longer to be seen as instrumentalities for the survival or greater development of the body or the entire personality. They become agencies for the organization and release of soul-power, that power which enables the reoriented and repolarized conscious ego to see itself operating in a new light and with a changed heart, for the single purpose of reaching, in a fully integrated and immortal, spirit-attuned form of con- sciousness, the Star which is man's permanent Identity.

This new form of consciousness is what European mystics have named the Christ-body or the Robe of Glory. During the Venus-phase of the Illumined Road, this body of light is being formed in seed. It is a solar seed, centered in the radiance of the Sun; and no longer a dark seed, propagating the compulsions of earth-nature. It is more than an electro-magnetic field and more than an expression of value. It is the means for the individual ego to comprehend the Star, goal of his journey along the path of the Solar Ray returning to its cosmic origin. Comprehension is based on a sense of value, but also on the ability to vibrate in sympathetic resonance with what is to be understood.

The revaluated Venus function builds, as it were, a spiritual resonator to the tone sounded forth through the greater cycle of human attainment by the Star, the individualized Father-in-Heaven. This resonator is a web of Solar light-substance. It is, one might say, like a radar-instrument revealing the topography of the approaches to the Star, and the character of all experiences on the Illumined Road. On the basis of what has thus been revealed, the individual can establish new standards of value. He can see, through the fog of earthly illusions and sense-confusion, the realities that count and are significant in terms of the goal of the Illumined Road. He can pierce the many veils of man-made glamor, be they in the field of culture, of religion or of social betterment. He can perceive the essential values of man's spirit-born quest through the confused array of humanitarian and primarily material ideals offered as ultimate goals to good and sensitive men; not denying these goals, but evaluating them in a different way, within a new frame of reference.

As the individual completes this third step on the Illumined Road the magnetism of his personality is fundamentally altered. Light shines through his eyes, in a strangely different way. There is in him, from him, a glow of spirit, a strength, a security, a knowingness which cannot be explained in terms of normal health, or of vigor of body or mind. This glow will increase as the Starward journey proceeds. It will prove itself in radiant acts, in new adjustments, in the power to renew all things. It will prove itself, slowly, gradually -- perhaps with temporary set-backs. But the glow of spirit must eventually win over all mental cloudiness and all instinctual glamors.

It will win in the furnace of works performed for and as the spirit. It will win through the ordeals of fire precipitated unconsciously by loves human, all too human. It will win in the light and by the power of light, as the individual revaluates the whole of his personality in terms of the bearing forth of light to a humanity still bound by geocentric values. As an ever-shining Morning Star of the spirit such an individual will radiate the subtle essence of his renewed personality beyond the need for sunsets and for the obscuration of sleep, beyond weariness and beyond pain. And he will go on, though scorned and misunderstood, laughed at or reviled, in the steady realization of purpose and truth, carrying aloft this purpose and truth as a light for all men to see and to orient themselves by, if they choose.

Fourth Phase: Re-energization

THE MARS STATION

To live means to expend energy. The pilgrim on the Illumined Road must make use of energy, as does the man preoccupied only with the maintenance, aggrandizement or reproduction of his body and his ego on the background of social competition and physical wants. Yet, at the beginning of the Starward path, a common experience is the sense of profound weariness of body and soul, as if the entire organism of personality found itself deprived of its customary supply of energy. Indeed, it is so deprived. A great drought comes upon the land of personality. The ancestral wells run dry. The water that raised the familiar crops and made the fields of earth-conditioned personality green and moist all but vanish. Is the desert to absorb all life within the man whose gaze is now being fixed upon the yet distant Star through clear perhaps, but lonely, midnights?

To the Woman of Samaria who had come to draw water from the ancestral well -- the earthly depths of unconscious and biological instinct -- Jesus promised the gift of "living water". And she asked, with all of us: "Whence cometh this living water, and with what can it be drawn?" If our biological and psychic life of personality has become arid, if our instincts and our glands have seemingly lost the power to preserve and maintain our organism of body and soul against the pressures and the shattering impacts of the world within and without, what source of power is there on earth or in heaven to fill our need?

The ancient Hindu Sage or spiritual Guide answered these questions by devising yoga disciplines, biopsychic techniques of breathing and of concentration, in an attempt to tap deeper and more secret wellsprings of vitality within the human organism. On the other hand the basic Christian solution stresses the power of faith. It is based upon the mystery-drama of the Incarnation, which in its true spiritual meaning does not refer to a unique act performed once for all by a "one and only" Son of God, but to the always renewable process of focalization of the universal "sea of spirit" into the "drop" which our individualized selfhood constitutes.

To live is not only to expend energy; more significantly, it is to use power; and power is energy released through form. Essentially, all energy is one; yet as the forms (or the "engines") through which energy is released differ greatly, so there are various kinds of power, at several levels of being. There is the power which can be released through (rather than from, as modern science believes) the atom's structure. There is power to be released through human organisms -- through the living body (a "generic" factor) and through the "collective" organisms of a society and culture. There is also a type of power which can be released through the integrated and completely formed selfhood of the individual person in whom his spiritual Identity has become "incarnated".

The manifestation of this latter kind of power begins with the display of what is commonly called "personality". This power of "personality" makes some individuals stand out from the mass in their ability to give magnificent "performances" -- whether these be theatrical, or political, or religious. We say that these individuals have a great amount of "personal magnetism", that they can sway the multitudes. From them emanates a mysterious and indefinable something which compels other men to give attention, respect and allegiance.

In some cases, these compelling personalities project a strong physical vitality; in others, the only evidence available to ordinary perception is that of a frail body, and perhaps of illness and pain. Even where great physical energy is displayed in maturity, in many cases the individual has had a sickly youth, but somehow was able to summon forth an apparently inexhaustible amount of driving power. What is the source of this power? Can every human being draw from it?

Actually, there is no "source" to that power, simply because the energy is everywhere. It is diffused through the whole of space. We live and have our being in an ocean of energy. Yet unless we can focus this diffuse energy and give it direction, it exists for us only in latency, as an un-activated and un-actualized potential of energy. To make it useable energy -- that is, power ready to be released according to purpose -- we must, first, be aware that it is all around and within us, then, establish a significant relationship to it, and lastly, reconvert our "engines" for the use of power, so that they might operate according to the rhythm and the universal purpose inherent in the character of the spirit.

Awareness here means "realization"; but one can only truly realize that which one has profoundly and completely desired. In order to realize spirit as power one must have desired spiritual power; and this desire is worthless except it be born out of an absolute and gripping need. The character and reality of the spirit as power can only be experienced in the darkest and most crucial hour of nearly total lack of all other power; for it is only as the organism of personality is hollowed out -- even if for an instant -- by a sense of dreadful emptiness that spirit may flow into the vacuum thus created.

Happy the soul whose gates do not shut tight in dismay and fear under the irruption of the universal energy that is of God. Happy is he who can hold himself open to the vivifying influx that renews utterly -- if it only can be received long enough -- the substance of individual Selfhood. Happy is he also who does not merely "take it for granted", and whose heart fills with gratitude in a transfigured sense of relatedness to the "Father" whence comes this Holy Spirit and the power to be in truth what one essentially is, and to love in understanding all that lives and breathes. And thrice blessed is he who with courage and conviction, in utter reliance upon the spirit, goes forth to perform the "works of the spirit" as a consecrated agent of divinity.

At this station on the Illumined Road, the essential need is to become clearly aware of the substantiality and concreteness of the spirit. To think of the spirit as an abstract or completely transcendent something will not allow its entrance into the concrete organism of personality. To picture it as an ideal and a dream, is to emasculate its transfiguring power, its reality. Spirit may be conceived in many and varied ways, but always it is power; power, however, indissolubly blended with purpose -- and this purpose utterly determined by the ultimate achievement of the greatest possible state of inclusiveness and creative or radiant harmony.

Impotency, at any level, can never be considered "spiritual"; nor is the lack of desire for power ever in itself a manifestation of the spirit. It is not the desire for power that condemns a man, but that which in him desires power, and the purpose for which power is desired. Not to desire power is simply a mark of inner fatigue and/or of the unwillingness to undertake a work and to assume responsibility for it; but we should not confuse a willingness to assume responsibility with the "personal concern over the fruits of action" against which the Bhagavat Gita warns the aspirant. Responsibility refers to the use which an individual makes of the power entrusted to him, whether it be by society or by the spirit. Responsibility does not imply a personal concern over the results of this use, provided the power has been used in truth and in understanding, and in complete consecration to the divinity within.

Spirit has substantiality, in as much as it is the substratum of all energy everywhere. There can be no energy without substance, no substance without energy; any more than there can be a universe in which time is without space or space without time. But energy and substance can be of two polarities and answer two essentially different purposes -- as different as the energy and substance of the "seed" are different from those of the "soil".

What we call soil is always the remains of a previous cycle of life-manifestation. Sand is composed of a multitude of shells that once held life; the rich humus of the forest is the result of the decomposition of myriads of leaves that were. But the substance of the seed, whether it be that of the seed's nucleus or of its cotyledons, is substance polarized futureward. Within it the creative energy of life and the purpose of rebirth operate -- rebirth in answer to the summons of the universal power of the sun, as spring opens the gates of a new cycle.

In man also we can distinguish at the spiritual level, a symbolical seed and soil. Individual selfhood is man's spiritual seed; the substance and energies of his bio-psychic organism are the soil in which this seed may be sown, yet which often, alas, contains only the bacteria and lower lives which, while they do serve the growth of seeds, of themselves can never reach skyward to the Star.

The process of re-energization on the Illumined Road is one in which the seed-powers of the spirit, locked in man's individual self, begin to operate, and operating compel gradually the reawakened energies of the ancestral soil of personality to serve the purpose of the self. At first the Illumined Road seems to be a road leading away from the vitality of the physical sun, and toward a remote and cold Star. Yet, as the purpose of the process of the transvolutionary journey to the Star becomes firmly established, the antiphony of sun and Star resounds through the vast spaces of the spiritual life. New powers are released. The vital forces of the "soil" feed the growth of the "seed" under the universal solvent that is "water" -- the compassion and love of universal Beings pouring of themselves upon those who tread the Illumined Road.

The positive act of rebirth and growth must nevertheless originate in the seed. All else contributes to the growth, but the seed must germinate of itself. Man finds the universe of spirit on his side as he steps on the Illumined Road, yet he must do the stepping on. It must be a decided step, and it is only to make certain that the "seed" within man is ready and vital with faith that tests and trials meet whomsoever passes the gates Starward.

The seed of man's individual selfhood must germinate when time and climate strike the tone of the new spring. And germination is self-denial, and the apparent death of the seed as a seed. Yet this death, this breaking asunder of the protective shell of egoism, this irruption of dark energies of the soil, this seeming pollution of virgin seed-substance by the manure of past cycles -- all these can be seen by him who has faith and courage as heralds of new powers, behind which can be glimpsed the brilliant shine of the Star.

There must also be faith and gratitude. Spirit is always a gift. Water is a gift. It is -- as the old Upanishads said significantly -- the product of sacrifice. There can be no spirit-energized growth without the cooperation of the universe of light. And light is a bestowal -- God, the bestower. Spirit is everywhere. It is the universal seed-substance of divinity. It is the Living Bread, as well as the Living Water. One should partake of it with gratitude and love.

The energies of the body and of life are to be "managed" wisely and efficiently, without waste or undue haste. But the power of spirit, being a gift and the result of sacrifice, should be met in an entirely different attitude. Without this attitude being held, there can be no deep reenergization, and the individual insulated against God is left stranded on the Illumined Road, unable to move, frozen by the fear of incommensurable space.

But if man's heart is warmed by faith and by gratitude, if he has realized that spirit is food and drink to him who is fully aware of its concrete reality throughout space, and who meets it as a gift of God, then man can begin his new task. He learns to use these new powers of the spirit, and not to waste them. He learns that he is to use them as a sacred trust -- to use them in answer to a need, so that an ever fuller state of harmony and inclusiveness be achieved wherever he passes -- to use them according to the rhythm of the spirit and for the purpose of God.

At this stage of the Illumined Road the individual is to act; but he must act in terms of new purposes, new values, and a new realization of the power of universal spirit. He must act in a new way, because the energy that enables him to act is a new kind of energy. He has left behind the unconscious or semi-conscious condition of instinctual activity in which he could draw from the generic energy of body and cells, or from the collective source of ancestral and cultural sustainment. He has known weariness, the inability to act under the surge of biological and social desires. Now, the individual, having emerged from a crisis of seeming sterility and utter lack of personal initiative or ambition, finds a new eagerness to act. But it is a much sobered eagerness. It should be a relaxed eagerness, freed from self-will, tenseness, haste; freed from the slightest shade of fear or inferiority.

The individual who has fully realized with the whole of his integrated self that the energy which now sustains him and from which he is to draw is the power of ubiquitous and all-enveloping spirit, cannot feel the lack of energy as a personal handicap. He is enfolded by inexhaustible energy as the fish by the sea. And yet... how is it that he finds himself, time and again unable to accomplish the miracles of creativeness or healing which he feels required of him?

The answer is that his realization of the spirit may still not be total enough, his faith may still be colored by doubts and fears, his ego desirous of acclaim and of a following. Energy, in order to become useable power must be focused and adjusted to the recipient of the release of power. It must pass through a transformer or engine: the engine of the true self, dynamic core of the integrated personality. Is this engine adequate for the work it is called upon to perform?

The total personality of the individual treading the Illumined Road must indeed become an engine for the release of spirit. The steps of reorientation, repolarization and revaluation have prepared the consciousness and transfigured the ego, its ruler. Yet, much remains to be done. Under the symbol of Mars, a new relationship to energy has been established, a new sense of creativeness and a new approach to action have been experienced. But the individual has yet to learn how to use effectively this energy, how to manage it as a trust in the name of that universal Harmony which is the substance of divinity -- thus, in terms of the needs which arise on his road and which it is his task and his responsibility to satisfy.

So many needs, alas, he encounters! And the first lesson he must learn is that of discrimination. He who is to manage the energy of spirit for God must come to know the limits of his function in the spirit. He must know his "place" in God -- the place the Star occupies within the Constellation in which It operates as a center of giving, as a lens through which God acts eternally. To know this is not only to know the limits of one's ability to act spiritually and to heal, the limits to one's effective and harmonic use of the unlimited energy of spirit; it is to know that one is not alone in this use. It is to experience, as a Star, one's companion Stars. It is to realize fully that each Star fulfills a function and a place in the spirit; and, knowing it, to perform that which it is one's spiritual destiny to perform -- serenely, joyously, calmly, undismayed by those needs one is not called upon to fill, secure in that all needs are always met by God in the way they can be met.

In the average man who is only superficially and hesitantly an "individual" and whose behavior, feelings and thoughts are largely controlled by the unconscious compulsions of generic instincts, collective traditions and mass-emotions, personality is an end-product. It is the flowering of a society and a culture, of a particular ancestry and a special environment; and as such, it is dependent for its energy and still more for its motives and goals upon the root-factors within the life of the human collectivity of which it is a differentiated expression. The personality of the man who is an integral part of his society and of his cultural group or class, and who feels -- consciously or unconsciously -- his rootedness in his collectivity is fundamentally similar to the work of art of a creative genius; and the creator, here, is the collectivity.

It is true that within this man and at the core of his personality there shines the flickering light of the Star which is his spiritual Identity; but this spiritual factor is far more latent than effective. The ego of the man -- his much cherished ego which is only a pseudo-individuality and a temporary scaffolding -- is n o t this Star. It is an opaque structure, casting usually a heavy shadow. It will, in practically all cases, decay after death, and often it becomes hopelessly crystallized before death. At best, the ego of a man is like the center of a beautiful and fragrant flower of personality; and all flowers are direct expressions of the plant's roots.

He who treads the Illumined Road must at first experience

an almost total sundering of his sharply differentiated personality from all racial and cultural roots. This will not ultimately mean actual isolation from humanity; for the Star-illumined individual living on earth participates always deeply in the struggles of his society. But this participation differs in nature, polarization and driving energy from that of the man whose personality develops along lines set by the images, idols and collective attitudes of his society. The right and power to participate in the work of civilization as a spirit-activated and Star-illumined person (or "personage") comes only to the man who has freed his consciousness from collective patterns and drives, and thus has become, for a time at least, an "isolated" individual. Reorientation, repolarization, revaluation imply this stage of "isolation"; but isolation does not mean, for us moderns, going to meditate, yogi-like, in a forest and "away from it all". It refers to a change of consciousness, which can take place in the very midst of crowds -- though solitude may make the process, for a while, much easier.

When this process is at least tentatively completed, the personality of the man who underwent the metamorphosis is basically different from that of the average man. It is "seed" rather than "flower". The seed is still an end-product of the plant, as long as it is developing on it, and the spirit-activated and Star-illumined individual is still a part of his society, as long as he lives in it; nevertheless, the entire polarization of the seed is futureward, and as it grows within the flower, it causes not only this flower but the whole ephemeral plant to die. Likewise the appearance of a certain type of highly individualized and spiritually illumined individuals in a society reveals the fact that this society has reached its apex as an earth-born cultural organism.

The new personality emerging from the crisis of metamorphosis is no longer energized, primarily or exclusively, by the generic energies inherent in the human race or by the cultural sustainment which any normal man gets from his tra-

dition and community. It is energized by the universal ocean
of spirit, by the interplay of Sun and Star. And the new personality's work or function is not to perpetuate or bring to
flowering the society and culture that conditioned the development of the old personality; but instead to lay the ideological foundations for a new society and culture, which will appear in due time. The old personality -- born of "Adam",
according to the Biblical symbolism -- was meant to bring to
fruition the energies of the earth and the values of cultivation
and culture. The purpose of the new personality, which is
born t h r o u g h Christ -- is to release the transforming and
creative power of the spirit; to release it as an engine releases power. The old personality, therefore, can be lik-
ened to an expression of art and culture, as one usually understands these terms. The new personality, instead, should
be considered an engine.

It is this change from an esthetical to an engineering product which we characterize here by the term "reconversion",
under the symbolism of Jupiter. Reconversion, and not conversion; because at the earliest stage of human social evolution personality can also be defined as an engine, but in this
case personality is to be understood as a collective factor.
In ancient times it is the tribe as a whole which can be said to
have personality; not the individual man or woman. The tribe
as a whole is the unit of human consciousness and activity; it
constitutes a complex engine whose purpose (instinctual and
compulsive) is the perpetuation and expansion of a particular
human group in a special environment. "Life" is the engineer
and it moulds from within the collective lives of all tribes-
men, energizing them by the power of deep and unconscious
bio-psychic roots.

On the Illumined Road, however, the individualized spirit
is the engineer; the Star fashions the engine of the metamorphosed personality. The spirit-energized personality is an
engine; but it is an engine built for an individualized and conscious purpose -- an engine of light-rays to perform the work

of the spirit. Personality is no longer the semi-conscious product of a collective culture or race tradition. It is the individualized and conscious agency through which spirit creates a new civilization by releasing great ideas and archetypal symbols (i. e. "forms of power") which will inspire, move and guide the future generations.

At the earth-conditioned level, Jupiter represents all that tends to bring a society to a stage of cultural blossoming and fruition -- the merchant or man of wealth as well as the priest or the arouser of group-realizations and collective enthusiasms. But at the level of the Illumined Road Jupiter symbolizes that power which leads the spirit-energized individual to realize that he can only reach his goal, the Star, by cooperating in faith, and in ever more lucid consciousness with, other agencies of the spirit animated by a similar purpose.

A religion and a certain type of social economy constitute the twofold basis upon which a culture develops. Both represent the collective response of a group of men to the basic challenges of their earth-environment; and this response reveals the mode of operation of the Jupiter function, within the collectivity and in all the men and women participating in this essentially collective activity. But, when man becomes a relatively isolated and uprooted individual intent upon expressing his ego and its differentiated viewpoint (or "uniqueness") he turns his back upon the Jupiterian drives in his personality -- the more so, the more isolated and unique he feels.

Then, the generic energies of human nature and the cultural powers of his society become c o n v e r t e d to his egocentric purpose. They feed his self-expression, or else his revolt against them gives him an emotional stimulus spent in repudiating them. The iconoclast or social revolutionist uses the Jupiter function in a negative way. In him Jupiterian factors turn "alcoholic"; that is, his social sense and his religious faith ferment and disintegrate. The energy which sustained his normal life as a man of the collectivity are now converted to war-production -- the war which he, as an ego, wages against a society, a religion and a culture which have become his enemies. When this war ceases to occupy the consciousness of the man who has passed through a crisis of ego-metamorphosis (or "catharsis") a process of r e c o n v e r-s i o n need be undergone.

This reconversion can never be a mere return to the pre-war s t a t u s   q u o, IF the crisis has been met successfully. The man who has stepped upon the Illumined Road c a n n o t reawaken his old allegiance to social, religious and cultural beliefs, any more than a seed can go back to stem or root. The only thing possible to a seed is to germinate into a new plant with root and stem -- when spring comes! To do this, for the seed, means to become an agent for the life of the species as a whole. The acorn's allegiance can only be to the oak species; not to the particular life of a particular oak on which it grew, however wonderful an oak this particular tree might be.

At the level of the human spirit, each individual who has become free from unconscious and compulsive bondage to his race and society is like a seed; but a seed that is fully conscious, individualized and unique in its immortal Identity. Yet all these "unique" individuals are participants in a spiritual community, whether they are clearly aware of it or not; just as stars are radiant units within the Galaxy, or, in astrological symbolism, within a Constellation -- and (in occultism) a seed-group or "Lodge".

The "reconversion" of which we speak is thus a process by which the Star-conscious individual learns that he, as a Star, belongs to a Constellation. He comes to acknowledge -- but at first only in terms of intellectual concepts and unsteady feelings -- the proximity, the companionship and the spiritual sustainment of his co-participants in the life and activity of this Constellation. Once more, thus, he feels himself one among a multitudinous whole. He is no longer able to pride himself in, or to bemoan his tragic loneliness, his isolation as an ego. He acquires very gradually and unsteadily a new sense of participation in a community; and both this sense and this community now have the characteristic of the spirit. They are no longer earth-conditioned and rooted in dark, instinctual nature.

When the personality begins to be renewed by such a feeling of communion with other beings who are of the spirit, and who work accordingly for the spirit, it can really concentrate upon an effectual work of reconversion. The clearer this feeling of communion and the more unmistakable and concrete the indications of a cooperation with great Beings upon whom the light of their individual Stars (and the joint power of the Constellation) radiate, the more rapid and thorough is the work of personality-reconversion. The main difficulty at the beginning stage of this work is that the individual must plan anew toward a goal, the precise character of which he cannot as yet understand clearly; and the power of habits and the tendency to automatism or routine performance along lines which have proven to be, if not safe, at least familiar in all respects, are very dominant indeed.

The problem is not unlike that of reconverting the production of a factory toward satisfying the needs of a new market, when neither the market nor its expectable requirements can be clearly known. Here, no normal instinct can help. Indeed the struggle is against instinctiveness and tradition. Vision, understanding, the rarely clear record of the experiences of individuals who have faced the same problems, and above all faith, are the engineers who alone can rebuild the tools of personality, adapting them to what is felt to be new needs. The new energy, represented by a transcendent Mars function, is available; yet there seems to be endless obstacles to its effective -- and perhaps safe -- use. The main stumbling block is unfamiliarity and lack of precedents. There must be improvisation of a sort at every step -- and the almost unavoidable consequence is tenseness and strain through worry over results, over-focalization of attention, and the inability to let things happen on their own momentum.

Obviously, this problem of reconversion of personality is paralleled today by its collective world-wide equivalent, the task of reconverting the economy, and as well the religious and moral thinking, of modern society. New sources of power have been revealed. Soon, mankind will no longer depend upon dark substances like coal or oil for the running of factories; and because of automation the un-enlightened toil of classes kept socially depressed by religious and color prejudices can be dispensed with. The global solidarity of all men and groups should be an incontrovertible evidence. We should be at the threshold of a global society, of the "One World" of Man -- though this surely does not mean necessarily a world dominated by one type of social and religious ideology or way of life (i. e. by one dominant mode of Jupiterian activity).

Yet what do we still see all around us, even long after the crucial tragedies of our last World War? Nationalism, collective pride, and class-greed for power, profit and position dominate everywhere the same old game of politics, or national production and international trade. Men without faith in the future still hope for a "return to normalcy" and worship with legalistic and insecure minds the status quo. And this, in one form or another, means the rule of social privileges and accumulated profits -- the social equivalents of egocentricity in the individual person. Each party to a constantly activated world-conflict of interests extolls its way of life, its approach to reality and religion, its culture and tradition -- and often its social excellence and exclusive claim to be the agent of history or evolution. Will our global crises be always in vain? Will atrocious suffering and death serve no purpose?

These questions (at the level of personality) no doubt arise in the troubled mind of everyone who follows the Illumined Road and is faced with the rebuilding of his personality after the ordeal which should have ended with the purification and reorientation of the consciousness, the will and the feelings. Underneath all superficial problems, and indeed their basic cause, is the fact that the very meaning and purpose of personality must be utterly renewed. Personality is -- I repeat -- no longer to be the flowering of a collective tradition or culture rooted in instinct and unconscious attitudes; neither can personality significantly endure on the basis of an egocentric rebellion and proud self-expression.

What is then to be done? Only one thing: to reconvert personality as a tool for the operation of the spirit. Human evolution is always a series of steps forward. Spirit is that which urges forward, which proposes new solutions to new needs or unresolved old needs. Spirit is a release of new l o g o s, of new creative "Words" that are God incarnate; for God's incarnations are solutions to the new needs of humanity. Reconversion on the Illumined Road makes it possible for these new solutions to become concrete and effective through personal example.

This is the true meaning of the Incarnation. Each man whose personality becomes an instrumentality through which the new word of creative spirit can be formulated effectively and convincingly is a divine incarnation, an "avatar". Jesus told us that he was "on his Father's business", and he bid us to do·likewise. The Father-Star in each man who is freed from bondage to human and cultural roots has a "business" for him to attend; and this business is that of the great Company to which the Father-Star belongs. Our task is to fulfill this work, as "sons" of our Father-Star; and this we can do only as we reconvert our personalities to new uses and new purposes -- and as we do it thoroughly.

The Sixth Phase: Re-incorporation
THE SATURN STATION

One of the main reasons for many confused and confusing statements found in writings on psychology is the apparent failure of the modern psychologist to take a realistic attitude toward the "ego". The Theosophist's distinction between a "lower", personal ego and a "higher" Ego does not help very much in clarifying the issue because it presents itself as part of an a priori and abstract classification which, however correct it might be in the last analysis, can hardly be called a solution to pressing and very concrete psychological confrontations experienced by the average man of our day. The problem every individual is facing when he seeks to overcome the narrow boundaries, the biases and the exclusiveness of a so-called self-centered or egocentric attitude can be understood in its true nature only if the validity of the very terms, self-centered and egocentric, is questioned and the ego (or personal self) is understood to be in practical, concrete reality a psychic structure, rather than a mysterious "subject".

The simplest way of approaching the problem is to analyze carefully and without prejudice the actual significance of the typical assertion made by every normal individual: "I am Mr. So-and-so". What does a person called Paul Smith actually mean to himself when he says: I am Paul Smith? Where is the emphasis? Where, the conscious focus of the statement? Which of these words (I, am, Paul Smith) really refers to the ego, as the modern psychologist understands the term "ego"?

The most likely answer to such questions would be that the primary and central fact in the statement "I am Paul Smith" is the sense of being "I"; that is, the feeling of subjective being, of identity. In some manner, the many experiences and reactions of the person (body, feelings, mind) known as Paul Smith are referred by himself to an inwardly sensed permanent factor: this factor is "I". The real problem, however, is whether this "I", to which all that a person experiences consciously is referred, is a c e n t e r of reference, or a f r a m e of reference; whether it is to be conceived as p o i n t or s t r u c t u r e.

The familiar use of such adjectives as egocentric or self-centered, together with Carl Jung's definition of the ego as the "centrum of my field of consciousness", tends almost inevitably to make the ego appear as a point or core; somewhat as an autocratic all-powerful king is the center of the state. There is a "field of consciousness" and this field has a ruling center. The element of structure, if it is considered, would then refer to the field of consciousness (i. e. the typical way in which the person thinks, feels, responds to sensations and to the challenges of everyday life.) This psychic structure would be the result of the activity and will of the ego, somewhat as the "law of the realm" is the expression of the decisions and will of the autocratic king, who is the one supreme authority in "his" realm or kingdom.

The above concepts, however, imply much that should appear today as "old fashioned" and naive psychology. If the king rules the kingdom and structures its many activities by decrees of all sorts, what is it that rules the king? What makes him will this rather than that? What conditions his choice and decisions?

The answer is that the king makes the new laws, but the old laws make the king. The traditions, the ancestral customs, the basic cultural-religious patterns and "primordial Images" of the nation out of which he emerged, as a child

conditioned by special training to become its king-- all these
many factors structure the consciousness of the king, and
thus determine basically, though not exclusively, his decisions. The usual king is a product of his national tradition and
way of life far more than the maker of laws that creates a new
tradition or structure of social behavior. When a king, like
the Egyptian pharaoh, Akh-na-ton, tries to alter completely
the social-religious structure of his kingdom, more likely than
not the attempt fails or is short-lived, and the old patterns
reassert themselves, proving thus to be more basic and powerful than the king.

Another approach will lead to similar conclusions. Does
the newborn child realize himself first as "I", or as "Paul"?
As far as experience usually shows, the child will first speak
in the third person, "Paul did this, Paul wants that", before
he very clearly states "I want" and still more "I am". Indeed
the clearly conscious feeling of "I am", in complete independence of the determining or conditioning qualification "Paul",
the person's name, is the goal of a very long and very difficult process of spiritual development; not the beginning.

If thus one can truly say that the name comes first into
the field of awareness of the child, then only later the realization, "I", the result is that as far as the unfolding consciousness of a person is concerned
the primary factor is a "structure"; the realization of a center to that structure, (i. e. the "I") is a subsequent experience.
Moreover, this so-called center is not to be considered essentially as a geometrical center, but rather as a center of
gravity -- that is, a point indicating the characteristic ba¹
ance of forces and tendencies within the field of consciousness as a whole; a balance which is expressed in terms of
"will". "Behind will stands desire" is an old occult max-
im. The direction of the will is determined by the balance of
often conflicting desires; the principle of "balance of power"
is the basic principle wherever will and decisions of will are
concerned.

Any man wills to do what he desires most -- provided we do not limit the word, "desire", to the so-called lower or most superficial elements of the personality. The religious ascetic starves himself because his desire to attain what he envisions as his greatest goal is stronger than the pressure of biological instincts. He "rules" his body's wants sternly; but behind this willfulness stands his desire for religious attainment or salvation, and behind this desire are the images or concepts of spiritual liberation and sin, images which have been aroused in his consciousness, in most cases, by the religious and moral teachings with which this consciousness was permeated during childhood and adolescence.

It is these teachings and ideals, the example of parents and neighbors -- or his rebellion against them and his "complexes" caused by frustration and pain -- which, together with still deeper inherited organic factors, have structured his consciousness. His ego did not structure the latter. The ego is rather a consolidation of consciousness, resulting from a realization of permanent individual characteristics, faculties and modes of response to life. It is a concentrate of those typical individual traits which differentiate the person from all other persons.

The ego, as a particular form of being, is a Saturnian factor, for Saturn is the lord of all particular forms or structures which are defined by their differences from all other forms; thus by a principle of exclusion. "Paul Smith" signifies the sum-total of a person's differences from all other human beings. And this sum-total of differences is established, not only socially, but in Paul Smith's consciousness as well, by his "name"; indeed, in modern societies it is normally established at two levels by two names: a family and a personal name. The former is meant to establish collective differences (of race, of family, etc.); the latter, personal differences (individuality).

When the man says to himself or to others, "I am Paul Smith", what he actually means to state is not that he is "I", but rather that here is "Paul Smith". Paul Smith is the ego, with its individual and group structural differences. The name is the symbol of the ego. And Jung knew this well when he wrote: "By ego, I understand a complex of representations which... appears to possess a very high degree of continuity and identity". He spoke of "ego-complex"; and every complex is a psychic structure (in our sense of the term, structure). But the ego-complex is not, as Jung added[*], "the centrum of my field of consciousness" as much as it is the structural factor in consciousness. Because there is structure and order in the field of consciousness of a normally mature person, the sense of permanent structural identity arises. This sense of permanent structural identity is what the average man today knows as the sense of "I".

To speak of it as a "center" tends to confuse the situation. It is both center and circumference; and it is, besides, the relationship of radius to circumference, the structural factor, Pi, which defines the form of the circle. More important still, in so far as practical psychological problems are concerned, is the fact that the ego is a state of concentrated attentiveness to structural problems. Indeed, the ego represents a condition of constant involvement in the business of keeping the structure of the field of consciousness intact against the pressure of internal as well as external agencies seeking to alter this structure; just as the State seeks forever to enforce its laws and regulations and to protect its boundaries and prestige.

The ego is truly the equivalent of the State in the realm of personality. The State may be controlled by a king, or by any other kind of official symbol of authority (like the Constitution of the United States); the ego may develop or fail to develop a sense of ruling "I"-feeling. The essential factor remains nevertheless the State-as-a-whole; and this State, being

---

* cf. "Psychological Types", page 540.

a structural factor, is found at work everywhere. A so-called egocentric, willful person is much like a modern "police State". The structural factor dominates and tends to stifle every part of the field of consciousness, regulating every function or sending every unwelcome thought or feeling into the "outer darkness" of the unconscious -- exile or concentration camp, as may be the case. The police State usually has an official dictator; but the dictator is a symbol and a symptom, far more than a cause -- except in special cases which we shall study presently. He becomes, at any rate -- even when he was not so at first -- a slave to the rigid structures he has evolved, and indeed had to evolve.

The average person, however, cannot be compared to a totalitarian police State. He is usually a very loosely integrated whole in which there is no a c t u a l strong central power, and psychic wants or drives (comparable to "special interests", monopolies, cartels, church organizations, workers unions, etc.) fight for the position of central authority. The ego of the average person is a differentiating structure within which the balance of power changes constantly (or at least periodically) and the "center" is merely a symbol -- a s e a l o f o f f i c e -- with which one powerful group after another identifies itself, and, through such an identification assumes the authority officially invested in the "center", in the realization: "I". The average man cannot truly say (save perhaps at rare moments of high realization) "I am" without any qualification of name; for to say simply "I am", with conviction and power, can only mean that the focus of consciousness is upon an "I" that is un-identified with particular traits, attitudes and complexes, all of which are products of changing responses to heredity and environment.

But, if the ego is a pattern of responses to heredity and environment -- the reader may retort -- must there not be That which does the responding? There is; and it is to this "responder" that the occultist-theosophist means to refer when speaking of the "higher self" or "Ego" with a capitalized E.

However, by failing to give a clear picture of what the lower or personal ego is in terms of the historical development of personality and of normal conscious experiences in modern man, the "esotericist" indulges but too often in psychological escapism. He is trying to escape from "Paul Smith" into a vague but exalted feeling-intuition of "I". By saying and repeating "I am" he is seeking to feel secure and established in a spiritual reality which nevertheless he cannot as yet incorporate into his consciousness -- which therefore remains vague and transcendent, a "cloud of light" perhaps, but not a "body of light", or the "Christ-Body".

Not yet, in most cases. The "I" that is actually meant in the statement "I am Paul" is a symbol rather than an experienced reality. It is, to the psychologist, the dimly divined goal of a process of personal integration and perhaps eventual transfiguration; while to the esotericist it is the reflected image of a transcendent reality. This reality has been called the Higher Self, Solar Angel, or Augoeides. It has indeed been given a multitude of names in the attempt to concretize the belief, which some men claim to be for them an actually experienced reality, that to every Paul Smith there corresponds a spiritual "He", an entity of Light, a God-like being. It is such a being that what is called here the "Star" -- one among millions within the Galaxy -- symbolizes.

What is not made usually clear enough is, however, that this spiritual entity is only in the consciousness of the average individual of today, a potentiality of being. It has been called the "divine Spark" or monad; but it may be wiser to think of it as a God-seed, from which a full-grown plant of spiritual substance and power may grow if it is sown in fertile soil at the right season, and under proper climateric conditions. The fertile soil is the heredity and environment of the actual person, Paul Smith. The right season and climate refer to the social and cosmic conditions under which Paul Smith lives on this earth. But, as Jesus tells us in the Gospel's parable, many seeds do not reach the stage of fully mature plants.

The I in the statement "I am Paul Smith" is not the God-seed. It is in most cases at best the anticipatory sense of a dimly felt inner stability and permanency. It is an uncertain intuition of what could be divinity at the core of Paul Smith's highest and most integrated experiences of actual living. The main goal of all true spiritual teachings is to bolster up this dim feeling-intuition by establishing it as a concept, as an intellectual corollary to the related idea of God's existence. "God is; I am" -- these are twin statements. If there is no universal "God", then the spiritual "I" would exist in absolute and essentially meaningless contrast to an alien and incomprehensible universe; and if there is no "I" as a potentially complete expression of divinity, then human life is an unbearable tragedy that leads nowhere.

In terms of astrological symbolism, the Star, that is still for the man on the Illumined Road a transcendent factor, is a focus or lens through which the universal being of God radiates as light and power. If the consciousness of that man can be made a clear mirror, then the universal organism of God can appear on this mirror, upon which the light of the Star is being focalized as a Ray of spirit. But the mirror must be clear and turned toward the Star! When these conditions are fulfilled, when the previously defined steps on the Illumined Road have been successfully taken, then the formless sense of "I" within Paul Smith's consciousness becomes a gradually clearer perception of a formed "He". The image of God is seen within the consciousness, carried, as it were, by the Ray of the Star.

It is more than a mere image or reflection. It is a God-seed, substantial and vibrant with power of growth and fulfillment. It is an incorporation of spirit in the likeness of God. Jesus is the symbol and actual prototype of such a full incorporation; the "likeness of God" is Christ. Christ was incorporated in Jesus; and this is what is meant by "divine Sonship" -- a potentiality inherent in all individuals. To tread the Illumined Road is to take effective steps to make the potentiality an actuality within and through one's total being. Because Jesus was, at least in the cycle of our present humanity, the first man to become in full actuality an incorporation of Christ, he is t h e Son of God. To the spirit, universal, all-pervading, everything that happens once had happened once-for-all in a "timeless" world. Yet to every man who functions consciously in a world of cycles and duration, the event of divine birth -- the incorporation of the spirit in the likeness of God -- is a potentiality in the process of becoming an actuality. It is "the Path". It is "the Way and the Life", which Jesus-Christ shows, toward the full and clearly conscious realization of "the Truth" -- the truth of the divine Sonship latent in every man.

Jesus answered to the questioning "woman of Samaria", who was seeking to draw vitality from the ancestral wellspring of human energy and wisdom, "I am He". In every Paul Smith there is also the possibility, however remote and incredible it may seem, that he too may be able to say to himself and perhaps to the world "I am He"; and saying this, to know with incontrovertible knowing that the Star is within his "heart" -- the Kingdom of heaven, the God-seed, the Christchild yet to be.

The Illumined Road takes a new turn when this process of incorporation begins. Before, the Star was known as a center of light-radiation to become oriented to, to value more than anything else, to seek power from, to commune with, in an attempt to recognize effectively all that one had to contribute to the "work of the world". But now, as this Saturn stage of the journey Starward is at last reached, an entirely new situation is faced. The Star is perceived within. A child is conceived of the Star. The future is incorporating at the vital core of the present. Now is being fecundated by "eternity", the consciousness of the Eon. "I" is in the process of becoming "He".

And what of Paul Smith? He becomes the mother of the

living God that is stirring within his consciousness. A mystery is being celebrated within him; a strange and often baffling ritual of gestation. Paul Smith now hesitates saying "I am Paul Smith". Can he even say truly: "I am"?

Until now, as he traveled through the first stages of the Illumined Road, he had sought strength and inner security in the realization "I am". He had striven to affirm his "I" as a permanent reality of spirit in contrast to the illusory complexities and conflicts that came to a sum total in Paul Smith -- in contrast to the constant flux of moods, desires and hopes of his "human, too human" existence among earth-conditioned, confused and greedy men and women. Yet, in his honest moments of clear perception, he knew fully well that this "I", which he claimed to be, was not substantial and actual in his experience. It was at best a presentiment or a threshold of experience. It was something hoped for, a presence as yet unveiled, a light, a power perhaps, but not yet a fact endowed with the incontrovertible power of all true facts -- the power of being experienced in fullness of conscious living and being.

To be fully experienced, the "I" had to be completely severed from the "Paul Smith" qualification. A negative process: a "not this, not this..." denial of earth-conditioning, of hereditary and environmental pulls, of bodily urges -- indeed, of the very power exerted by the structural ego and its constant concentration upon, or attentiveness to, the problems of maintaining this structure of personality under all possible circumstances. The individual, Paul Smith, had to be nameless, before he could truly feel, "I am". And even then, it was only a feeling, an intuition of beyond, an irruption of light perhaps, as if one was thrown into a sea of formless splendor and timeless ecstasy -- the mystic's experience, cosmic consciousness, glory and light; nevertheless not reality, because no effective organism for action -- no new body or personality -- had as yet been concretely formed.

Until the new stage began. Until Saturn spoke on the Illumined Road. Until the Star came to be known within the consciousness: "He"! At this stage, the mystic proclaims: God lives me. At this stage, the great wonder is: He is I. The subject, I, has become the expression of a vaster consciousness, of a more cosmic organism. "I" has become an utterance of "He". In that moment "I" takes birth as an organic, a living reality, and not merely a feeling-intuition of some transcendent power which has to remain formless.

He is I -- and that, I am. The I am-ness of the individual that was known to himself and to others as Paul Smith is now re-established, re-incorporated in seed in the realization "He is I". One day, still far distant, the transfigured personality will be able to say, with Jesus: "I am He".

With the Saturn stage of the Illumined Road the first part of the process which makes of a man a living God closes, and the second part begins. Saturn, the spiritual seed, is both end and beginning. The phase of "reincorporation" is the sixth in sequence; it is also the first in a new series of six phases. The distant Star in the sky toward which the illumined individual was seeking to reorient his total being and consciousness has come to be known within the "heart" of the individual, as the God-seed. The "I" which was a "threshold realization" -- a mere feeling of transcendent identity -- for the personality whose consciousness was structured by an ego concentrating upon keeping this structure intact and powerful is now, as it were, turned around. "I" becomes an expression, a power, a prolongation or offspring, of "Him", the God whose countenance is now at least dimly perceived. "God lives me" says the Christian mystic, whose personality has become a mother, a womb within which the divine embryo is developing as an organism of spirit. The Star in the sky has become the pulsating heart of the Christ-child within the utterly renewed human person.

What we have to witness thereafter is the slow process of gestation of this divine embryo, until a phase of spiritual unfoldment is reached which parallels that of viability, then of actual birth, in the realm of life. In astrological symbolism Saturn marks the impregnation of the ego by the Ray that emanates from the Star, the definite formation or the activation of the God-seed. Uranus and Neptune refer to the mystic processes of transfiguration and trans-substantiation; while in Pluto and the planet beyond Pluto we find symbols for the last phases of the gestation of the Christ-being. The ultimate event is birth itself, the "entrance into" the Companionship of the Stars: the real Initiation.

At the usual level of astro-psychological interpretation, Uranus is seen as a stirring, upsetting, revolutionizing and dynamically transforming power. Its profoundly disturbing effect has destructive connotations whenever man is so intent upon the preservation of the structure of his consciousness and of his typical responses to life -- the preservation of his ego -- that any power challenging the excellence of this ego-structure appears to him and indeed factually becomes completely negative and disruptive. Uranian events are thus to the ego what violent social revolutions are to the upper classes clinging with stubbornness to their obsolete and anachronistic privileges.

In other cases, however, the Uranian challenge to ego-structures and social-religious privileges, instead of manifesting outwardly as an upheaval from the repressed and undifferentiated depths of the person's unconscious -- or of the people at large -- is perceived as a kind of Visitation from the spirit. It may come as a frightening Presence of light and power, or as a lightning from the sky. It may be a vision, a summons to action, a sudden realization of the next step to be taken or of the distant goal. These too may arouse such a sense of insecurity, of fear, or of utter dismay at the spiritual emptiness of years gone by, that the ego shuts tight its structures of consciousness, refusing to see, unable to withstand the power or the implications of the revelation; and the shock may be so great at times as to bring hopeless deterioration to the ego, at least f ~ a period.

But, for the individual who has already advanced upon the Illumined Road to the point where Saturn has actually meant the incorporation of spirit within his own being as a divine seed, Uranus needs no longer be regarded as a power of negative disruption, even though its Visitations may still shake the reoriented personality to the very core of its being, and may be annunciations of eventual liberation from the earth-born body. Uranus, at this stage of the Illumined Road, is a power of transfiguration. It releases light through the personality aglow with the mystery of spiritual gestation—the light of fulfillment. The Star is focusing its rays upon the God-seed within, and this seed is an organism of light created in the likeness of that God Whose Body is universal Space: Space filled with the creative Energy-Substance which, when focused through multitudinous lenses, the Stars, men perceive as light.

The Star is the cosmic lens; but the Image of God is within the individual in whom "ego" has now become "soul". The ego was the manager-ruler of the structural responses of consciousness to life experiences -- a typical masculine entity concerned with the problems of form, technique and mastery over matter and society. But when this ego ceases to strain its attention and power in the direction of structural and material factors -- when he begins to turn inward the Star-ward seeking to envision the Divine Countenance, the Perfect Form and Archetype of Man created in the likeness of God -- and when at last the rays of the Star are able to reach the core of his being, and project upon it or awaken within it this Divine Image, then, the man-ego becomes the woman-soul, filled with the light of potential divinity, great with Christ-child.

Uranus thereafter operates as a universal power surrounding the divine seed within the personality and establishing it within a spiritual frame of reference, in somewhat the same sense in which the embryo within the mother's womb is surrounded with a magnetic field of life radiations, interpreted by many clairvoyants as a host of elemental forces or entities directing the complex process of gestation. The personality that has become a "mother of the Living God", being

thus pervaded with this Uranian field of creative spirit, shines
with light. And this is the Transfiguration: not merely a mysterious event that happened to one man alone, but a state
of being reached after the turning point in the Illumined
Road, the Saturn event, following which the individual experiences himself as a temple for the unfolding God-seed.

The Transfiguration of Jesus is a symbolic expression of
what is implied in this "state of being" in as much as it pictures the various elements of the new situation. It has been
interpreted as the record of one of Jesus' "Initiations"; and
it may well have been the culminating moment when Jesus,
Son of Man, became fully identified or integrated with Christ,
Son of God. But, as we seek to understand here as clearly as
possible a spiritual process potentially experienceable by every individual having passed through a particular crisis of
total reorientation, it is more significant to consider, not only what happened to Jesus, but the entire scene "on the Mount"
and all the participants in this mystical event.

The key to its interpretation is provided by what the Syn-
optic Gospels record as previous to the Transfiguration. Jesus had asked of his disciples: "Whom say ye that I am?"
and Peter had come forth impetuously with the answer: "Thou
art the Christ, the Son of the living God" (Matthew 16:16).
But when Jesus soon after spoke of his coming tribulations,
the same Peter protested that this should not happen; and Jesus rebuked him in extremely strong language implying that
Peter had, in this protest, been the very tool of the Tempter.

This interplay of forces between Peter and Jesus is most
significant, because Peter here represents the typical "disciple" with an intense urge toward the spiritual life, yet with
a still strong mental dependence upon ordinary earthly values. And, in every individual following the Illumined Road
there is a Peter as well as a Jesus. Peter, here, is the symbol of the ego-consciousness suddenly able to recognize at
its innermost core the reality of the God-seed, but as yet

unwilling to change the frame of reference within which this seed is to unfold its power. Peter is thus the aspirant at the Saturn stage of the Road -- Peter, the Rock. He is the first to utter the new "Name", to proclaim the new fact of the incorporation of God as Christ in the individual man, Jesus. Yet he can only visualize and interpret this new fact with reference to the old kind of ego-structured consciousness. Yes, God has come among us; but God should behave as a man. "He is I", this disciple admits; but "I", to his mind, is still conditioning the ways of "Him".

Jesus' answer to Peter, "Get thee behind me, Satan", suggests that Jesus himself may have been tempted to evade the destiny implied in the very fact of his being the Christ; but he rejects this fourth temptation, as strongly as he had rejected the three temptations in the desert following his Baptism. He accepts fully his Christhood, and with it the Crucifixion. The plant which bears the seed within the protective envelope of the fruit realizes that, once the seed is fully mature, the plant itself must disintegrate according to the seasonal rhythm. The seed, indeed, actually "kills" the ephemeral plant that bears it. Christ's Ascension is predicated upon Jesus' Crucifixion. Likewise, one stretch of the Illumined Road must be experienced as the Path to Golgotha.

To realize this fully and to accept it irrevocably is the meaning of the transition from the Saturn to the Uranus stages of the journey Star-ward. He who makes this transition successfully passes symbolically from the Peter to the Jesus state of consciousness. He is then ready for the Transfiguration, which seals, at the same time, the glorious destiny of the God-seed (the Christ within) and the final surrender (Crucifixion) of the ego; a surrender necessary to the development, out of the God-seed, of the new organism of spirit, the immortal vehicle of the celestial Self, the "Risen Body of Christ".

The scene on the Mount of Transfiguration consecrates

the victory of Jesus over this fourth and Saturnian temptation. And, for this reason, Peter the Tempter has to be present; and he reacts to the glorious event in his typically Saturnian way. "Let us make three tabernacles... " which means
"Let us establish this great event within the framework of our
usual ego-structured and formalistic world". In polar contrast to Peter, Jesus, the Victorious, becomes transfigured;
"his face did shine as the sun, and his raiment was white as
the light" (Matthew 17:2). And with him talk "Moses and Elias, who appeared in glory and spoke of his decease; which he
should accomplish in Jerusalem" (Luke 9; 30); and the Voice
of God is heard, out of the cloud which soon after enfolds the
whole Mount, saying: "This is my beloved Son, hear him".

In this mystical scene the human and super-human protagonists are evenly balanced in a strangely polar relationship. Not only Peter balances Christ Jesus; but the two disciples, James and John (the sons of Zebedee whom Jesus called also "sons of the thunder" in order to establish symbolically their spiritual station), are the earthly counterparts respectively of Moses and Elijah (Elias) -- Moses, the Law Giv-
er, and Elijah (meaning, Jehovah in God), the greatest of the
old Prophets, who was taken up to heaven in a whirlwind.
The Voice of God completes the Septenary. Thus the whole of
"Man" is represented: lower trinity (the disciples), higher
trinity, and Christ Jesus, the Link, in whom divine and human natures are integrated.

The light that radiates through Jesus' countenance is the
Uranian light and his shining vesture symbolizes the now developing "organism of spirit", the Robe of Glory spoken of by.
the Gnostics. Yet this is not the final step of the complete
Initiation; indeed, it is, in a sense, only the definite beginning. What happens is that a new relationship between the
inner world of spirit and the outer world of human society is
dramatically or ritualistically established.

The individual who reaches this Uranus stage on the Illumined Road is now more than man. He not only has experi-

enced the reality of the God-seed within him; now this seed of light shines through the flesh. It speaks out its divinity in poems of light, and the Voice of God commands: "Hear him". The transfigured individual has become a focal center for the release of the power of the Universal Mind, Ouranos, the creative god of universal Space. Men are called upon to listen to him, to catch from his radiance the contagious fervor of one in whom God is being brought to birth, whose soul is being filled to overflowing by spirit -- as, often, a pregnant woman seems to overflow with a strange power of glowing life.

The mystery of the unfoldment of the God-seed within the man whose ego has become transformed into soul is rooted in the spiritual manifestation of Saturn; but it begins to radiate outward only after the Uranus energy is released. Uranus is lightning, but it is also the creative power of the mystic Sound that, according to the old tradition of India, pervades all spaces -- the Akasha or (higher) Astral Light. This Sound, like lightning, may kill; but it is also the Voice of God within the spirit-impregnated soul. It must be heard; because spirit is always and forever that which fills all needs, which restores harmony wherever the ego-mind and matter have pulled apart. Indeed, there can be no real manifestation of spirit except two polarities are present and, being present, are integrated.

Thus on the Mount of Transfiguration the realm of spirit and the realm of aspiring humanity are polarized to each other; and Christ the Son is the integrative light that binds spiritually the two realms, while the Voice of the Father arouses and summons earthly man -- man at the disciple stage, but still overshadowed by fear.

This great drama is one that takes place within the highest realm of the individual consciousness (the "Mount") of the man having reached the Uranus stage of the Illumined Road. What occurs within the individual soul need still be performed at the collective level of society. This performance is the

Passion -- the confrontation with the violent inertia of obsolete social and religious structures; the opportunistic judgment of Pilate, agent of an imperial society which, when confronted with the need to transform the very spirit and quality of its basic relationship, can only evade the real issues and wash its collective hands of any sense of guilt; then, the public Crucifixion.

In this phase of the drama between the transfigured individual and the materialistic power-greedy rulers of a soulless society we must see the logical working-out of the Transfiguration; and it is on the sacred Mount of Transfiguration that Moses and Elijah announce to the Christed Jesus his death in Jerusalem on the Mount of Calvary (meaning, skull). What is crucified is the whole past of the individual -- that which supported the formation of the seed of man's divinity, the mother of the living God. The transfigured individual must arise from all sense of subservience and inner bondage to any "mother" that enfolded his growth as an organism of consciousness. He has to prove his Sonship to the Father, by dying to all earthly "mothers" -- to all that is collective and unindividualized, traditional and binding.

But in this death it is the collectivity that finally does the repudiating. The privileged classes repudiate the transfigured individual whose spirit-radiating and contagious example menaces their privilege, but whose spiritual being is now energized and sustained by another power -- the power of Uranus, of creative Space. The Crucifixion frees the Christ-being from the society that rejects him; it frees him from the past. Henceforth he can be solely a precipitate of the future into the evolving present. He can be an unhindered creative power of spirit. He can be the creative future focused in and through an "organism" of light and spirit -- the Risen Body. He has won immortality through death...thanks to Judas.

This is the great mystery, or spiritual paradox, at the core of Uranus' activity. To ordinary egocentric man, Uranus is the revolutionist, the arouser, the peace-shattering power that destroys the attitude of unquestioned reliance upon the seemingly secure past. Then, Uranus appears to the freer mind as the inspirer, the revealer, the spiritual fecundator, the transfigurer. Finally one more function needs to be accomplished. Uranus must evoke the Adversary of the individual he has transfigured.

There are always elements in any personality which cannot become transfigured, which resist metamorphosis until the very last crisis. Even the "Peter" aspect of the individual's consciousness seeks forever to materialize and to organize what is of the spirit; even Peter will thrice deny his Master when to say "Yes" to his divinity menaces his personal security; and he will flee from persecution, in later days in Rome, until the vision of Christ shames him into returning to meet his own crucifixion.

At the Saturn stage of the journey toward the Star, there often arises within the traveler's consciousness a sense of spiritual satisfaction with himself. Has not God been found to dwell like a seed of light within his soul? Has he not recognized the divine Presence, and given up many things to "follow" this Christ within? It is this sense of spiritual achievement and self-complacency which Uranus will shake and destroy -- and this is the work of the Adversary, whom Uranus evokes.

To all Peters seemingly secure in their fervent discipleship to Christ must come the shattering of hope, the sense that they have devoted their all to one who has failed, the tragedy of denial of the most cherished Ideal. Their Saturnian inertia must once more be broken; now at the seemingly spiritual level. The power of the God within must overcome the fear and insecurity of whatever is left of the old ego dismayed at the prospect of seeing the structures of personality which it built crucified.

Jesus says: "Nevertheless thy will be done, not mine". But Peter takes his puny physical sword (his ego will) and, even after the experience on the Mount of Transfiguration, he fails to understand, and he fights against the inevitability of the Crucifixion. He has still to learn how to rely totally upon the power of the spirit -- how impossible it is for the immortal spiritual organism to be free to function, unless the body of earth-substance is completely purified and re-made of spirit-substance. Peter might have understood, had he had the power not to fear on the Mount of Transfiguration. But his fear and his materialistic attitude of traditional worship forced the entire Mount to be enveloped in a cloud; just as, in the Garden of Olives, his mortal weariness made him unable to stand, awake, by his divine Master, while Jesus made his ultimate prayer to the Father.

The cloud, the weary sleep -- when the spirit demanded of Peter with extraordinary urgency complete wakefulness as a conscious participant in the Mystery: these are the negative manifestations of Neptune on the Illumined Road. But, beyond and through these, the traveler should see unfolding a new power of the spirit; and to him who can pierce all mental clouds and overcome all soul-weariness there comes the new mastery: the Neptunian transsubstantiation of earth-born personal elements into divine gifts -- whose symbol is the Eucharist.

Eighth Phase: Transsubstantiation
THE NEPTUNE STATION

The Saturn phase of the Illumined Road marks the impregnation, by the universal spirit, of the ego of the individual who has irrevocably reoriented his personality toward the celestial light of the Star. The realization of new values, new goals and new sources of energy has prepared the way for the great moment when the individual comes to recognize the presence within him of the living seed of his divinity. His inner life, now repolarized to become a soul-tabernacle enfolding the growth of the God-seed, gradually becomes attuned to the reality of the all-encompassing spirit filling in all space. His consciousness is being transformed, his mind transfigured, by the focusing of the Uranian electric flow which shatters and burns away all inertia and fear, all reliance upon tribal, social or religious security, all sense of satisfaction with self and achievements of self, even those which appear most "spiritual".

This flow of universal "waters" from the upturned urn of the sky poured upon the soul in gestation of the living God is nevertheless strange and disturbing. It brings to the consciousness nothing that is familiar, nothing that one can become oriented to, according to known values or standards. And the mystics of all lands have recorded for us, travelers on the Illumined Road, the bafflement, the confusion and the fright that comes to one seemingly lost within what seems as a cloud condensing from celestial realms of the spirit. It is this cloud that enveloped the Mount of Transfiguration, as the three disciples faced the apparition of Moses and Elias conversing with the transfigured Jesus whose countenance was shining as the sun and whose raiment was white as the light. And the disciples were afraid.

Mystics speak of "the Cloud of Unknowing"; but whence can this cloud come, actually, if not from w r o n g k n o w-i n g? When the cloud overshadowed the disciples on the Mount what had happened? The confused Peter faced with the vision of Jesus' transfiguration had uttered these typical words: "Master, it is good for us to be here: and let us make three tabernacles; one for thee, and one for Moses, and one for Elias" (Mark 9:5). Two of the Evangelists add passingly, as a sort of excuse, that Peter did not know what he said, for he was sorely afraid. But this "not knowing what to say" and this fear are factors of profound and decisive significance in the process of spiritual unfoldment, when they manifest at crucial turning points or crises of destiny! They it is which actually cause the "cloud" to envelop the consciousness of the aspirant or disciple pitched at the highest point it can reach -- the sacred "Mount".

Peter had hardly uttered his words, in response to his spiritual experience of the Transfiguration, when the cloud blotted out the vision. The vision vanished simply because Peter -- symbol of man's ego, able to recognize the divinity within his being (the Christ-being, the Son of God), but as yet bound to Saturnian values -- had met this transcendent experience with an inadequately oriented mind. He had had his "inner ego" opened; but, confused by what he saw and unable to stand the glory and majesty of it at the level of the spirit, he had to bring the experience to the plane of religious and tribal custom -- the only plane with which he was as yet familiar. Peter (the Saturn-individual, the "Rock") felt psychologically compelled to materialize the spiritual experience, to o r g a n i z e it.

Peter all through his life is seen struggling against his need for psychological or physical security. And this need, so hard for him to overcome, is the very cause of the Neptunian cloud that hides from his sight the final mystery of the Transfiguration. The Voice of God is heard; but the final consecration (or Initiation) of Jesus as the Christ is obscured. Neptune must always turn negative for the consciousness still bound by the Saturnian yearning for security and logic at all cost; for, if this yearning is unsatisfied, fear must develop, and fear makes the supreme vision vanish. Spiritual knowledge is lost in the Cloud of Unknowing; it may even be destroyed utterly by the Neptunian glamor which substitutes intellectual or devotional mirages for the reality of the spirit.

At the Neptune stage of the Illumined Road the one great obstacle for the traveler to overcome is the fear of the unknown. The road-way may seem lost; the Star above may be dimmed by an utterly confusing light-mist, as the God-seed within seemingly draws all vitality, hollows out the soul as if a center of positive emptiness; there is nothing to be oriented to -- nothing but some incomprehensible Mystery. Even the Master within is lost in glory; and the world below is dimly sensed, disintegrating in the shadow of an exhausted society. This exhaustion rises up from the human plains and as well from every cell of the disciple's body. Weariness summons fear out of dark ancestral depths. The cloud enveloping the once illumined path may last, who knows how long! Will there be sufficient strength to pierce through its perhaps limitless expanse with bleeding feet and harrowed mind? Or will the soul dissolve into the Neptunian mist, drawn in by the God-seed as by a whirlpool?

It is under such elusive yet frightening pressures that the "Peter" in every traveler on the Illumined Road comes not to know what he says. It is the Shadow in him that speaks -- the Shadow of Peter and also of the Church built upon his failings as well as upon his virtues. And more and more tabernacles are built, stone-monuments to the Neptunian cloud that forever hides or distorts the final rite of the Transfiguration. The Shadow speaks words of unknowing; words which do not fit the majestic occurrence; words that suddenly render the situation small and meaningless; words that seek to salvage a past spiritually obsolete and disintegrating; words unleavened by the new spirit which is always substantiated by courage, daring and fearless faith; words that betray self-satisfaction and lack of creative imagination.

"It is good for us to be here", says Peter. But there is no "good", but God. Where great spiritual experiences confront the consciousness, God only matters -- not "good". God and spirit are the facts to experience; not traditional goodness and what men call morality, fulfilling which they "feel good" and build more tabernacles -- to stifle the divine seed with piety and unknowing. What is to be faced, understood, assimilated are the creative electrical "Waters" of Ouranos, the Sky -- the abode of God the Father: Our Father. If we assimilate these creative energies, the Living Bread of Christhood or divine Sonship, we are able to build our "body of immortality", the Christ-Body, the fully grown plant risen from the God-seed. If we do not, because of fear and soul-weariness, the creative Waters turn into a Neptunian mist that utterly confuses and disorients the mind. The Wine, that is the Blood of Christ, becomes a power of self-destroying inebriatedness which evokes lurid shapes and evil phantasmagories. Even the very substance of the Love of Christ, the Living Bread of divine Grace, sours in the soul ulcerated by doubt and anguish.

Uranus is the creative power of the universal spirit. If it is met with faith and spiritual vitality by the Saturnian ego of the traveler on the Illumined Road, this power becomes food for the soul and for the growth of the God-seed within it; and the result is the Neptune-built Christ-Body, vehicle of man's immortal Essence. If the Uranus downflow is received with fear and weariness, it becomes atomicized and it dissipates into the Neptunian cloud, in which spiritual values become lost and the God-seed disintegrates. The issue therefore is clear. Neptune can either be positive or negative. It can feed the concrete and organic growth of man's divinity; or it can dissolve it utterly, as a strong acid. The determining factor is the individual's inner attitude toward Uranian creativity. If he accepts the mystery and the spiritual responsibility of creative acts performed in the name of the spirit, he will find Neptune a source of divine abundance; if he rejects or falters in his approach to creativity, Neptune will envelop him into a deleterious or intoxicating cloud, and eventually lead him to a Plutonian death.

What this means to the individual is illustrated today by the way in which a similar type of collective all-human confrontation is making history for modern society. At this collective social-cultural level, the Uranus influx has expressed itself as the intellectual and technological Revolution of the last two hundred years. New forms of combustion, the release of electrical and now atomic energy, and all kinds of social stimulations have compelled humanity to face a tremendous potential of creative action. There is almost nothing that global man could not build or transform on earth, no general obstacle or hindrance that a concerted all-human creative effort could not remove or utilize constructively. The potentiality of Uranian transformation of human society has been immense and glorious to consider.

What has mankind done with it? Its ruling class has become drunk with power; its Saturnian nationalism and imperialism have made of the globe a field of carnage and starvation; the fanatic subservience to old religions or new ideologies have created emotional hatred and mental confusion everywhere; mankind is lost in a Neptunian cloud -- and what it breathes in it is poisoned by smog or drugged by an immense variety of chemicals which all carry the signature of Neptune, the glamor of Neptune.

Why? Because modern society, as a collective entity, has lacked the imagination and the courage to create a new world; because the obsolete Saturnian structures of the past have choked nearly every new spiritual growth; because the Uranus power released during the Revolutionary Era of nearly two hundred years ago had at once become deviated by minds that, fearing the glory of a radically reconstructed society, translated feudalism and privilege from the Courts to the Market Place; because the Uranian bestowal of the power to create and to imagine the "more abundant life" once promised by Christ, was stopped by the men of the Age of (false) Enlightenment (18th century) at the level of the intellect and of an uncreative and verbal equalitarianism.

The Neptunian era that followed during the nineteenth century actually built the substance of our modern society (its machines, its industries, its commerce and travel); but it built upon the intellectual foundations of scientific materialism. It built upon spiritual scarcity and upon the power vested in the remnants of ancient feudalism to corner the more abundant life under the cloak of rugged individualism. Neptune is the wholesale builder of collective substance. Its power of proliferation is immense; but it builds only according to man's attitude toward Uranian creativeness. If this attitude is one of resistance to the unfamiliar New, of fear before the revealed Glory, of weary withdrawal into the Saturnian shells of social security and privilege, then, Neptune's power of growth leads to the senseless mushrooming forth of hectic cities, tabloid newspapers, glamor-crazy motion pictures, murder-storied radios, hallucigenic drugs -- and to generalized cancerous conditions due to unorganic living and un-natural habits of feeding, physical or psychological.

Neptune, nevertheless, is, in its true positive being, the substantiality of the spirit. Neptune is the substance of creative Space, the "Astral Light", the Ocean of spiritual Sound, the encompassing "Gift-Waves" of divine Grace, the all-inclusive charity of the Compassionate Ones. It is the divine Substance which feeds what the Uranian spirit has aroused into creative being. It is the Eucharist, the Bread and the Wine that give everlasting life -- to those who have exp-

erienced within their souls the God-seed, and have not re-
coiled in fear before the glory and the responsibility. It is,
at every level, the healing and sustaining power of the wholeness of the whole.

This power is, at the physical level of the body, the source
whence are derived the antibodies, white corpuscles, and special hormones or enzymes which are sent through the blood to
heal and purify whatever part of the organism has been injured
or exhausted. At the level of the great spiritual organism
that may be called "Man", this Neptunian power is "Grace"
(C h a r i s) -- Grace which comes to every soul that has recognized and accepted its participation in the "works of the spirit", -- and its companionship, in the mystic Christ, with all
that is of the spirit.

To the individual limited and bound within the structures
of his ego, the universe as a whole answers as K a r m a: the
Mosaic Law of exact compensation. But to him whose soul
has become a hallowed shrine for the Living God, whose circumference of self includes potentially the whole universe,
whose mind establishes its formulations in terms of the reconciliation of all opposites, leaving nothing outside of its all-
inclusive multi-dimensional logic -- to him God answers as
Grace. Though his path be strewn with collective obstacles
and harsh memories of his individual past, he is nevertheless
secure -- with the only security that is of value, t h e   s e c-
u r i t y   t h a t   c o m e s   f r o m   b e i n g   t h e   W h o l e   in ac-
t i v e   e x p r e s s i o n   a t   o n e   p o i n t;   a n d   t h i s   p o i n t,
o n e ' s   i m m o r t a l   s e l f.

This faith in Grace is the Neptunian consequence of a cou-
rageously met and assimilated confrontation with Uranus and
its creative transfigurations. The two factors cannot be separated, and both are expressions of an utterly changed conscious relationship to spirit and to God, its cosmic Source.
Spirit is the "universal creative" -- not in the sense of it being the builder of worlds and physical organisms, but because
it is that constant h a r m o n i c   M o t i o n which emanates and

releases incessantly whatever is necessary to compensate for and to harmonize any disturbance in the equilibrium of the universal Whole. Spirit "creates" solutions to every need -- including that vast solution to the need of chaos which we understand as a universe or solar system. Every human birth, considered as the release of an individual l o g o s (or pattern of destiny) through which the past of an immortal self can be harmonized and balanced by the potentiality of a victorious future, is a solution presented by the spirit. Every birth-chart is a plan for regeneration, an individual creation of the spirit, a l o g o s sent by the Father to "save" a portion of humanity.

To him who takes such an attitude, not only intellectually but with the whole of his being, the Uranian revelation of his own divine Image on the inner "Mount of Transfiguration" must be the fulfillment of his most intense expectations. In this experience he sees at last with utmost clarity the w o r k i n g s of the creative spirit behind and through the core of his selfhood. He sees his divine Self ("Christ") radiating through, because finally incorporated in, his ego now transformed into soul, the "Jesus" within him. He sees, not as a Peter reducing spiritual experiences to a Saturnian level, but as a "son of thunder" -- a "John the Beloved" -- meeting, with the power of identification born of exalted love, the downpour of Grace; for the glow that he saw enveloping the entire being of the transfigured Jesus was indeed the substance of Grace.

Grace comes to pervade the "soul" that has left behind the sense of individual lack inherent in the nature of the "ego". As an ego, man knows himself a p a r t f r o m the spiritual Whole; as a soul, he experiences himself a p a r t o f this spiritual Whole. And as he does so experience he becomes actually and consciously suffused with the vitality of the Whole. He partakes of the "Blood" of the Whole, of the creative substance of the spirit -- the mystic Wine and Bread. He partakes of the divine Eucharist -- the perfect gift of Grace --

as the cell of the body partakes of the vital essences and the healing chemicals of the forever flowing blood in which it "lives and has its being".

This is "the life more abundant", the life in Grace; a life from which has vanished the gnawing sense of frustration and lack, and the regrets or remorse of ego-bondage, ego-unful-fillment and ego-conditioned tragedies; a life now filled with the presence of the unfolding God-seed within the soul and with the downflow of Grace this unfoldment summons because it requires it. And this must be likewise the life of charity; for charity is man's only true way of responding to the char-ismal gift of the spirit, Grace. F a i t h in the creative power of the spirit; H o p e that the Transfiguration shall come and find us fully awake to behold this "marriage of heaven and earth"; and, "the greatest of all", C h a r i t y to men every-where -- in the name of the spirit.

True charity (a g a p e) can only be the pouring out, at the level of still ego-bound men and women, of what the traveler on the Illumined Road has received as Grace. The man flood-ed with Grace must give charity, which is perfect love, if he is to receive greater spiritual abundance i n h i s s o u l; but that charity can only be true to the spirit, if it comes indeed f r o m the divine spirit, even though it be released t h r o u g h the individual man. To give out true charity means, first of all, to experience oneself as an agent of the spirit, as a foc-using of the divine Whole. Charity is not of the ego, but of God through the ego transformed into soul. It is as the soul overflows with Grace that the whole organism of the spirit-illumined man or woman is able also to radiate charity. The gifts of a privileged nation filled with earthly goods, egocen-tricity and collective self-complacency can be bitter to the peoples ravaged by a catastrophy for which the whole of hu-manity is responsible.

Yet, it was as the presence of Neptune became revealed to Western man that society at large began to respond to the call of mercy and humanitarianism; and even the most ego-

centric "business baron" found it necessary henceforth to bestow the social semblance of charity to the victims of the system that had enthroned him -- as the Congress of the United
States has found it necessary since the last War to bestow
many earthly gifts so as to protect its ideological frontiers
and the system which places it in power. How could one think
of these things, except as Neptunian reflections on the troubled waters of a Western Society that knows actually as little
about Grace as it experiences the Transfiguration in its individuals! And from the Neptunian cloud filled with glamor, illusions, and mirages of spiritual reality, how few are the
"Peters" able to bear, even in fear, the Voice of God! All
that can be heard, among men in palaces or men in neat gad-
get-filled bungalows, is the sound of splitting atoms -- the
voice of uranium whistling words of death and terror.

Is this the heralding sound of the Second Coming? Is the
Christ-reality to be born in our tortured and mentally dis-
traught world of bigger and better egos? Is true Neptunian
compassion to heal these ranting egos, perhaps soon to break
down in a global crisis? Is wintry snow thereafter to enman-
tle with white peace the ravaged earthliness of millions of
men, women and children in preparation for a new spring?

The answer is with the seeds that lie in the ground amidst
autumnal decay -- in the decay, yet not of it. The answer
is with individuals whose faith has made of them travelers on
the Illumined Road and, to ever so little an extent, partakers
of divine Grace for the sake of the God-seeds slowly -- oh,
so slowly -- unfolding within their souls. New social solutions, new religious organizations, new political integrations
will no doubt emerge from this present death of the old. Yet
these can only be sustained and fed with the vision and the
power that individuals, who work them out concretely, can
pour into them. There can be an illumined or a very dark future for humanity. It will be either in proportion as enough
men and women will have had the emotional stability, the courage, the wakefulness, the enduring strength, the clear mind
necessary to meet positively the confrontations of Uranus and
Neptune in their inner lives.

The experience of death must come to every individual on the Illumined Road; but, as it comes, the man who has passed successfully through the stages symbolized by the Uranian transfiguration and the Neptunian transsubstantiation of the very contents of selfhood is ready to meet this experience of death in a way impossible to the ordinary person still controlled by the power of the ego and the energies of earth nature -- in a c o n s c i o u s way.

To die in full and lucid consciousness; to retain throughout this dying an objective awareness of the process of relinquishment of the bio-psychic structures which until then conditioned the experience of living; to enter deliberately and purposefully into what to other human beings seems to be at least temporary darkness and loss of identity -- these are possibilities to which great occultists and sages have given the weight of their testimony. When these possibilities are clearly defined within a truly philosophical frame of reference unencumbered with fears, illusions or dogmatic preconceptions, they should not appear fantastic or nonsensical. They become logical necessities of human evolution which eventually individuals who are prepared and ready for them will experience as actual facts. Death need have no terror for anyone who understands the nature and character of the ego, its formation and its purpose. What has beginning must of necessity have an end in a universe in which all motions are cyclic. But no man has to identify his essential self with a n y o n e p a r t i c u l a r b e g i n n i n g; and thus no man needs to lose his identity through the corresponding end.

The understanding of death implies an equal understanding of birth. He who knows how and why any one thing begins knows likewise how and why it ends; and, thus knowing, can transform this end into a new and greater beginning. This is the secret of "personal immortality". Death, however, is not a simple or single event, because the conscious and individualized man is not only one thing. The formation of his ego is a process distinct from the generation of his physical organism; and whenever entities have different beginnings, they must likewise end differently. And "end" does not have to mean cessation and annihilation; it can signify transition and re-organization.

A physical organism, seen in the world of forces, which is by far the more "real" world, is the field of operation of various types of electro-magnetic (and other) energies differentiated for specific organic purposes. The various systems of the body (blood circulation, nerves, muscles, digestive apparatus, endocrine glands, etc.) depend upon the interaction of these energies in order to function healthily. The energies themselves are differentiated manifestations of what we might call for lack of a better word, the life-force. Throughout the process of fecundation and gestation they acquire their specialized characteristics by energizing and integrating the substance of cells and organs which are made available to the new growth within the mother's womb.

After the body is completely formed and has reached its full maturity these energies begin slowly to lose something of their intensity or precise tone, while various kinds of toxins accumulate in the cells. They tend to give up their differentiated traits, to become unclear rhythms. Eventually they return to the undifferentiated character of the life-force; and this is the death of the body. The universal homogeneous life-force has won back to itself the differentiated heterogeneous energies which operated in the various functional systems of the organism. The many energies have been reabsorbed into the vast unity of the ocean of the life-force. The body which these many energies animated and operated has become disintegrated under the pressure of this life-force.

Thus it is universal life that destroys the separated living organisms. This is no difficult paradox, for consider the fish of the ocean: they are actually a pocket of transformed sea-water separated from the ocean by skin and muscles. But, when they die, the differentiated sea-water within returns to the great sea, and the tissues of skin and flesh also decay into this sea-substance. Man's body likewise is differentiated earth-substance (including water and air), and at death this substance decomposes into the earth; while the energies animating the body return to the electro-magnetic ocean of the one life-force which permeates our whole planet, and presumably its entire orbital field.

A not too dissimilar process should be found operating in the case of the ego which is a structure of psychic and mental elements differentiated through the formative years of the life of personality. These psycho-mental elements do not come out of nothing. They are actually the results of the generic evolution of humanity and of the collective harvest of feeling-images, meanings, concepts, ideals, and purposes produced by a society, a culture, a community. This collective psycho-mental sea of human values is not only a vast collection of images and ideas; it is a vast reservoir of energy -- human energy in a collective un-individualized state, psychic-mental energy. It is from this reservoir that any individual person draws in order to give substance to his slowly crystallizing and differentiating ego. It is the collective unconscious from which progressively emerges the individualized conscious, which gives form and substance to the realization, "I am this particular person". It is the evolving one Mind of humanity.

Death leads, in time, to the final victory of the collective unconscious over the conscious ego -- the reabsorption of the latter into the former -- unless the ego has been able to become a prepared field for the descent and individualization, of the spiritual Essence (its Star) belonging to a more encompassing cycle of being; unless man has experienced the Transfiguration, the "Divine Marriage of Heaven and Earth" within his personality.

These alternatives however do not begin to present themselves only at the time of physical death. They outline themselves gradually during the last years and even decades of the life. We see the average individual person of our time and society losing little by little after maturity the expansive aggressiveness of his individuality and the sharpness of his "difference" from his fellow-men. Especially after forty, the collective power of his race, his tradition, his culture asserts itself ever more strongly in most cases, subduing his rebelliousness and his strictly individualistic attitudes.

This may mean a d e e p e n i n g of self through the assimilation of communal values and energies which, in the heat of his youthful attempts at self-individualization and originality, he had repudiated or to which he had failed to give conscious attention and personal significance. It may mean also a s u r r e n d e r of the individualized attitude, born of personal experiences and inner realizations, to the collective sea of the race's past. In most cases, it means far more a progressive surrender to, than a conscious "assimilation" of, collective values; and death merely puts its final seal upon the process. Society, civilization and humanity overcome the individual ego which thereafter remains only a m e m o r y (perhaps a very potent one), a latent focus of future crystallization in the collective unconscious; or a "shade" -- sometimes a very talkative one, if some extraneous stream of psychic energy is made to reanimate its patterns for a show of fictitious personality!

This is not, however, an absolutely inevitable ending to the individualizing process of ego-formation within the lifespan of a human personality. If this personality has developed clear-cut and distinct ego-structures through socially significant and personally creative behavior and thought, these structures can become the focus for the incorporation of the Star-Self (the Saturn phase of the Illumined Road); and as this occurs the power of this incorporation may overcome the inevitable pull toward reabsorption into the psychic and mental ocean of collective humanity. The transfigured ego, filled with Neptunian spirit-released substance (the "Living Bread that descendeth from Heaven"), can withstand the pressure of the return of the energies and the chemicals of the body to universal nature. He escapes the whirlpool of disintegrating forces, and remains a focus of individual consciousness, serving now the purpose of the greater self -- the "He" that has become "I". And this is what has been called "personal immortality", represented, in our culture, by the risen Christ able to demonstrate his glorious immortal being in and through a "body of light", the Risen Body of Christ -- known to Eastern occultists as the Nirmanakaya Body of the perfected Adept.

This condition of consciousness and being can be at least approximately understood by comparing it to what would happen to a man who, after falling asleep, would find himself still in full consciousness of his individual identity and able to operate in some trans-substantial realm of activity, beyond (or rather "through") the physical. To fall asleep is indeed, for all practical purposes of personal existence, to die temporarily as a conscious ego aware of self and of an objective world. Sleep takes place as the differentiated and individualized elements of the total personality (body and psyche) are overcome by the pressure of the collective and generic factors of human nature. Symbolically speaking, the "sea" presses so heavily upon the "fish" that the membranes separating the fish's organs from the sea collapse temporarily, and a state of suspended animation results which we call sleep.

During this period of suspended animation the individualizing energy of the organism regains strength, the strength once more to withstand the all-around pressure of the undifferentiated sea of the life-force in which we live and have our separated being. In sleep, then, the "individual" is forced to become subservient to, and to be temporarily absorbed by the "generic". Human nature operates in and through the sleeping individual without he being able to resist its rhythms and dictates. The "prodigal son", returned home, is once more part of the collective entity, the family.

Another illustration, easily understandable, is presented by what occurs in trees during winter. The living fluids of trees withdraw, as it were, into the roots. The sap hibernates within the great womb of the soil, from which it originally emerged under the individualizing and stem-producing power of springtime. Likewise the ego-consciousness of the individual person withdraws during sleep into its "roots" and within the vast all-human wombs of the g e n e r i c unconscious (i.e. human nature) and of the c o l l e c t i v e unconscious, (the collective past and tradition of the individual's culture, religion, nation, etc.).

The ego is compelled to withdraw; he cannot maintain his individualized separate rhythms of existence against the incessant pressure of the collective. He must give up consciousness and activity in an objective world, until he regains the power to reassert himself as a separate individual entity in control of an awakened body.

This is why the Hindu yogi, whose intense struggles of will aim at the full individualization of consciousness and the retention of individuality through and beyond death, strives eagerly to overcome sleep and the need for sleep. He r e f u s e s   t o   d i e   e v e r y d a y ,   a s   a n   i n d i v i d u a l ,   i n t o   t h e   c o l l e c t i v e   b e i n g   o f   h u m a n i t y   a n d   o f   h i s   c u l t u r e ; and he seeks to build for his self a permanent vehicle of consciousness (an immortal organization of psycho-mental energies) which the death of the physical organism will not be able to shatter or slowly to disintegrate.

The average person of our present humanity does die as an individual every night, and he lets human nature and the collective energies of his community take control of his physical and psychic instrumentalities for action. This control of the collective unconscious over the mechanisms of consciousness manifests often in what we call "dreams". The voice of the collective wisdom of the mother-race and mother-culture speaks, in the usually confused language of dream-images, to the wayward child-ego who has asserted in too eccentric, too differentiated and thus too dangerous ways his will to be a unique and original individual. It is a normative voice, that seeks to c o m p e n s a t e f o r the abnormalities of individualized human existence, especially in our artificial city environment. It is the voice of the "roots" of human existence; a conservative power stressing, n o t the new ways of evolution, but rather the old wisdom of collective experience and of age, the secure path of long-tested tradition and wholesome living.

This "descent into the root" of humanity, performed at the close of the day's activity and, more conclusively, at the end of the cycle of life in an objective body of earth-substances, is expressed in the astrological symbolism of Pluto. So Pluto has been associated with the idea of death; and it should have been likewise linked with the act of falling asleep. Pluto is indeed to be understood as the power which compels all separate individualizations (egos, national entities, particular cultures, etc.) to return to their collective roots or foundations of being.

However, this return to the roots, however inevitable it be at the close of any cycle of individualized existence, can be performed in either of two ways. It can be an unconscious and compulsive collapse and a more or less final disintegration of that which had achieved individual form and differentiated consciousness; but it can also be, in some rare instances, a conscious and deliberate act of repudiation of, and liberation from, a p a r t i c u l a r l a y e r o f c o l l e c t i v e b e i n g from which the individual once emerged and to which he need no longer be attached.

In the first case, death is truly the end of the cycle of individual personal existence. What remains of this cycle is, on one hand, a spiritual harvest (the seed-essence of truly assimilated individual experiences which had spiritual value) and the "manure" of all strictly materialistic tendencies and impulses in which the spirit had no concern; on the other hand, the more or less persistent imprint of the person's deeds, thoughts, feelings and spiritual radiations in the collective memory of those who loved him, were touched, inspired, stimulated by him -- or even forced to hate him unforgettably!

In the second case, death, experienced in full consciousness on the Illumined Road, means freedom from bondage to forms and substances no longer useful to the individualized spirit and reintegration within a greater spiritual Whole.

The first alternative is that which is today the destiny of most personal egos; the second is experienced by the individual who has transferred his allegiance to the Star, his celestial and permanent Identity, through the three stages of the Illumined Road which have been symbolized by Saturn, Uranus and Neptune. This individual having experienced a new sense of conscious identity (Saturn), a new release of spiritual-celestial power (Uranus) and the growth within his inner being of a new type of substantial-dynamic organization (Neptune) is ready to repudiate and relinquish utterly all that had been previously in the place of these three new factors of being: that is, his old sense of self, his old type of earth-conditioned energies, and the earth-born organism itself, the physical body. This phase of repudiation is symbolized in the life of Jesus by the Crucifixion -- the symbol of conscious and deliberate dying to the "common humanity" of earth-born men and to the patterns, biases, greeds and purposes of a disintegrating society and civilization (represented by the Jewish High-Priest bound to tribal dogmas, and by Pilate, the Roman Administrator, his hands tied by political expediency and intellectual confusion).

It is a Plutonian step because, even though its result will

be the Resurrection, nevertheless in this step is implied the "descent into hell". The Star-transfigured individual must touch bottom in man's common humanity, he must meet, assimilate and bless the collective evils of the race and civilization from which he once emerged as a struggling individual. No one can completely relinquish what he has not experienced down to the deepest depths -- not only in his individual nature, but in terms of the collective memory of humanity. "Hell" is the imprint of all past human evil in the collective memory of the Mind of Man. To face this and not to sink in horror or fear is the final price to pay for personal immortality. Such a confrontation is the ultimate Pluto-experience.

The meaning of this experience should be more easily understood if we consider what has been taking place this century in the realm of Western civilization, especially since the discovery of Pluto. The cycle of European Western Society is ending; the collective "ego"-structures (the culture, traditions and set values) of this Society, born some 1200 years ago, are breaking down in death. Can this death become a Crucifixion, prelude to a Resurrection?

It can only be so if the human collectivities which have emerged from the European cycle and established themselves as national entities in other lands succeed in focusing clearly within their own collective consciousness the power and light of the spirit that shone only dimly through the lifespan of the European Society. This European Society experienced a Uranian visitation in the eighteenth century and a Neptunian re-organization of its substance (the Industrial Revolution) in the nineteenth. But what did it do with them? What did we, of the United States, having emerged from mother-Europe, do with them?

The United States, as a national collectivity, is potentially the Risen Body of Europe. Our federal organization of States, peoples and faiths is potentially the embryo of

this glorious Body that might be. We c o u l d become symbolically, in relation to the Europe of the Gothic age and the
Renaissance, what the Risen Christ was to Jesus, the Galilean Adept. We could become a light-giving universalistic God-
revealing civilization, gradually superseding or absorbing the
European culture which, while nobly striving and inspired,
nevertheless was still filled with conflict and bound by old tribal and feudal patterns. We could; yet, in order to fulfill this
glorious future we would have not only to become a c t u a l l y,
not only theoretically, free from Europe's ancient forms of
bondage (and from new ones of our own!) but we would have
to face the confrontation with Europe's "hells" far more intelligently and creatively than we have done so far.

The progressive decline of European culture and traditions (and before Europe of older civilizations) can only mean
Crucifixion in a Jesus-like sense if we of America can "des-
cend into hell" and consciously meet, assimilate and bless
the collective evils of Western civilization; and having done
so, "arise on the third Day" in a Body of Glory, focal field
for a global civilization that need not die, as all civilizations
have so far died.

It is indeed much to ask of "these United States"; for how
tragically we have failed, in so many instances, to live up to
the occasion! Yet this is our potential destiny; as it was the
potential destiny of the Alexandria of the first centuries B. C.
and A. D. with regard to the dying Hellenized Mediterranean
Society of the day. Always, as a human cycle ends, there is
something born in and from this cycle which has the p o t e n-
t i a l i t y of becoming an immortal organism, gathering-in all
that was spiritual in this cycle and re-incorporating w i t h-
o u t b r e a k o f c o n s c i o u s i d e n t i t y the essence of the
cycle into a larger and more universal one. The potentiality
only; for in all but rare instances the Plutonian confrontation
with the shock of death and with the accumulated evil of the
past shatters the sense of personal identity.

Man "falls" asleep, much as he "falls" in love and "falls"

into the hells he has summoned. Man dies in his ego, and the image of the Star within his soul (if at all present!) is much too weak to serve as a pulsating heart-center for the actual re-integration of self in terms of celestial vitality (Uranus) and of divine substance (Neptune). Thus Pluto means death and the loss of conscious identity. He is the ultimate Tester -- not like Saturn whose tests deal with the everyday confrontations of organic ego-controlled existence, but in a far deeper sense. What Pluto tests is the capacity in every individual to transfer his sense of personal identity from the realm of earth-objectivity and bio-psychic attachments to that of "celestial" activity -- the realm where, as a Star, he finds himself one in purpose and in being with his Companions, within a symbolical Constellation (a "spiritual Brotherhood").

Pluto guards the path that leads through unconscious death or conscious Crucifixion to some type of celestial re-integration. Alas, the awesome character of the confrontations he summons as necessary conditions for re-integration in conscious Selfhood is such that only but a very few men can face them and retain their full individual consciousness and their contact with the Star. Unless one has truly experienced this Star within one's self, the Plutonian tests can only mean disintegration and unconscious dying; for, during them, the darkness of "hell" shuts out all the sky and the Stars that are above. But, if the divine Presence remains vibrant within the soul temporarily submerged by the ancient evil, then, this Presence can act as the core of the new "Body of light", the celestial body, the Christ-Body. And the Resurrection follows.

Tenth Phase: The Resurrection and the Ascension

THE PROSERPINE MYTH

Anything that begins must end; but there are ends which are made points of emergence into larger cycles, and there are "deaths" which channel the harvest of individual selfhood into the patterns of more-than-individual living. To him who has experienced the Transfiguration; to him who has assimilated the Neptunian "gift-waves" of the spirit, death can become -- if he passes successfully through the tests of Pluto and the "descent to hell" -- a reorganization of the dynamic and ideo-spiritual elements of his illumined personality. The bio-structural framework which the racial ancestry had built and filled with compulsive instincts and collective idols collapses; the warp and woof of the ego-ruled psyche vanish, and the many colored shapes of personal existence are dispersed, as a neat jig-saw puzzle being shaken loose violently. But, from the very substance of Space itself, from nowhere and everywhere, a condensation of power and purpose is felt, and the scattered elements are reintegrated into an "organism of light". Space itself is now the warp and woof -- a new kind of space, an expression of the purpose and power of the spirit. The tapestry of self is woven by the Star into a "Robe of Glory", a "Risen Body" of spirit-substance.

The Hindu philosopher speaks of the s v a r u p a, the concrete and operative form of selfhood (s v a, meaning "self"); the Buddhist, of the n i r m a n a k a y a body, a protean organism which is beyond or without (n i r) the principle of ego-individualization (m a n a s). The Gospels record the mysterious appearance of Christ after the Crucifixion in what, in every respect, was a physical body, able to take food, susceptible of being touched by Thomas' doubting hands, holding converse with pilgrims on the road in a most normal way -- yet, also capable of materializing in the midst of a room, passing through walls and closed doors as if these were open lanes of space.

The devotee bows in stunned worship as before a unique never-to-be-repeated miracle, and finds it convenient and far easier not to think further. The intellectual believer, who has need of Christ as a teacher of ethics or psychological wisdom, seeks to dismiss what he cannot explain with his ego-structured mind compelled to think in terms of absolutely separate bodies and discrete concepts. It is all symbolism, he claims; and he too fails to meet the challenge of a potential fact, around the existence of which he might have to reorganize his data of insecure knowledge. How could one understand Christ's Resurrection, who is not ready to reintegrate his consciousness around the potentiality of his own eventual resurrection? How could one conceive of the "Body of Glory" who has not realized the substantiality of the spirit and the possibility that space itself might have an entirely new meaning and character in terms of the activity of the spirit?

That the spirit might be said to have substance should not disconcert the modern mind now accustomed to behold the transformation of matter into energy. But while all that modern man can do is to decompose and disintegrate, the essential nature of the activity of the spirit is to harmonize and to integrate, to bring forth new concrete manifestation in terms of a divine purpose -- thus, to create. This activity of the spirit occurs in answer to the needs of all separate entities, of humanity as a whole as well as of all relatively isolated egos striving through lives of discord and want. It is a harmonic response to every disharmony, a compensatory (thus healing, whole-making) activity welling up from the absolute Harmony which we call God, and whose manifestation men witness as the heavens.

For most modern intellectuals these heavens still constitute the immensities of a space which extends infinitely in all dimensions, as the limitless container of celestial bodies; yet the Einsteinian concept of space already negates such an image, as space is made to curve and to become bent or modified by the presence of material aggregates, of planets and suns. The synthesis of the concepts of space and substance can be carried much further, at two different levels. Space considered as a framework of emptiness inside of which separate objects move and extend the one next to the other is space conditioned by matter; it is "discrete" space, space as e x t e n s i o n. But space can be conceived also as a manifestation of the being and power of God; emerging as a result of the activity of the spirit, each act of spirit generating as it were its own space. Space, so understood, is "concrete" (which means etymologically "growing together"); it is space as i n t e n t i o n, and not as "extension".

If spirit is "intent" upon being active in any particular field where there is need of its activity, s p i r i t i s t h e r e. The intention creates the space. It is not for the spiritual act a matter of "going from one place to another" in a space which extends "between" things. The space covered by the act of spirit can only be conceived in terms of the intention and purpose of the act; not in terms of material "distance". This space is an expression or attribute of the purposeful activity of the spirit -- and fundamentally of God's i n t e n t. Thus, in Biblical symbolism, God says: "Let there be light!" And there is light. Modern science now recognizes that light is both energy and substance. But, more than this, light is, in essence, an expression of spiritual space; or we might say the link between the space of spirit-activity and the space of material objects, the link between God's "intention" and the "extension" of the world men perceive through this very light.

The main characteristic of spiritual space, as we understand it, is that it is "ideo-plastic". If the disharmony of an illness is present in a person, and if the healing action of the spirit seeks to reestablish the disturbed harmony, the spirit's intent condenses, as it were, spiritual space at the point where the disharmony exists. The spirit is there, in that space; and it is there precisely, concretely, as a "healing image" of harmony, compensating for and harmonizing the diseased condition. This healing image is not a mere phantasm. It is substantial in a spiritual sense. It is a manifestation of the "concrete" space in which all acts of the spirit occur. Besides, it should be clear that, as this healing image is intended as a compensation and cure for the disharmonic material condition, it bears a definite relationship to that condition. It is, in a general sense, the positive and radiant counterpart of the negative and darkened organism being healed. It is as soul is to ego, as the Risen Body of Christ (and of all true Sons of God) is to the material organism of Adamic man in bondage to the disharmonic condition of earth-nature.

Indeed the Risen Body of Christ was, and is, a healing answer to the need of humanity. It is an effective and infinitely potent act of the spirit intent upon revealing to the men of a new era the purpose of God for them and the era. It is an act of spirit expressed ideo-plastically; that is, in the form of the divine idea and purpose of the act. And it manifests in spiritual space, in a space that is concrete and substantial in as much as it can condense in substantial objectivity, at whatever point of our material space the healing and revealing act of the spirit is intent upon reaching. The intent of the act, the condensing ideo-plastic image, and the spatial substantiality of it, are all indissolubly related factors in the spirit's act itself; and the expected result of the event is a healing or stirring effect upon the human beings confronted with the Christ-Body, or with any similar manifestations and revelations of the harmonizing power of the spirit.

The appearance of Christ in his Risen Body was made necessary by the poignant need of his disciples and of the civil-

ization to which they were to convey the Glad News of the individualization and incorporation of God in a perfected individual of the Adamic race. What this News conveyed was the
birth of a vast cycle of human evolution in which the power of
divine Sonship was to be released in such a manner that every
person in whom the God-seed had reached sufficient development as an organism of individualized spirit could assume
this power and become transfigured by it. Every Risen Body
-- every Adept or Master -- is an answer to a need, the need
of humanity as a whole, or of a section of it to which the resurrected individual is specifically linked by his ancient karma overcome by the power of perfect love and sublime compassion. This Body, for the man who overcame the Plutonian confrontation with the accumulated collective failure of
all mankind, is the vehicle of his personal immortality; but it
is also a super-personal answer to this collective failure (the
state of "hell"), the shadow of which blinds human beings everywhere.

The risen individual is no longer bound by the cycle which
his birth on earth as a person had opened. He has emerged at
long last as a center of divinity, as a Source of spirit-activity,
as a "Celestial", as a Star in the Constellation which is the
sacred Company of Those who like him are servants of the
Great Orphan, humanity. He has become the component part
of a vaster cycle, bound by "Man", rather than by an individual ego. He has transformed the conscious death of his Crucifixion into the prelude to a final entrance (i. e. Initiation) into
the realm of divinity. He has made of an end a beginning -- a
beginning which need have no end. For, as the end of the new
cycle will come near, it can once more be made into a greater beginning; this, for ever and ever, from cycle to always
vaster cycle. Immortality is the power to make of every conscious and significant end the beginning of a larger cycle.

Beyond the planet Pluto, symbol of the Guardian at the
Gates of Immortality, we may already distinguish the pres-

ence of a new orb. I have suggested long ago the name Proserpine for the yet unknown planet; for in that name lies hidden the symbol of all resurrections. And the stage beyond Pluto can only be that of the Resurrection.

But resurrection can be the unconscious and fate-ordained resurgence of life in a framework of "material space" and earth-bondage, or the conscious, radiant and healing service of the triumphant Christ to humanity in the "spiritual space" of his Risen Body. In the ancient myth of Proserpine (or in the Greek Eleusinian Mysteries, K o r e) one can find references to both types of resurrection, though by far the more explicit and obvious meaning is that according to which Proserpine symbolized the spirit of ever-renascent vegetable life, the so-called Corn Spirit.

There is little doubt that the story of the abduction of Proserpine by Pluto, god of the Underworld, and of her return to the surface of the earth for two-thirds of each year, was in its earliest form a mythological representation of the yearly cycle of vegetation in temperate regions. Proserpine during her yearly stay in the realm of Pluto is vegetable life in the condition of seed; while through the remaining months of the year she is life in the condition of leaf, stem, flower and fruit. Thus the story tells of the constant rhythm of seasonal life in its below-the-horizon and above-the-horizon states; and throughout the vitalistic stage of human culture, particularly in evidence during the Taurus precessional Age and in agricultural societies built along the banks of great rivers, this yearly life-rhythm was the substance of the "cults of fertility", about which much was written last century, but not always with great understanding.

However the myth, at least in its latter-day versions, contains some features which point to a deeper and spirit-revealing meaning -- a meaning dealing with the development of spiritual individuality and with the more conscious aspect of the "descent to hell". Characteristic is the division of the cycle of Proserpine into one-third and two-thirds, rather than

into two halves -- the more obvious astrological pattern. It
may correspond to the alternation of seed-period and leaf-
period in the vegetation cycle of almost semi-tropical countries; but it also refers no doubt to the sequence of sleep-
period and of hours of wakeful activity (one-third and two-
thirds of the day cycle). Thus the abduction of Proserpine by
Pluto represents the unconscious process of falling asleep,
which (we saw previously) comes under the symbolism of Pluto.

The story in which Proserpine picks a black narcissus,
after which the earth opens and she is ravished by Pluto, is
deeply significant; for the black narcissus symbolizes the shadow image of the self, the dark form of the psyche, made up
of all the fears and frustrations of the ego. It is the pull (or
"perfume") of these psychic failures which forces the ego to
let go of individualized consciousness and to blend its energies with those of man's common humanity. The threshold of
consciousness (the "earth-surface") opens and Pluto draws
Proserpine to the world of roots and of the disintegrating humus of ancient cycles, the realm of instinctive memories and
of bondage to the past.

The name Pluto comes from a Greek radical signifying
"rich". This god rules over all earthly wealth, because all
wealth is the product of earth-conditioned activity, and his
realm, Hades (the collective unconscious of psychology), is
the repository of the collective past of mankind. Hades however is not a place of torment (the latter being Tartarus, still
farther below); it is a place of unconscious identification (Proserpine "marries" Pluto) with the collective root-principle or
substratum of human consciousness. Its denizens wander aim-
lessly -- without real (i. e. creative) individuality or purpose.
Thus the human soul in this condition is undifferentiated and
ghostly.

However, thanks to the plea of Proserpine's mother, Demeter (the Great Mother, Goddess of the fruitful earth), the
gods of the Sky intervene and Proserpine is made to return to

the earth-surface which becomes once more green and fruitful; and the alternation of above-the-earth and below-the-earth
conditions begins for Proserpine. The important fact here is
that Demeter's plea represents the conscious formulation of
a need. Everything on earth needs Proserpine and her life-
giving presence. The high gods answer to this need in compassion for mankind and for the Earth-Mother disconsolate in
her barrenness.

The entire process becomes then a purposeful ritual in
which the individualized consciousness, having assimilated
the experience of man's common roots, rises under the call
of the tragic need it has witnessed w i t h i n the Great Mother, while being summoned by the celestial spirit, the Fatherhood of the Sky (Zeus-Jupiter being Proserpine's father).
And this ritual was indeed the central theme of the Eleusian
Mysteries, the spiritual legacy to Greece of her parent-cul-
ture, the Cretan culture.

Yet Proserpine's cycle journey, even if related to consciousness rather than to the yearly phases of vegetation, refers to a compulsive and non-deliberate process. Proserpine culls the black narcissus unaware of what will befall her;
and she carries into Hades no living remembrance of her
celestial father. On the contrary, in the case of the Christ-
mythos, Jesus meets his Crucifixion deliberately and in full
consciousness. And he can do so b e c a u s e he had experienced the Transfiguration; because the God-seed was germinating within him; because the Star had been realized by him
as "heaven within". He can therefore carry to hell his own
heaven, his own spiritual space -- and rise through the levi-
tating power of his own spiritual intent, in the fullness of his
spiritual fruition, the Christ Body.

The normal individual returns to earth, like the Proserpine of the popular myth, through the power of that over which
he has no conscious or individual control; he falls asleep and
awakens, he dies and is reborn, in unconsciousness. Only he
who has realized fully the power of divine Sonship within his

transfigured being, he who has not shrunk from the Crucifixion and who did accept his responsibility to humanity and the
era to come, can succeed in experiencing death and the descent to hell in a consciousness illumined by the presence of
the Star within. Only he can rise in the spiritual space of
heaven-within and, as need arises, can condense the substantiality of this space into a Risen Body that will communi-
cate to his disciples the message of his immortality within
the realm of the "Celestials".

The Ascension concludes the process of transference from
the lesser to the greater cycle. It symbolizes the final Initiation into the Spiritual Brotherhood, whose celestial representation is the Constellation in which the Star of the risen individual is a center of light and power. There, individuality
still exists; but it is now "celestial" individuality -- the uniqueness of the Star, that perhaps is now a Sun radiating light
and spirit upon planets and myriads of emergent lives.

It is said that when the Illumined Road is thus consummated, there are several paths open to the Son of God, some of
which lead him entirely beyond all possible contacts with our
humanity. Symbolically, likewise, there are various types
of star-systems: binary stars, star-groups, solar systems,
and probably many others. Yet every star that radiates light
-- and there are range upon range of light! -- can be understood as a condensed nucleus of that creative divine Potency
which forever emanates and differentiates Itself as light. To
us, bound by our conception of space as a framework for objects (celestial or otherwise) to extend in and move through,
this creative Potency appears to be, as it were, beyónd or
behind space; and poet-mystics have thought of stars and suns
as "holes in the sky" through which the creative energies of a
transcendent world of divine Beings stream forth, or as lenses focusing the one divine Potency in an infinity of directions, differentiating it into a multitude of cosmic forces and
powers.

The concept seems to have, however, a static character

still bound to the idea of extension of material objects. God is not beyond some infinitely extensive universal space, or beyond a dark sky shutting him from our mortal eyes. God is where God acts; and God acts where there is disharmony and need for the restoring of equilibrium. Spiritual space is where a center of divinity acts. It is a characteristic manifestation of the act of spirit, and this manifestation occurs wherever there is a polarizing need for it. Thus "heaven" is potentially everywhere in so far as our material space is concerned. Heaven is a unity -- and thus symbolically a "kingdom". Spiritual space is a unity. An organism of spirit does not travel through it. The spirit creates it, as mind creates ideas and images which have no material extension, yet which, if the mind is spirit-energized, can condense into concrete bodily manifestations.

Indeed mind, in this sense, is essentially the substantiality of spirit. The associative power of the human intellect generalizing upon the perception of the senses is a shadowy and but materially significant manifestation of this cosmic and harmonic Mind which is the spiritual substance of the universal Whole. Initiation is the entrance into this realm of ideo-spiritual substantiality, the harmonic universal Mind -- entrance as a conscious individual established in permanent Identity. It is thus symbolically the Ascension from the realm of earth-substance to that of spirit-substantiality, from the disharmonic mentality of mostly unconscious, instinct-bound and passionate men to the creative Mind of divine Harmony in which transfigured individuals act as nuclei of divine compassion and as agents for the release of the forever harmonizing and healing spirit within, yet beyond, all existence.

The cloud that enfolds the ascending Christ-Body and hides it from the disciples' perception is that ever-shifting threshold of consciousness which appears to separate the Mind of divine Harmony from that of intellectual and ego-constrained human beings. The Illumined Road is a bridge between these two realms of consciousness. It is the path of the light-ray returning to its divine source; for light is the link between spiritual space and material space -- and, in man, the path of this returning light-ray is the path of unconditional service and of an unwavering will to harmony.

Following that path the individual person passes through all the stations of the Illumined Road. That they become nearly similar to the last "Stations of the Cross" means simply that at all times the would-be Christ-Individual must act in the midst of a humanity still estranged from God and confused by its own intellectual achievements. The Crucifixion is the drama of the release of the spirit-impelled individual from the o u t e r collective mind of the society of his day and age. The Resurrection from hell is the release of this individual from the i n n e r collectivity of mankind's ancient memories of fear and failures.

Thus released, the Christ-individual is free -- free to accomplish forever the acts of the spirit in terms of that divine "necessity" which is the essence of absolute Harmony. He is free to integrate his unwearied efforts with those of the Companions seeking forever to lift the cloud on the Mount of the Ascension, so that men may commune, in understanding and in truth, with the vast Mind whose source is God, and whose substantiality sustains and embodies the ever-present manifestations of Those whose countenance is light, whose hearts beat in unison with the rhythm of divine Purpose.